Ancient
Zionism

THE FREE PRESS
New York   London   Toronto   Sydney   Tokyo   Singapore

Ancient Zionism

The Biblical Origins of the National Idea

AVI ERLICH

5\10

The Free Press
A Division of Simon & Schuster Inc.
866 Third Avenue, New York, N.Y. 10022

Printed in the United States of America

printing number

1 2 3 4 5 6 7 8 9 10

Library of Congress Cataloging-in-Publication Data

Erlich, Avi, 1944–
    Ancient Zionism : the Biblical origins of the national idea / Avi Erlich.
        p.   cm.
    ISBN 0-02-902352-1
    1. Palestine in the Bible. 2. Bible. O.T.—Criticism, interpretation, etc.   I. Title.
BS1199.P26E75   1995
296.3'11—dc20   94-36617
                                                                        CIP

For

SHALA, AARON, AND MARGARET ERLICH

and

RACHEL HALLOTE

and

JONATHAN ROSEN AND ANNA ROSEN

For Zion's sake will I not hold my peace, and for Jerusalem's sake I will not rest, until the righteousness thereof go forth as brightness.

—Isaiah 62

Contents

Introduction: The Beginnings of Intellectual Nationalism

We speak of a "national concept" when a people makes its unity, spiritual coherence, historical character, traditions, origins and evolution, destiny and vocation the objects of its conscious life and the motive power behind its actions.

—Martin Buber, *On Zion*

Behold, I make a covenant: . . . for it is a terrible thing that I will do with thee. Observe thou that which I command thee this day: behold, I drive out before thee the Amorite, and the Canaanite, and the Hittite, and the Perizzite, and the Hivite, and the Jebusite. Take heed to thyself, lest thou make a covenant with the inhabitants of the land whither thou goest, lest it be for a snare in the midst of thee: But ye shall destroy their altars, break their images, and cut down their groves: For thou shalt worship no other god.

—Exodus 34

MONOTHEISM WAS ANCIENT ISRAEL'S FIRST ACHIEVEMENT, THREE AND A half millenia ago. The second achievement, following immediately, was Abraham's invention of the Land, a place that was both a territory and a literary construct, a landscape meant to be read for the monotheistic civilization it would come to represent. The ancient Hebrews took this second idea as the only possible justification for their seizure of lands that had formerly belonged to the Canaanite tribes. Yes, they believed God gave them the lands of Canaan, but only on condition that these lands be used to represent a set of ideas. The Hebrews also told themselves that God explicitly forbade them *other* lands—so there could be no empire—and they told themselves that if they failed to use the lands of Canaan to represent monotheism, they would lose both the signifying Land and the civilization for which it stood. The Canaanites, or their like, would get these lands back.

The ancient Hebrews may be the only people who preserved stories that present ancestors as intruders in their own land. They told detailed stories of how Abraham, a native of Ur in Sumeria, ingratiated his way into Canaan and then bought his first toehold; they also faced squarely the bloody details of Joshua's conquest of lands that had once belonged to others. In modern as well as ancient times, the Hebrew words for "to conquer" and "conquest" (*lichbosh* and *kiboosh*, respectively) refer primarily to the Hebrew conquest of Israel, not the conquest of foreign territory.

This insistence that the Land was not a natural possession but an emblem that had to be self-consciously acquired was necessary to the Hebrew view that nationalism required diligence, with the intensity of physical combat providing some measure of the intellectual effort that was also demanded. The Land was not to be taken for granted. Its terms were rigorous: The ancient Hebrew had to apprehend the Land in order to conquer and hold it. (Modern Zionists of the militaristic school, such as Vladimir Jabotinsky, who led Jewish brigades in Palestine during both world wars and in between, could be forthright or cagey about the enterprise of reconquering the Land, but they were understandably reluctant to employ the old terms of conquest. In a secular age that shows little patience for the expression of a thoughtful nationalism from which civilized people can in fact draw their being, ancient Zionism would appear fanatical and imperialistic, even when its enemies were fanatics and imperialists.)

3

Where the Canaanites were materialists and literalists who immersed themselves in the fearful cycles of the land's fertility, throwing their babies into Molech's fiery maw in exchange for a dubious guarantee against famine, the Hebrews at their best read into the Land a higher God, a living God who had created the entire universe and thus did not seek the mindless sacrifice of children. Created in this God's image, the Hebrews would read from the Land the possibility of elevating the human mind above bloody fantasy. In the great civilizations that flourished to Israel's east and west, in Sumeria and Egypt, men became gods when they died, and the gods of men were dead. In Israel, however, the Land recalled the radical distinction between the everlasting creator and the mortals of His creation, thus freeing human beings from the pretense that in death they might become gods or that in life they must dispatch dead babies to plead on their behalf.

This use of the Land created the foundations of Israel's intellectual nationalism and led to our modern expectation that nations will represent ideas and values, not merely powers and interests. The Hebrew Land became the object of imagination and poetry, and from this experience a rich national literature emerged. Its chief purpose was to charge the Land's people with lively thought, about monotheism particularly but also about the intellectual life in general. Since, as we shall see, a cultivated mind was necessary to grasp the unseen God of monotheism, the cultivation of the Land came to signify the need to cultivate intellect. Conversely, the failure to use the Land to stimulate intellect would remove the justification for having evicted the original idolators. In the event of intellectual backsliding, the desiccated Land would revert to the Canaanite tribes, who would again soak the earth with the blood of babies chosen to appease Molech. The Canaanites would never be a nation, never rise above slavery to local gods and landscapes. Only the Hebrews saw these lands as unifiable, because only the Hebrews possessed a unifying idea that made a Land out of disparate territories.

That the Land must be *read* is a preoccupation of a major portion of Tanach, the Hebrew Bible. The emphasis falls on the distinction between the brutality associated with illiterate submission to the local pantheon and the literate use of the Land which engendered the civilization of monotheism. In the following chapters I will try to describe in detail this relationship between culture and Land, to which the ancient Hebrews gave the name Zion. Before I do so, I should say a word about my approach by offering a representative story. We can recognize the biblical redactors' demands on their readers, because these demands form the basis of our own literary sensibility.

The story is a small part of the familiar narrative about Moses receiving the Law on Sinai while the restless Hebrews below seek a visible god in a golden calf. Already we are caught up in the text's ironic tone, in its distinction between the enlightened view of Moses, high on the mountain, and the stooping of the Hebrews, who remain in the lowlands in every sense:

> And when the people saw that Moses delayed to come down out of the mount, the people gathered themselves together unto Aaron, and said unto him, Up, make us gods, which shall go before us; for as for this Moses, the man that brought us up out of the land of Egypt, we wot not what is become of him. . . . And all the people brake off the golden earrings which were in their ears, and brought them unto Aaron. And he received them at their hand, and fashioned it with a graving tool, after he had made it a molten calf: and they said, These be thy gods, O Israel, which brought thee up out of the land of Egypt. . . . And the Lord said unto Moses, Go, get thee down: for thy people, which thou broughtest out of the land of Egypt, have corrupted themselves: They have turned aside quickly out of the way which I commanded them: they have made them a molten calf, and have worshipped it, and have sacrificed thereunto, and said, These be thy gods, O Israel, which have brought thee up out of the land of Egypt. And the Lord said unto Moses, I have seen this people, and, behold, it is a stiffnecked people: Now therefore let me alone, that my wrath may wax hot against them, and that I may consume them: and I will make thee a great nation. And Moses besought the Lord his God . . . Remember Abraham, Isaac, and Israel, thy servants, to whom thou swarest by thine own self, and saidst unto them, I will multiply your seed as the stars of heaven, and all this land that I have spoken of will I give unto your seed, and they shall inherit it for ever. And the Lord repented of the evil which he thought to do unto his people. And Moses turned, and went down from the mount, and the two tables of the testimony were in his hand: the tables were written on both their sides; on the one side and on the other were they written. And the tables were the work of God, and

the writing was the writing of God, graven upon the tables. And when Joshua heard the noise of the people as they shouted, he said unto Moses, There is a noise of war in the camp. And he [Moses] said, It is not the voice of them that shout for mastery, neither is it the voice of them that cry for being overcome: but the noise of them that sing do I hear. And it came to pass, as soon as he came nigh unto the camp, that he saw the calf, and the dancing: and Moses' anger waxed hot, and he cast the tables out of his hands, and brake them beneath the mount. (Exodus 32)

Here is the source of the pious idea that God wrote the Bible, handing it to Moses divinely engraved, "the work of God." But notice that the text makes no claim that all the Five Books of Moses, including this very story, were engraved on these tablets, the first version of the written law. It seems simplistic to reduce the complex weave of this story to the bald assertion that God wrote it all, especially when the text asks us to pay attention to a rich pattern of human telling and reading. In any case, what God has written, Moses is free to break. In fact, Moses becomes in this passage an author himself, a man of verbal power who diverts God's wrath by telling Him the story of the covenant. Our passage also sets in parallel Moses's breaking of the divine tablets with the inept allegorical reading of the Hebrews, who mistakenly interpret the golden calf as the god who raised them out of Egypt. Joshua too is a misreader, thinking the noise in the camp a sign of battle. He is an overeager version of his later self, the leader-to-be of the conquest of Canaan, hearing sounds of battle when the problem is, if anything, more dangerous. The text, then, contrasts the literacy of Moses with the God who has forgotten His own covenant, with the Hebrews who have forgotten their God, and with the youthful Joshua, who misses the moral significance of the riot in the camp. If the text insists on divine authorship, however ambiguously, it also emphasizes mortal telling, human reading and misreading.

This is so, I think, because reading and misreading are crucial ideas in Hebrew civilization. Leaving literacy to God does not suffice. True, Moses knows how to read from afar the noise in the camp because God has already told him what is happening. But his reading of the Hebrew camp is active and attentive. He alone is able to recall and retell the covenant. He alone understands its civilizing power to restore harmony and forestall the "evil which [God] thought to do unto his people." Joshua, standing apart from the camp at the bottom of the mount, a promising lad who holds himself back from the debasement of the golden calf, is still green in understanding, not yet ready to lead the physical conquest of the Land, let alone to master its significance. Likewise, the Hebrew idolators have a long road to literate maturity. They fulfill their promise when they are able to read from the Land the civilization of Moses. Now they are in the wilderness, illiterate.

At the heart of our passage is the covenant regarding "this land," recognizable as the Land of Israel even when the phrase is uttered in the desert. In Hebrew culture to this day, "the land," or "this land," is the Land. What is this covenant?

> Now the Lord had said unto Abram, Get thee out of thy country, and from thy kindred, and from thy father's house, unto a land that I will shew thee: And I will make of thee a great nation, and I will bless thee, and make thy name great; and thou shalt be a blessing: And I will bless them that bless thee, and curse him that curseth thee: and in thee shall all families of the earth be blessed. (Genesis 12)

Most simply, the covenant is God's promise to make from Abraham's seed a great nation, as numerous as the stars and rooted in the specific soil of Canaan. In exchange, God is to be acknowledged as the only God of the creation. But surely this is not a bargain that God requires, nor one that interests the redactors of the Bible *as a bargain*. In fact God immediately transforms the covenant into a blessing, not a bargain but a gift. The covenant allows its human beneficiaries to enlarge their vision from the ownership of fields to the intellectual scale of the Creator. The blessing is the opportunity to escape idolatry, which is presented in the Bible as enslavement to mindless magic and an exile to the desert of literal-minded materialism. It is as a blessing that Moses recalls the covenant to God on Sinai, and it is also as a blessing that the redactors recall the right reading of the Land in the midst of this wild scene of the Hebrews worshiping the golden calf. The metal forming it—so recently plucked from their own ears—is soon to be returned to their bodies, when Moses grinds up the calf and makes the idolaters drink the dust.

In our story of Moses receiving the tablets as the Hebrews dance (the root Hebrew word for *dance* is *tablet* spelt backwards), the covenant meets its opposite, which is idolatry. Idolatry is to be despised not only because it is blasphemous but because it senselessly undermines both the clear mind and the national soul. The idolatrous mind mires itself in the local field, reducing thought and life itself to physical fertility. Thus, the idolatrous mind can have no national culture, no idea larger than the fertile plot of ground. All must be sacrificed to the field, including children. The Hebrew readers of the story of the golden calf would recognize in the melting of the golden ornaments the related idolatrous urge to throw babies into the fire for the sake of this primitive fertility. In the idolator's world, the appeasement of the local gods becomes the supreme cultural value, but in the Land every valley and every high place unite as a reminder of the living Creator.

Abraham, whom Moses evokes on Sinai, wished to separate himself from the idolators of Sumeria, but the real problem for the Hebrews was to eradicate the idolatry from their own breasts, to maintain instead the culture of literacy. Time and again they failed, just as they did in the episode of the golden calf. Instead of climbing the Land's high places to renew their intellectual purpose, they rededicated the hilltops to the old cults again and again. According to God in Ezekiel 23, the Hebrews "caused their sons, whom they bare unto me, to pass for them through the fire, to devour them. . . . For when they had slain their children to their idols, then they came the same day into my sanctuary to profane it." In throwing children into the fire as if they were earrings, the Hebrews reduced themselves to so much base spiritual metal.

Indeed, the redactors most likely harmonized the stories of Moses with the prophecies of Ezekiel, even though the two lived centuries apart, Moses at the beginning of national life (the Exodus from Egypt occurred around 1250 B.C.E.) and Ezekiel almost seven hundred years later at the time of the first exile from Israel. The collation of the Bible as we have it today took place largely in Babylonia, where the Hebrews were transported by their conquerors in 586 B.C.E. Thus Ezekiel is made to allude to Moses's view of the golden calf: "Because ye are all become dross, behold, therefore I will gather you into the midst of Jerusalem," thunders Ezekiel. "As they gather silver, and brass, and iron, and lead, and tin, into the midst of the furnace, to blow the fire upon it, to melt it; so will I gather you in mine anger and in my fury, and I will leave you there, and melt you" (Ezekiel 22). In alluding to the making of the golden calf from molten metals, Ezekiel insists that the failure to read the Land for its monotheism results in the awful reduction of mind to metal; God has only to leave the Hebrews' melted minds where they were in order to punish them.

For the ancient Hebrews, the intricate story of the golden calf shows this melting of minds as much as it demonstrates impiety. I try to read the Bible as it begs to be read: a sophisticated, self-referential, literary narrative about the Hebrew mind and the relationship to the Land. The Bible demands a literary response now, just as it demanded a literary consciousness of the Hebrews in the past. Literacy was mandatory in Hebrew civilization, for without it their culture could not survive and they could have no God. We are able to see this because Hebrew literacy in fact has shaped our own literary culture. Those who seek a pietist's view in this book will be disappointed, as will those who believe that the Bible, while charming, hardly counts as a source of ideas. On the contrary, the Bible treats nationalism as a literary idea that is able to serve as a summation of the intellectual life. As we shall see, the Hebrew writers knew that their nationalism often degenerated into a vicious materialism, but they would have dismissed the current notion that nationalism necessarily corrupts and rots the mind. The Hebrews and their literary Bible see intellectual nationalism as the antidote to self-preoccupation, because, like poetry itself, the Land can be made to stand for the reach of human consciousness.

I view the Bible as an artfully edited compendium of ancestral texts compiled by unknown redactors in the period of the Babylonian captivity. These exiled Jewish editors took as their chief theme the grand narrative of the invention, establishment, loss, and restoration of Zion. By focusing on the idea of intellectual nationalism, and demonstrating how the Land of Canaan came to symbolize the culture of monotheism, the redactors of the Bible achieved a powerful imaginative unity. In my reading, then, Tanach is not a loosely organized "canon" of divinely authored texts but a book with a specific human purpose. It is the Bible's redactors and not the voice of God in Moses's ear that allows the great lawgiver to foretell the exile of the Hebrews, when God "would scatter them into corners" and "make the remembrance of them to cease from among men" (Deuteronomy 32). Similarly, it seems part of an editorial plan to emphasize the overarching story of Zion that Ezekiel looks back to Eden as an early version of the lost Jerusalem and forward to the restoration of Zion as a recultivated Eden: "And they shall say, This land that was desolate is become like the garden of Eden" (Ezekiel 36). Like all great literary works, the Bible everywhere alludes to itself—sometimes indeed with more than human artfulness. This is so because it was made that way, by skillful hands in Babylon, where the literary output of the Jews undoubtedly exceeded their weeping.

Of course this view does not exclude the fact that the Hebrew redactors in Babylonia were working with texts that were alredy ancient, nor does it exclude the likelihood that the redactors believed these materials to be divinely influenced, if not divinely composed. They may very well have accepted the Five Books of Moses as revelation, but this did not stop them from supplying emphasis and perspective. Indeed it seems that the Bible we have contains texts that were as much as a thousand years old at the time of the Babylonian exile, yet we see the old texts through the redactors' concerns.

Consider this passage, in which Moses predicts the future history of Zion; from Sinai he foresees the time of Joshua's conquest of Canaan, the later time of the early kings, and, by implication, the still later time of lapsed kings, whose failure to heed Moses's warnings would send the Hebrews into exile:

> When thou art come unto the land which the Lord thy God giveth thee, and shalt possess it, and shalt dwell therein, and shalt say, I will set a king over me, like as all the nations that are about me; Thou shalt in any wise set him king over thee, whom the Lord thy God shall choose: . . . But he shall not multiply horses to himself . . . neither shall he multiply wives to himself, that his heart turn not away: neither shall he greatly multiply to himself silver and gold. And it shall be that he shall write him a copy of this law in a book . . . and he shall read therein all the days of his life: that he may learn to fear the Lord his God, to the end that he may prolong his days in his kingdom. (Deuteronomy 17)

The redactors made Moses agree with Samuel's warnings, some two centuries later, that the Hebrews would not get a king "whom the Lord thy God shall choose" but one quite different: "He will take your menservants, and your maidservants, and your goodliest young men, and your asses, and put them to his work" (1 Samuel 8). And Moses's warnings are made to evoke the future outcome—known to those in Babylonia—that Israel's kings would not in fact spend "all the days" of their lives reading the Law but would instead provoke the exile, from which return to Zion was nevertheless possible, if the original Hebrew judgment could be reconstituted:

> Thy princes are rebellious, and companions of thieves: every one loveth gifts, and followeth after rewards: they judge not the fatherless, neither doth the cause of the widow come unto them. Therefore saith the Lord, the Lord of hosts, the mighty One of Israel, Ah, I will ease me of mine adversaries, and avenge me of mine enemies: And I will turn my hand upon thee, and purely purge away thy dross, and take away all thy tin: And I will restore thy judges as at the first, and thy counsellors as at the beginning: afterward thou shalt be called, The city of righteousness, the faithful city. Zion shall be redeemed with judgment. (Isaiah1)

I attend to the literary placement of the arc that connects Moses and Samuel and Isaiah—and other actors in the story of Zion from its inception in the mind of Abraham to its redemption as imagined in the poetry of Ezekiel and in the stories of still later poets. I greatly admire Robert Alter's *The Art of Biblical Narrative* (Basic Books, 1981). But rereading Alter's impressive book now, I see how far we still are from appreciating the Hebrew synthesis, which demonstrates that a national civilization and its literary culture can in fact be one. "I do not think," writes Alter, atypically missing the mark,

> that every nuance of characterization and every turning of the plot in these stories can be justified in either moral-theological or national-historical terms. Perhaps this is the ultimate difference between any hermeneutic approach to the Bible and the literary approach that I am proposing: in the literary perspective there is a latitude for the exercise of pleasurable invention for its own sake. (p. 46)

In my view, the Bible both adopts Zionism as its overarching theme and engages in infinitely varied play, which rarely departs from the biblical writers' grasp of the national picture. There is no reason to brand criticism along national lines as ugly national-historical hermeneutics. In fact, the biblical fusion of nationalism and literacy is part of the air all educated peoples of the West have breathed for two millenia, perhaps once not discussed because so thoroughly taken for granted; perhaps now not taken for granted because we have forgotten that the fusion is possible.

During fourteen hundred years in the Land, monotheistic culture grew so rooted that not even two thousand years of subsequent Diaspora could uproot the culture of Israel from the Land of Israel. Zion is the name David gave to the fusion between the Land and the culture of the Land; it is the name used by Israel's prophets to inspire a return to that synthesis. Zionism is thus the use of the Land of Israel to represent the civilization of Israel. Had Zionism not been complete and intellectually satisfying in ancient times, and had the ancient Hebrews not bequeathed the idea, modern Israel would never have reemerged, no matter what later Zionists thought or did. In any case, Zionism is not a modern invention, nor is it an idea still trying to define itself, as some of Israel's friends and enemies imagine. Notions about Israel becoming a nonspecific moral beacon to the world and venomous barbs equating Zionism and racism both fail to recognize the introspective culture that laid the foundations on which enlightened nations now use land to build civilizations rather than empires.

The term *Zionism* smacks of modern ideologies, hardly the stuff of the Bible, whose poetic language is too rich to tolerate the dry abstraction of any "ism." Yet Zionism was alive in ancient Israel and portrayed by the old Hebrew writers, although without use of the term. In the Bible we find no word for messianism either, and no term for materialism or imperialism, though these conditions were recognized and presented directly. In the Book of Esther, for example, the materialism and imperialism of Ahasuerus are graphically rendered, while messianism hovers closely over the surface of this tale of national salvation. Though the term *Zionism* may seem at first a somewhat shocking anachronism thrown back on the Bible, it accurately summarizes the intellectual relationship between Zion and the civilization it signified.

The Bible's self-conscious development of Zionism as a literary and national theme has not won the exposition it deserves. Martin Buber recognized that a "unique relationship between a people and a land" arose in ancient Israel, and he saw the grandeur of naming that "national concept" not after the people themselves or their country, but after a real and idealized mountain that is at once David's fortress and the repository for the poetry that makes life worth living. But Buber's *On Zion* does not focus on ancient Zionism, following instead its subtitle, *The History of an Idea*, into centuries less rigorously poetic and more mystical. This obscures the initial Hebrew achievement, the invention of the very idea of a "national concept."

Other Jewish historians have also refrained from detailed analysis of the ancient Hebrew invention of using Land to represent culture. The great Salo Baron, writing in 1937 in the introduction to the first edition of his monumental *Social and Religious History of the Jews*, appreciated this invention and its modern implications:

> It has come to pass that, through a perverse irony of history, the Jewish nationality, the first nationality (in the modern ethnic rather than political sense) to appear on the historical scene, was long denied the right to be classified as a national entity altogether. That this happened in the period of modern nationalism, at a time when, one might say, the ancient Jewish conception of nationality was finally accepted by the world at large, makes this paradox even more poignant. (Vol. 1, 28)

Baron was so fearful of nationalist movements afoot in Europe and among Jews themselves that he downplayed this idea of "the first nationality." The ancient Hebrews saw nationalism and religion as one, but Baron chose not to explore this synthesis, fearing that modern Zionism and "secular nationalism," as interpreted by his contemporaries, "would divorce the Jewish people from its religion."

Even if we put Baron's fears aside and look back at the Hebrew synthesis of literacy and nationalism, three bright distractions blind us to the idea of ancient Zionism. Herzl's modern Zionism, the romantic and messianic Zionism of the centuries before Herzl, and the legal culture of the *Talmud* obscure the Hebrews' ancient achievement. The word *Zion* is ancient, but almost nobody now thinks of Zionism as anything but what Herzl (or his detractors) said it was. A. B. Yehoshua, for instance, in a now somewhat dated defense of Zionism, reveals how even a supple mind may neglect Zionism's deepest roots in favor of Herzl:

> The word "Zionism" has become a dirty word in New Left and other progressive circles. There are of course justifiable reasons for the opposition

to many manifestations of Zionism, to certain mystical undertones and its various expansionsist trends. We should therefore go back to the pure notion of Zionism, stripping it of the coverings and additions it has accumulated over the years. We should restore to the term its meaning of returning to origins. ("The New Left and Zionism," in *Who is Left? Zionism Answers Back*, The Zionist Library, Jerusalem, 1971)

But what Yehoshua has in mind as "origins" is "the context of the Jewish problem as it appeared in its severest form towards the end of the nineteenth century." This misses, I think, a true understanding of Zionism and undercuts the defense Yehoshua means to offer. Actually, Zionism needs less a defense than a clear exposition of the original article. Biblical Zionism lights Herzl's torch, whose lesser light, standing in the foreground, outshines the brighter beam.

Behind Herzl shines the lamp of romanitic and messianic Zionism, which was the culture of Jews in the great Diaspora, of those who suffered through centuries of exile in hostile Christian Europe and in the unreliable Islamic empire. Into their daily liturgy, these Jews incorporated a ritualized longing to return to Zion, but as they struggled for subsistence in Spain, North Africa, Yemen, and Eastern Europe they never believed they or their descendants would see Israel rise again— that is, not until the Messiah came. This longing for their homeland produced a culture and a poetry of great beauty and power, but the poetry was mystical and the Land that was its subject metaphysical, very different from the Israel of ancient Zionism, which offered an achievable and achieved reality. The culture of landless longing, founded on unrealistic expectations, also stands closer to us than does the Bible, so its dimmer light joins that of Herzl to obscure the original brilliance.

For all the poignancy of the prayer for Zion's restoration that is part of the Jewish grace after meals—recited after *every* Jewish meal for centuries—for all the lyricism of Israel ben Moses Najara, a sixteenth-century rabbi and poet whose hymns are traditionally sung at the Sabbath table to this day, the Zionism of the prayer book and of the medieval poets was not rooted in a possessed and possessable Land. Even though Rabbi Najara wrote in Safed and died as the rabbi of Gaza, these two cities were then in the Ottoman empire and Zion was in another world. "Turn to thy city, Zion's sacred shrine!/On yon fair mount again let beauty shine/There happy throngs their voices shall combine,/There present joy all former ill shall ban!" Thus sang Rabbi Najara in "Yah Ribbon" and thus sang the Jews in their dispersion, but the language was archaic and Aramaic, and the "fair mount" was otherworldly, not the actual city of Jerusalem where Hebrew was once spoken and would be again in a future remote to Rabbi Najara. The actual Jerusalem of the song was still crumbling in the Judean hills, some forty miles from Gaza, in Rabbi Najara's time, but it might as well have been nowhere.

"No joy in sunny Spain mine eyes can ever see,/For Zion, desolate, alone hath charms for me," sang Judah Halevi in *Zionides*, written in early twelfth-century Spain, but the great Hebraicist and philosopher had only a foggy notion of the real place. He died in Alexandria on his way to the Promised Land, having undertaken an ill-conceived journey to Zion as an old man in the midst of the Second Crusade. This kind of dreamy Zionism continued up to the present century. Shaul Tchernichovsky, a practicing physician who settled in hardscrabble Palestine in 1931, repudiated mystical Judaism, yet even he could write the poem "They Say There Is a Land," which contains these lines (perhaps meant ironically): "A land where is fulfilled/All a man can hope." Undoubtedly he, too, had sung "Yah Ribbon" many a time. Tchernichovsky himself rejected the spiritual Zionism of "Yah Ribbon" as a corruption of the Zionism of the original conquerors of Canaan, but like all thoughtful Jews he found it hard to shake the dreams of centuries. I try to turn aside the distorting light of those dreams and recapture the world view of the original conquerors.

And as we look beyond Herzl and beyond Judah Halevi, further back toward the period of the Bible, we encounter the lamp of rabbinic Judaism as set forth in the *Talmud*. With its enlightened emphasis on law and ritual, the *Talmud* draws attention away from the Bible's poetic achievement. Since the compilation of the *Talmud*, the light of law gleams so brightly in the traditional Jewish scholar's eye that he hardly can see the older flame, from which law and national song shine as one. The fact that the Jews managed to survive with the *Talmud* but without Zion makes it even harder to see the Bible's bright union of law, literacy, and Land.

The *Talmud* is made up of two great parts, each a compilation of centuries of commentary. The first is the *Mishna,* a codification in

Hebrew of oral law derived from the Five Books of Moses; the second, the *Gemara,* is a commentary in Aramaic on the *Mishna.* The *Mishna* was completed by 200 C.E., the *Gemara* by 500 C.E. Thus the rabbis of the Talmud lived over several centuries, removed variously from the vision of the Babylonian redactors. It is an irony of history that the rabbis of the *Talmud* themselves lived in Babylonia (another, lesser *Talmud* was compiled in Jersualem over the same centuries). Their world view was so altered that the poetics of the redactors of the Bible, who preceded them by as much as a thousand years, no longer resonated in quite the original way. In fact, the rabbis of the *Talmud,* though they perfected a meticulous technique for decoding the ancient texts, were less interested in discovering literary nuance than in establishing clear guidelines for behavior. Their methodology was highly cerebral, but it was not supple or deeply imaginative. The national poetry of the Bible is thus obscured by their achievements. However essential to Jewish life the rabbis' rendition of the Law has been, one cannot get from talmudic sources an adequate appreciation of the Hebrew invention of intellectual and literary nationalism.

Consider the rabbinic interpretation of the commandment to return lost property, a law Moses deliberately sets within the context of Hebrew national culture, rooted in the Land. In Deuteronomy 16, Moses reminds the Hebrews that they must commit themselves to the Law, as this will remind them of their purpose on the Land. Both the Law and the Land go beyond practicality to serve as reminders of monotheistic civilization: "That which is altogether just shalt thou follow, that thou mayest live, and inherit the land which the Lord thy God giveth thee." In Deuteronomy 21, Moses recalls this theme, "that thy land be not defiled, which the Lord thy God giveth thee for an inheritance," and then in the very next verses gives the law of returning lost objects as an example of doing "that which is altogether just":

> Thou shalt not see thy brother's ox or his sheep go astray, and hide thyself from them: thou shalt in any case bring them again unto thy brother . . . In like manner shalt thou do with his ass; and so shalt thou do with his raiment: and with all lost things of thy brother's which he hath lost, and thou hast found.

The talmudic rabbis ignored the governing context of protecting the civilization of the Land. Their goal was practical. With commendable care, they determined what a lost article is (for example, objects of negligible value, worth less that one *prutah,* do not count), they defined "finding" (merely *seeing* the lost object counts), and they made clear what constitutes a valid identifying mark. They adopted the principle that every word of Moses must be interpreted, thus providing one root of our own literary criticism, but they did not really *read* the passage. Instead they plodded along, and thus they got bogged down. They rightfully assumed that the ox, the lamb, the ass, and the garment illustrate the range of objects that must be returned if found, but then they took off on a tangent regarding the need to ruturn even the hair clippings from a found ox's tail, which are nowhere mentioned or implied by the text. Stuck at this level of detail, the rabbis could not determine what meaning the lamb adds to the passage, let alone comment on the larger picture of preserving the inheritance of the Land. Here is an excerpt from the long and convoluted discussion, as amplified by Adin Steinsaltz (*The Talmud* [Random House, 1990], Vol. II: *Tractate Bava Metzia,* part II, pp. 97–99):

> The Torah teaches us that if the finder shears the ox's tail, he must return even those shearings to the ox's owner. In other words, the seemingly superfluous example of the ox informs us that a finder is obliged to return a lost object in the condition in which he found it. Even something as trivial as the shearings of an ox's tail cannot be withheld . . . Just as a garment is special, in that it has identifying marks and claimants, thus obliging the finder to announce it, so too must everything that has identifying marks and claimants be announced. Hence we may conclude . . . that the word "lamb" did not come to teach us about identifying marks. This concept can only be derived from the word "garment." Rather, the word "lamb" was written in the Torah to teach us something else, but unfortunately we do not know what.

In my view the poetry of the lamb and the ox links the ethical activity required to identify and return lost objects with the similarly vigorous intellectual activity required to read the Land and to grasp an abstract God. One must return easily identified objects such as a garment or an ass (the rabbis noted that a lost garment can be identified because it is handmade and unique, while an ass can be identified by its saddle), and one must also return objects whose owners are difficult to identify, be they highly valuable like an ox (usually one of

its kind on a farm) or of less value like a lamb (usually one of many
and perhaps not even immediately missed when lost). Unmarked
oxen and lambs can in fact be identified and returned if care is taken.
It is this kind of care that Moses wished to cultivate. Moses would
not be interested in the clippings of an ox's tail unless these would
help represent the culture of the Land (it is unlikely that they would),
but he was interested in the way the poetic overtones of the Law and
the abstract attributes of the Land might nourish each other in the literate mind of the monotheistic Hebrew, "that thy land be not
defiled." I try to look over the rabbis' shoulders at the civilization that
was present in Israel for two millenia before many of the talmudic
rabbis ruminated. Perhaps the rabbis assumed this civilization in their
discussions or perhaps they were already losing the old literacy; in any
case they did not pass it on to us, and in some measure they inter-
fered with its transmission.

What follows, then, is an essay on biblical Zionism, on the ancient
links between Land and culture that constitute the intellectual heritage of modern Israel. I treat the ancient Hebrews as if they all
belonged to a homogenous civilization, despite the changes during the
long period between Joshua's conquest and the razing of the Second
Temple; this is a useful fiction that the Bible itself employs. Though
the Hebrews helped invent history, the Bible treats Zionism as a literary ideal, a structure that was complete from the beginning, as in
Isaiah 66: "Who hath heard of such a thing? who hath seen such
things? Shall the earth be made to bring forth in one day? or shall a
nation be born at once? for as soon as Zion travailed, she brought
forth her children." Thus, though I keep the history of ancient Israel in
view, my aim is not the history of an idea but its structure.

I have little to say here about modern Zionism, though my argument, insofar as it succeeds, accords respect to the living civilization
whose foundations were laid by the literate inventors of ancient
Zionism. I also have little to say about other modern nationalisms,
though my argument suggests that every national culture worth our
respect, now or at any time, must develop its own poetics, offering
more than the mouthings of street ruffians. We want to know, for
example, what ideas, if any, are represented by the claims of greater
Serbia and by the outrages committed in its name. Similarly, we want
to know what specific national concept, if any, stands behind the

Palestinian Arab claim, which was long associated with hatred of the Hebrew civilization that created the idea of nationhood. If peace indeed takes hold in the Middle East, more will be needed than an Israeli recognition of the Palestine Liberation Organization and a PLO recognition of Israel. There will have to be a forthright squaring of competing national ideas, and a drawing of borders between peoples who can state and honor each other's idea of homeland. The substance of ancient Zionism provides a standard that might be matched by those who have hoped in the past to throw Zionists into the sea. Peaceful coexistence will fail if Israel's former enemies recognize no national idea, or if Jews forget their own civilization.

The value of ancient Hebrew ideas, rather than their mere longevity, constitutes the strongest part of modern Israelis' attachment to Israel. Inherited values form the basis of any thinking person's attachment to his or her national culture, assuming that one can still be, in the twentieth century, so attached. As a reminder that the Zionist graft of Land and culture flowers in the West, I have used, unless otherwise noted, the Authorized Version of the translation of King James, a weighted bough whose fruits taste of the old roots.

Chapter 1

Land and Intellect

Remember the days of old, consider the years of many generations: ask thy father, and he will shew thee; thy elders, and they will tell thee. When the Most High divided to the nations their inheritance, when he separated the sons of Adam, he set the bounds of the people according to the number of the children of Israel

—Deuteronomy 32

For, lo, the winter is past, the rain is over and gone; The flowers appear on the earth; the time of the singing of birds is come, and the voice of the turtle is heard in our land; The fig tree putteth forth her green figs, and the vines with the tender grape give a good smell.

—Song of Solomon 2

ABRAHAM IS THE INVENTOR OF INTELLECTUAL NATIONALISM. HE IS THE person who made it possible to sing of the turtledove "heard in our land," to sing of national meaning and purpose. He invented the idea of assigning cultural meaning to land, to Zion in particular, but also to any land that can be made to stand for a specific civilization. Abraham is the father of national poetry, the begetter of the psalms of David and the Song of Solomon. He is the person who made it possible *to think* about what a nation might be.

Of Abraham's origins, we know little. He grew up in the sophisticated civilization of Sumeria, in a land with science and architecture, commerce and law, mythology and poetry. The Sumerians invented cuneiform writing, the city-state, the codification of law, the potter's wheel, the art of fine measuring, which they established on a system of sixty parts, the basis for our division of the hour into sixty minutes. By the time of Abraham in the seventeenth century B.C.E. Sumeria, weakened by internecine warfare, was already slipping, but it is difficult to imagine that a young man like Abraham would think it possible to find a better place to live from a material point of view. Nor would Abraham's father, Terah, be likely to improve his lot by leaving Ur of the Chaldees, Sumeria's choicest city-state. Some of its neighbors might be more vigorous, but none were more cultivated.

Yet Terah, apparently unaware that he was motivated by God, picked up and left for Canaan, then a squalid outpost on the edge of the Mediterranean, in the no-man's-land between the great centers of Egypt and Sumeria. Terah took along his son Abraham, his daughter-in-law Sarah, and his nephew Lot. But he died on the road in Haran, a strategic place because it was at the headwaters of the Euphrates and because it was on the frontier, at the intersection of trade routes important to Sumeria's well-being—a no-place crucial to the defense of a someplace. For Terah the someplace that needed defense was Sumeria, but that was his blindness. In the Hebrew view, Haran was a step toward Canaan, which the Hebrews came to believe was a special place, worth defending. Terah missed this. He did not look forward to Canaan but backward to Sumeria.

Terah probably was not aware that he was making anything more than a physical journey. He had no knowledge that there was intellectual cause to leave Sumeria. The Bible leaves us with the impression that he thought himself driven by whim. True, he set himself the goal "to go into the land of Canaan" (Genesis 11), but he did not seem to intend this with any seriousness, appearing content to stop in Haran, where "he dwelt" until he died. Somehow Sumeria failed him, despite its enamelwork and its vast public buildings, but he would not have been able to articulate why. He certainly would not have known what God later tells Abraham: "I am the Lord that brought thee out of Ur of the Chaldees, to give thee this land to inherit it" (Genesis 15).

The Bible seems to play on the resemblance between the place called Haran and Haran the son of Terah who died in Ur. In Hebrew the names are not identical, but they are close enough to make the point that in Haran Terah came to a dead end as had his son, the Sumerian son without a future. It is doubtful that Terah had an inkling that he had taken the first steps toward a national consciousness based not on Sumeria's sumptuousness but on a mind-enlarging idea. This realization was left for Abraham, the son who became a patriarch. Abraham could grasp the reason for forsaking the palaces of Sumeria, guarded as they were by golden lions without spirit.

The rabbis tell us that Terah was an idolator in the manner of Ur of the Chaldees but that Abraham saw through his father's empty spiritual life. We are told that Abraham smashed the idols in Terah's idol-making shop, then blamed the wreckage on the figures themselves, answering his father's scepticism about the idols' power to destroy themselves with the observation that since idols cannot create or destroy they should not be worshipped.

But this charming rabbinic tale is not in the Bible. The Bible offers us instead a better story, one not so smug about Abraham's brilliance, yet showing us much more of his subtlety. After Terah dies in Haran, having never learned why God transported him there, Abraham rises to a vision, showing us an astonishing mind far superior to that of a mere iconoclast:

> Now the Lord had said unto Abram, Get thee out of thy country, and from thy kindred, and from thy father's house, unto a land that I will shew thee: And I will make of thee a great nation, and I will bless thee, and make thy name great; and thou shalt be a blessing: And I will bless them that bless thee, and curse him that curseth thee: and in thee shall all families of the earth be blessed. So Abram departed, as the Lord had spoken unto him . . .

into the land of Canaan. . . . And the Canaanite was then in the land. And the Lord appeared unto Abram, and said, Unto thy seed will I give this land: and there he builded an altar unto the Lord . . . and called upon the name of the Lord. And Abram journeyed, going on still toward the south. And there was a famine in the land: and Abram went down into Egypt to sojourn there; for the famine was grievous in the land. (Genesis 12)

God tells Abraham to leave his homeland, his kindred, and his father's house, as if he had not yet gone anywhere, even though he has gotten as far as Haran. But in a sense Abraham really has not gone anywhere, since Haran itself is nowhere. It's just a place with no idea to distinguish it.

This passage, in which the invention of intellectual Zionism is first announced, is careful to characterize the ancient Hebrew attachment to the Land as primarily cerebral. In fact, at the beginning of Zionism, there is hardly a land there at all, just an idea. No attempt is made to present the Promised Land as a physical location rivaling the charms of Sumeria. God does not even mention the name of the place he means Abraham to inherit, nor is the homeland of Sumeria evoked to measure the physical loss. This moment of Abraham's realization of the universal God is kept on a higher plane. Even as Abraham arrives in the Land, the redactors' emphasis falls on Abraham's invention of a double idea, not on the acquisition of land. Abraham's dawning awareness that there can be no more than one Creator of the universe immediately begets a second idea, that it would be wise to root the monotheistic abstraction in a special soil. It is this double idea, much richer than the mere impulse to smash idols or acquire farmland, that drives Abraham from his idol-worshiping family on an intellectual pilgrimage to the Land of Canaan.

At first, the place is not much good for anything but intellect. Abraham does not know where he's going as he sets out to the unnamed place God will show him, and in the beginning he does not spend very much time there after he arrives. As soon as he has built an altar to his Idea, to the appearance of the Lord in his mind's eye, to the promise of an emblematic nation-to-be, he moves on to a more practical place, to Egypt. Thus the ancient Hebrew redactors make clear at the outset that the Land was more a cornerstone of Abraham's intellectual life than the object of a claim. Initially, Abraham goes on to

Egypt without making any claim to physical land. Egypt, like Sumeria, had food, while the Land was food for thought.

The Bible is careful to show us Abraham's mind. Only selected incidents in Abraham's life earned a record, and all of these reveal intellectual qualities of far greater interest than his unrecorded exploits as an idol-smasher. Through Abraham we are shown the idealized national mind of Hebrew civilization.

The canonizers of the Books of Moses, working a thousand years after the death of Abraham, were trained in the tradition of David's court to seek an exquisite compactness. Though David himself had been dead five hundred years, the seminaries and colleges he founded had preserved and transmitted the national literary heritage, which was carried into exile in Babylonia—the Hebrews having been flung back to the place that Abraham fled. David's progeny now distilled the intellectual history of the ancient Hebrews into the legends of Abraham as seen from the perspective of the exile. Looking backward from Babylonia, then, backward from Abraham's birthplace as it flourished a thousand years later under a new name, backward from a new empire at the mouth of the Tigris and Euphrates, we look on the stories of Abraham's intellectual achievement.

God's covenant with Abraham won an obvious place in the redactors' canon, since it captures the moment in which monotheism and intellectual nationalism were invented simultaneously. The binding of Isaac, set in a deceptively simple fable, won a telling for its exploration of the persistent will to human sacrifice and for the distinction it makes between a thoughtful relationship with God and blind obedience. The search for an appropriate bride for Isaac emphasized the need to transmit Abraham's unprecedented vision. The editors chose carefullly.

One story of Abraham's early years in the Land of Canaan stands out for its seeming triviality. Yet this story may tell us most about Abraham's mind and the Hebrew ideal it manifested. The story records a quarrel and a parting. From its apparent banality there shines the fire of ancient Hebrew culture, an intellectual and literary *attitude*, applied to monotheism and to nationalism alike:

> And there was a strife between the herdmen of Abram's cattle and the
> herdmen of Lot's cattle: and the Canaanite and the Perizzite dwelled then

in the land. And Abram said unto Lot, Let there be no strife, I pray thee, between my herdmen and thy herdmen; for we be brethren. Is not the whole land before thee? separate thyself, I pray thee, from me: if thou will take the left hand, then I will go to the right; or if thou depart to the right hand, then I will go to the left. And Lot lifted up his eyes, and beheld all the plain of Jordan, that it was well watered every where, before the Lord destroyed Sodom and Gomorrah, even as the garden of the Lord, like the land of Egypt, as thou comest unto Zoar. Then Lot chose him all the plain of Jordan; and Lot journeyed east: and they separated themselves the one from the other. . . . And the Lord said unto Abram, after that Lot was separated from him, Lift up now thine eyes, and look from the place where thou art northward, and southward, and eastward, and westward: For all the land which thou seest, to thee will I give it, and to thy seed for ever. (Genesis 13)

This passage probably condenses all that one need know about ancient Zionism. The reading of the story entails an unpacking of ideas.

Perhaps one should begin with Abraham's disingenuousness. We have seen that Abraham has already been promised the *entire* land, and that promise is repeated here. His offer to Lot to choose the left or right hand and leave him the other affects a magnanimity that Lot is meant to appreciate and the reader to penetrate. In fact, Abraham does not care which way his nephew goes, since he expects to be master everywhere in Canaan. He does not share this view with Lot because that would defeat the momentary purpose of making peace, but the literary editors expected their readers to note that there is more to Abraham's generosity than meets Lot's eye.

Abraham's ability to play a role, even to deceive, is linked to the first requirement of monotheism. Only an inventive mind, an imagination able to conceive ideas previously unthought, can grasp the concept of a single Creator who has no more representation in His creation than does a potter in his pot. A more flagrant falsehood is recorded in the chapter preceding our passage in the story of Abraham's trip to Egypt, where he presented Sarah as his sister to prevent being killed by a Pharoah who lusted after his beautiful wife. This lie, actually recorded *twice* in two different moments of Abraham's sparse history, was thought so central to the patriarchal character that it was also attributed to Isaac in a third telling (Genesis 20 and 26).

A mere teller of lies, of course, has no value. The liar must be encouraged, allowed a certain play to develop his fabrications into something nobler. The inventive mind is necessary to the monotheist, who cannot exist if he cannot fasten the mind's eye on the unseen. And, indeed, ancient Hebrew culture took as its chief purpose the elevation of imagination, through poetry, history, and law, through teaching the contents of the Bible. One begins with a mind able to prevaricate, a capacity for cleverness, like the playacting of Jacob, who puts on the clothes of his brother Esau to steal the firstborn's blessing from the dying Isaac (we will consider this story from Genesis 27 later). Then the intellectual task is to warn against mere duplicity by telling the story of Simeon and Levi, who used one aspect of the covenant as a mere trick to get the residents of Shechem to hobble themselves with circumcision on the eve of a surprise attack on them (Genesis 34; we will return to this story, too). Finally, the object is to raise the gift of ruse to the level of prophetic vision.

By easing Lot out of his hair Abraham reveals not only a wily disingenuousness but a higher, more literary, understanding of the function of the Land. Where Lot sees land as pastures, more or less fit for grazing, Abraham sees the Land as a marker of his spiritual and intellectual life. He is indifferent as to which pasture Lot leaves him not only because he will eventually acquire all but also because he understands that the purpose of his being in Canaan is to rise above rich grass and to emblemize a rich relationship. He knows what his descendants will learn all too painfully, that if one wants good pasture the best place is "the land of Egypt, as thou comest unto Zoar," the land of materialism and, ultimately, of physical and intellectual slavery. If one wants an intellectual life one must lift up one's eyes and see the covenant, worth more than the cow pens of Lot's vision.

Abraham sees the Land as whole and as representational. For him, geography is symbolic, intellectual, sublime. Lot, whose name means "enclosed," limits himself to the lowlands—to the "plain of Jordan"—to which he journeys, taking a symbolically downward course to Sodom from the promontory on which the two cousins overlook the land, the one with eyes and the other with the mind's eye. In fact, at this moment, Abraham is at once the only person on earth who holds in his mind the monotheistic vision and the only person in Canaan who knows he is in one Land, whole and inseparable despite its gradations of pasture, a Land which can be made to stand for an idea. The reference in our passage to "the Canaanite and the Perizzite" is shorthand for the Bible's usual listing of all the tribes ("the Amorite, and the Canaanite, and the Hittite, and the Perizzite, and the Hivite, and the Jebusite," as well as others) who lived in the area without any awareness that the lands they variously occupied could coalesce in somebody's imagination as a single place. The editors march the *other* tribes into this passage to join Lot in providing contrast with Abraham, whose mind is capable of seeing a single Land and a single God, making the one represent the other.

The capacity to see many adjacent places as one place and the poetry to make that one place nourish and represent an entire culture constitute the basis of intellectual nationalism. It took Europe two thousand years to achieve this fusion of place and idea, for example to make a union out of Calais and Marseilles and make that union represent French culture. Along the way, there was great confusion; either French culture grew while French national unity fell into battles between local duchies, or Napoleonic patriotism degenerated into a bullying of other cultures. For Abraham, the idea that a union of lands could be made to represent a specific way of being was born whole and mature in a single, dazzling instant.

Abraham's idea is antiliteralist and explicitly anti-imperialist. Since the Land's function is to represent monotheism, there is no need for it to be particularly large. It must be large enough to be a self-sustaining nation, large enough to notice that its intellectual lapses led to disintegration into the old tribal areas, but not an empire. Our passage continues to delineate a land that—though it radiates large metaphorical meanings to the lifted eye—is limited to the magnitude of territory encompassed by ocular vision: "Arise, walk through the land in the length of it and in the breadth of it; for I will give it unto thee" (Genesis 13).

From the beginning, Abraham foresaw a distinct nation with defined and confined borders. The Land was fixed, no bigger than what was walkable; there would never be an empire. Empires are built by great but obtuse warlords, Ozymandiases for whom land stands only for land and for whom glory is exactly proportional to the size of conquered territory. In the ancient world, empires waxed and waned without anyone realizing that conquest can be sated if land is made to represent more than the carnage of the last battle.*

Once the Hebrews grasped the intellectual use of land, they understood the idea of empire as a destroyer of intellect, empire's natural enemy. Empires, gobbling all, undermine the sharp distinctions that intellectuals must make, dimming the view especially of monotheists, who must draw their lines carefully to exclude idol worship. The emphasis in our passage on Abraham's separating himself from Lot points up the large obligation felt by ancient Hebrews to separate themselves from other people, both as an exercise in making distinctions and as a way of keeping their idea separate from the idolatry of others. The former inhabitants of the Land were to be expelled, and the Hebrews were not to reach out for new lands with new idolators; to do so was to practice a double idolatry. Conquest both treats land as if it were itself an idol and requires a willful mingling with foreign idolators:

---

*The boundaries of the Land, "from the river of Egypt unto the great river" (Genesis 15), are ambiguous in the Bible, deliberately so. The "river of Egypt" is certainly not the Nile and the "great river," if it is the Euphrates as given in translation, can refer only to headwaters in what is now Syria, not the the waterway of ancient Babylonia. Both Egypt and Babylonia are *definitively* not in the Land. Perhaps other rivers are meant (cf. Exodus 23). The poets of ancient Israel placed their emphasis on the significance of a bordered Land, not on the exact location of the borders. Though the boundaries of ancient Israel changed, the idea that Israel was to be small, bordered, and emblematic never changed.

In Moses's dying song, the Land's extent was to be fixed "according to the number of the children of Israel" (Deuteronomy 32). What number is that? Rashi, the great exegete of eleventh-century France, thought the Land's size met the needs of the seventy descendants of Jacob numbered in Genesis 46. But Moses implies that the Land would *change* in size (as it did) according to the number of Hebrews who could hold the monotheistic vision; he immediately links the idea that the Land is the Hebrews' inheritance with the idea that the Hebrews are God's inheritance: "For the Lord's portion is his people." Presumably, if no Hebrew saw what Abraham saw, the Hebrews would have no Land and the Lord saw no portion. The integrity of the Land's borders depended on intellectual integrity. Eventually, tribes dwindled in numbers and disappeared, and then the whole Land was lost. "The whole head is sick," diagnosed Isaiah, "Your land, strangers devour it in your presence" (Isaiah 1).

But I have said unto you, Ye shall inherit their land, and I will give it unto you to possess it, a land that floweth with milk and honey: I am the Lord, your God, which have separated you from other people. (Leviticus 20)

And I will set thy bounds from the Red sea even unto the sea of the Philistines, and from the desert unto the river: for I will deliver the inhabitants of the land into your hand; and thou shalt drive them out before thee. Thou shalt make no covenant with them, nor with their gods. They shall not dwell in thy land, lest they make thee sin against me: for if thou serve their gods, it will surely be a snare unto thee. (Exodus 23)

. . . the children of Esau, which dwell in Seir . . . shall be afraid of you: take ye good heed unto yourselves therefore: Meddle not with them; for I will not give you of their land, no, not so much as a foot breadth; because I have given mount Seir unto Esau for a possession. . . . And when thou comest nigh over against the children of Ammon, distress them not, nor meddle with them: for I will not give thee of the land of the children of Ammon any possession; because I have given it unto the children of Lot for a possession. (Deuteronomy 2)

Allowing the original inhabitants to continue in the Land and absorbing idolatrous neighbors ensnares the mind. The same imagination required to hold an invisible God in mind could invent river nymphs as easily. Imagination had to be cultivated because monotheism could not exist without it, but it also had to have borders, its fantasies fenced. Separating oneself from other people was part of the complex culture of distinction making, which was practiced at every turn to assure the differentiation of monotheism from idolatry. The Hebrews made intellect muscular, made it capable of monotheism, by distinguishing clean from unclean food, weekday from Sabbath, legal guilt from innocence, our Land from *not ours*. This culture of discernment was not to be sacrificed for the blur and cheap thrill of conquest, not even at the expense of the children of Lot and Esau, who were thought of as obtuse and not respectable. Those who malign modern Zionists with the charge of empire building might notice that in almost four thousand years, while Assyria, Babylonia, Greece, Rome, Turkey, Britain, and Russia won or lost vast empires, while Alexander penetrated to the banks of the Ganges, while Islam waved its sword over the Danube and Napoleon waved the tricolor on the Nile, while the

United States Navy landed in the Philippines, Israel yearned for no land beyond a narrow strip on a corner of the Mediterranean. Having swallowed much land only to suffer the bloated ennui of Suleiman the Magnificent and the incrassation of Pizarro, Christendom and Islam accuse little Israel of empty conquest.

For the ancient Hebrews, then, the story of Abraham's separation from Lot is a complex literary event that helps define ancient Zionism. Abraham's achievement is primarily intellectual and literary and recognized as such by his intellectual successors, who cast the story of God's covenant with Abraham in literary form. For neither Abraham nor his successors did the Land function primarily as a "Holy Land"— the phrase is never mentioned in the Bible—but rather as a rich literary symbol, an occasion for thought and for intellectual ritual, not for pietism or salvationism. For the ancient Hebrews, God was holy, the Sabbath was holy, but the Land was a signifier. Like a skullcap, the Land signaled an attitude. Its function was to give the intellectual life—on which monotheism depends—a local habitation, to provide it an objective correlative. In ancient Hebrew culture, the Land is an invention imposed on nature, representing monotheism and the imagination capable of its formulation; as a carefully distinguished place, it represents the distinction making required to exorcise idolatry; as the subject of poetry, it represents the literary culture that established Israel as part of the foundation of Western culture.

Similarly, the Land *represented* holiness while Egypt *had* holiness, that is conventional holiness—magicians, golden calves, a divine river, all-powerful pharaohs. The bleak Land was chosen because it stood for holiness, which was thought to reside outside the creation. One encounters so many references to the Holy Land it seems hardly possible that Abraham would object to the term; but he would have, even given these passages from the prophets themselves, who reimagine the lost Zion that Abraham invented and David named:

> Sing and rejoice, O daughter of Zion: for, lo, I come, and I will dwell in the midst of thee, saith the Lord. . . . And the Lord shall inherit Judah his portion in the holy land, and shall choose Jerusalem again. (Zechariah, 2)

> And it shall come to pass in that day, that the great trumpet shall be blown, and they shall come which were ready to perish in the land of Assyria, and

the outcasts in the land of Egypt, and shall worship the Lord in the holy mount at Jerusalem. (Isaiah 27)

The translations obscure the Hebrew emphasis. In the Hebrew the "land" is not holy, nor is the "mount"; rather, Zechariah speaks of "the land of the Holy One" and Isaiah of "the mount of the Holy One" (the grammar of the construction is clear). Nor is Zechariah or Isaiah imagining a God who would literally "dwell in the midst of thee." Both foresee a time when the Hebrew people will again use the Land in general and Mount Zion in particular as reminders of Abraham's covenant with the Creator. In so doing they will have brought God back into their midst cerebrally, following the lead of Abraham, who journeyed to a place that was not in itself holy.

In fact, the Bible goes out of its way to mock those who think the Land literally holy. In 2 Kings 5, Naaman, "captain of the host of the king of Syria," is plagued by leprosy. Consulting the Hebrew prophet Elisha, he is instructed to bathe seven times in the Jordan. Indignantly he follows the prescription, having expected more dazzling magic. If bathing is all that is needed, surely river baths in swift Syrian currents would provide a better treatment than wallowing in the sluggish and muddy Jordan River. Amazingly, Naaman is cured. The practical captain, realizing that he may have been mistaken about the Syrian gods and the Syrian rivers, now embraces the God of Israel. After Elisha refuses his gift of thanks, Naaman then requests a further favor for himself: "Shall there not then, I pray thee, be given to thy servant two mules' burden of earth: for thy servant will henceforth offer neither burnt-offering nor sacrifice unto other gods, but unto the Lord." Naaman, a good but overly literal man, like many a Jew and non-Jew who follow him, thinks he cannot worship the Hebrew Lord without two mules' load of holy dirt on which to kneel. This silliness—in a man sophisticated enough to disclaim his forced bowings to false gods in the future (Naaman's faked groveling to the Syrian god Rimmon became proverbial)—can only be waved away by Elisha, who merely wishes him, "Go in peace." Elisha knows that either you grasp *the* idea or you do not; and if you do not, you take the dirt-laden mules. The Land, in its rich cultural context, signifies the holiness of the Creator, but there is no holiness in the dirt.

The Hebrews, of course, would not have thought it possible to function without the earth at all. They meant not to deny the need for land but to elevate the function of the Land. They created a culture in which laws and rituals had representational power. Their chief and central symbol was the Land, and they could not regard it as dispensable. They thought the Land should be small, but they were convinced it had to exist, to remind them of their God and their values. They were poets who believed there was no such thing as poetry without a concrete poem.

Against my argument that the Hebrews did not regard dirt as itself holy, one might point to the zealous attachment of many modern Jews to the fields of Judea and Samaria, the so-called territories of the West Bank. This is a complicated issue, one which cannot be satisfied here. However, let me observe that the Jewish part of the conflict arises not from a fanatical snatching at dirt, but from the old idea of Zion—that the particular and small Land of Israel, of which Judea and Samaria happen to be the tiny heart, represents the civilization of Israel, just as France represents French civilization. The Arab part of the conflict arises from the Arab seizure twelve hundred years ago of this very Land of Israel, of the Temple Mount, of Mount Zion, of Judea, thus raising the question of whether fanaticism might more likely arise from attachment to another people's lands than to one's own Land.

Anton Shammas is an Israeli Arab and writer who believes Israel belongs to the Arabs. He reminds us in the *New York Times Magazine* of December 26, 1993 that the Arab attachment to Jerusalem is exactly parallel to the Arab attachment to Granada. Both cities are trophies whose return to nations once conquered by Islam is to be mourned. Shammas believes that Israel is "the map of Palestine that Zionism drew a hundred years ago." He must believe something similar about Spain:

> The fall of Granada has always marked for the Arabs the last glimmer of their golden centuries, an everlasting tombstone for their irretrievable cultural defeat. Mourning over the loss of Granada, however, has always been almost metaphorical for them, because it happened so far away from the Mashriq, the East, far from the traditional center of Islamic civilization. . . . The map of Palestine, in contrast, was a branding iron that scorched the actual image of the lost paradise, from the Jordan to the sea,

onto the memories of all Arabs. . . . Palestine, like the other paradise that the Arabs lost, will become a mapless country.

Shammas writes with no regard for what Jews or Spaniards might think, no awareness that Granada and Jerusalem have other functions than the searing of Arab memory. If Arabs do not dominate Palestine, it becomes in his view a "mapless country." Presumably, if Arabs regain their "lost paradise" in Palestine it will be mapped, not because it represents a specific Palestinian idea on the model of Spain or Israel but because it is part of the Arab empire, whose "traditional center" in Mecca and Medina maintains the antediluvian notion that national greatness depends on maintaining distant conquests. That Arabs long to regain hegemony over Granada and Jerusalem itself raises the question of fanaticism, while the Jewish people's ancient rooting into the Land of Israel—and nowhere else—may not be fanatical at all. Jews root into Judea as the Spanish root into Spain; Jews do not mourn their former houses in Granada or their former houses in Baghdad. That kind of longing, and that kind of fanaticism, belongs to Arab ideologues like Anton Shammas.

I am not saying that Judea and Samaria are indispensable to modern Israel, but it should not be hard to see why some Jews reasonably regard them as such, especially when they look at the countervailing claims of thinkers like Shammas. However, since the children of Abraham are already committed to a small Israel, since they are enjoined not to take alien populations into their midst, and since they are committed to drawing a border between themselves and surrounding peoples, it is probably true that the vast majority of Jews inside and outside Israel would accept a border placing large parts of Judea and Samaria in Arab hands in exchange for a true peace. This would have to include Arab recognition of the ancient idea of Zion, with the corollary that Jerusalem is in Israel as Granada is in Spain and Mecca is in Arabia. The power of this recognition lies in its making possible the flowering of intellectual nationalism in Arab nations and in the Jewish nation, where the idea of using land to represent an idea began.

Chapter 2

Land and Literacy

The Blessing can be realized only in Canaan; indeed, in one sense the Blessing is Canaan. All of the Blessing is equivocal. . . . Yahweh, at Sinai and later in the Wilderness, is concerned to fix boundaries between himself and the Israelites, lest they trespass and be destroyed by him. Without boundaries separating them from the incommensurate they cannot survive. Yet Yahweh's Blessing intends to award a temporal freedom from the bounded. Can the Adamic dust sustain the Blessing?

—Harold Bloom, *The Book of J*

ABRAHAM GOES TO CANAAN IN GOOD FAITH, STANDS IN THIS UNSEEMLY gutter between two great material civilizations, and reads from the scantily bearing valleys the great idea of monotheism. There is no food to eat, but he stays as long as he can. After feeding himself and Sarah in Egypt, Abraham returns to Canaan as soon as he can, again willing to live on the yield of lean fields because these are the lands chosen by God to represent the idea of God. He is the only person in the world capable of such an undertaking. God promises him that he will be rich, but in the early going he is driven only by his idea.

Abraham keeps his end of the bargain. But for ten years on the Land he and Sarah are barren. Moreover, he is distracted from the terms of the covenant, fighting wars with Amraphel and other kings, as noted in the seemingly interpolated chronicles of Genesis 14, whose narration forces the high-minded covenant into the mess of history. When he is eighty-five, Abraham desperately appoints his steward Eliezer as heir, but God repeats, reassuringly, "Unto thy seed have I given this land." When he is eighty-six, Abraham is presented with Ishmael, his son by Hagar, Sarah's maidservant. But this is still not the promised heir, though Abraham is again reassured: "He that shall come forth out of thine own bowels shall be thine heir. . . . Look now toward heaven, and tell the stars, if thou be able to number them: . . . So shall thy seed be."

Still, the repeated promise of a future produces no heir, and the story of the covenant becomes equivocal, ambiguous as poetry, which in fact it is. There is nothing in the present for Abraham but ambiguous poetry. Furthermore, he is told of an amendment to the covenant that will mar his children's future in a way that he has not bargained for, having accepted God's seemingly straightforward promise. Abraham learns that his children will only inherit the Land after serving as slaves in Egypt for four hundred years! Of course this complicates the way we read the covenant, which is what the redactors intend; they mean to anatomize the difficulty of mastering a culture that places literacy at its center. Reading the Land is no simple business.

Noting that "to me thou hast given no seed," Abraham begins to wonder what God means by this delayed delivery of heirs to the Land: "Whereby shall I know that I shall inherit it?" The answer comes in a poetic ritual and in an eerie dream:

39

And [God] said unto him, Take me an heifer of three years old, and a she goat of three years old, and a ram of three years old, and a turtle-dove, and a young pigeon. And he took unto him all these and divided them in the midst, and laid each piece one against another: but the birds divided he not. And when the fowls came down upon the carcasses, Abram drove them away. And when the sun was going down, a deep sleep fell upon Abram; and lo, an horror of great darkness fell upon him. And he said unto Abram, Know for a surety that thy seed shall be a stranger in a land that is not theirs, and shall serve them; and they shall afflict them four hundred years. And also that nation, whom they shall serve, will I judge: and afterward shall they come out with great substance. (Genesis 15)

Abraham dreams history, and he dreams poetry, two parts of a complex whole for the Hebrews. The ravens that are chased away clearly represent the obstacles to the fulfillment of the covenant, which was born of an instant but will ripen only with the development of a national poetics and a people who can understand the language of poetry and ritual, even the language of dreams.

The rabbis in the period of the *Talmud* and afterward, already distant from ancient Israel's culture of poetry, found the meaning of Abraham's ritual and the "horror" of his dream difficult to understand. They were particularly puzzled by the ritual and the dream as an answer to Abraham's reasonable request for a sign that he would inherit the Land. And the rabbis thought God's message that Abraham's descendants would be slaves after the time of Joseph a peculiar response to a man who is asking for reassurance about his direct heirs, the still unknown Isaac and Jacob. The whole passage seems bizarre, a divine puzzle, with the ritual, dream, and puzzle making a muddle of what should have been a clear bargain. In the ancient world, the division of pottery shards or carcasses was a common and straightforward sign of a deal made, but in this passage a deal seems to be unmade, or at least frustrated and radically complicated.

And that, I think, is the Hebrews' idea of poetry, close to our own sense that poetry taps dark recesses of the imagination, for which ravens and gruesome carcasses are only mild representatives. Hebrew readers were expected to note that the demands made on them as readers of texts resembled the demands made on Abraham to decode ritual and dream. There would be no inheritance until these demands were met, not for the first reader of the Land and not for later readers of texts celebrating the Land. Abraham did not have any written texts to read, but he was expected to develop full literacy using the materials at hand—rituals and dreams, and the Land itself. That Abraham acquired a divine literacy is signified by God's adding a divine syllable to Abraham's original name, Abram, the *ha* taken from God's own name.

Again the covenant is repeated, with still more complications:

> Neither shall thy name any more be called Abram, but thy name shall be Abraham. . . . And I will establish my covenant between me and thee and thy seed after thee in their generations for an everlasting covenant, to be a God unto thee, and to thy seed after thee. And I will give unto thee, and to thy seed after thee, the land wherein thou art a stranger, all the land of Canaan, for an everlasting possessesion; and I will be their God. . . . This is my covenant, which ye shall keep, between me and you and thy seed after thee; Every man child among you shall be circumcised. And ye shall circumcise the flesh of your foreskin; and it shall be a token to the covenant betwixt me and you. (Genesis 17)

Just as the Land becomes the national marker of a commitment to the One God, circumcision becomes the personal marker, the "token" of a relationship, a sign to be read—the Hebrew for "token" is *oht*, a letter of the alphabet and a marker. Abraham does not flinch as he circumcises himself, deeply aware that reading the covenant requires sacrifice and surrender, dedication of one's seed, fortitude, and a cutting literacy.

And there is still more waiting for Abraham, more training in literacy. When he is ninety-nine he is told that the following year he and Sarah will have a son, though he is withered and she no longer menstruating. Again the promise is repeated, and again fulfillment is delayed. "And I will give unto the, and to thy seed after thee, the land wherein thou art a stranger, all the land of Canaan, for an everlasting possession." Then, when Abraham is one hundred years old, Isaac is born, but that this be the promised heir is far from certain. There remains the matter of God's demand that Isaac be offered as a child sacrifice, just the Sodom-like abomination that monotheism was supposed to prevent. That Abraham is willing to submit even to this, in the name of monotheism, signals his trust in a future under monotheism, no matter what. The paradox of Abraham's willingness to sacrifice the heir of the covenant to the God of the covenant is probably unresolvable, but the larger point is clear. The mind that masters the dark poetry of monotheism is finally freed from the illiteracy of child-sacrifice. All this accumulating history and poetry that steps between the covenant and its fulfillment teaches that monotheism must enter history and transform it, just as its poetry enters minds and transforms them. The process is long and fearful, as long as four hundred years of slavery and as fearful as ravens in the mind.

Isaac surviving, Abraham's future is finally present. As the promise is again repeated, his history is finally national history, now as an idea ready to enter the history of the world, as a blessing:

> . . . because thou hast done this thing, and hast not withheld thy son, thine only son: . . . I will multiply thy seed as the stars of the heaven, and as the sand which is upon the sea shore; and thy seed shall possess the gate of his enemies; And in thy seed shall all the nations of the earth be blessed; because thou has obeyed my voice. (Genesis 22)

We are free here to understand that God is praising Abraham not for his literal obedience to the command that Isaac be sacrificed but for his obedience to God's latent "voice," which forbids the crassness of literalness just as it forbids child-sacrifice. Abraham is praised for his deep literacy, just as the young Joshua is mocked for his naive misinterpretation of the roar in the Hebrew camp. Joshua did not recognize idolatry when he heard it, but Abraham did, even when the idolatry came disguised in God's own command.

Another early episode in Abraham's life illustrates his sophisticated literacy and connects it to the Land. Sarah has died, and Abraham must acquire a place to bury her. Like the story of Abraham's separation from Lot, this episode turns on the distinction between land as wealth and Land as the center of a literary culture. This time we pause to relish a technique as modern and as ancient as literature itself, the weave of the figure in the carpet. Indeed, this story of Abraham's first acquisition of a tiny part of the Land has as its ultimate subject the literary sensibility:

> And Sarah died in Kirjath-arba; the same is Hebron in the land of Canaan: and Abraham came to mourn for Sarah, and to weep for her. And Abraham stood up from before his dead, and spake unto the sons of Heth, saying, I am a stranger and a sojourner with you: give me a possession of a buryingplace with you, that I may bury my dead out of my sight. And the children of Heth answered Abraham, saying unto him, Hear us, my lord: thou art a mighty prince among us: in the choice of our sepulchres bury thy dead; none of us shall withhold from thee his sepulchre, but that thou mayest bury thy dead. And Abraham stood up, and bowed himself to the people of the land, even to the children of Heth. And he communed with them, saying, If it be your mind that I should bury my dead out of my sight; hear me, and entreat for me to Ephron the son of Zohar, That he may give me the cave of Machpelah, which he hath, which is in the end of his field; for as much money as it is worth he shall give it me for a possession of a buryingplace amongst you. And Ephron dwelt among the children of Heth: and Ephron the Hittite answered Abraham in the audience of the children of Heth, even of all that went in at the gate of his city, saying, Nay, my lord, hear me: the field give I thee, and the cave that is therein, I give it thee; in the presence of the sons of my people give I it thee: bury thy dead. And Abraham bowed down himself before the people of the land. And he spake unto Ephron in the audience of the people of the land, saying, But if thou will give it, I pray thee, hear me: I will give thee money for the field; take it of me and I will bury my dead there. And Ephron answered Abraham, saying unto him, My lord, hearken unto me; the land is worth four hundred shekels of silver; what is that betwixt me and thee? bury therefore thy dead. And Abraham hearkened unto Ephron; and Abraham weighed to Ephron the silver, which he had named in the audience of the sons of Heth, four hundred shekels of silver, current money with the merchant. (Genesis 23)

This meticulous story, surprising in the quantity of detail devoted to the acquisition of Sarah's grave, works by innuendo. Ephron's character emerges. He is a shrewd businessman, ready to give up a worthless cave (the land is ridden with caves, useful in a passing way to shepherds in the rain but hardly of economic value to farmers and keepers of livestock) to win good will from a powerful foreigner, a "mighty prince." If Abraham wants the cave, let him have it; someday I may need a favor from him—something like this seems to be in Ephron's mind, initially. Then he learns that Abraham will not accept the cave as a gift. Puzzled, Ephron sizes up Abraham. *Why* does the prince insist on paying? Ephron realizes Abraham will pay any price, not just "as much money as it is worth." Ephron doesn't know what Abraham is up to, but the practical man knows that it is not everyday that the rich prince will squander money.

Ephron demands an outrageous sum. Four hundred shekels pays the yearly wages of fifty laborers. The redactors thought this so greedy, so self-diminishing, that they dropped a letter from the Hebrew spelling of Ephron's name immediately after he quotes his price (this is not reflected in English translation, which does not have the Hebrew's flexibility with vowels, like this: "Ephrn"). The diminished Ephron reveals himself. He shows us that he has business sense, quick to make a killing when he can do so legally. He is normative man. There is even a hint in his obsequiousness that he is embarrassed by his greed, bantering even while insisting, via a Levantine wink, that he be paid in silver (no IOUs, for the giddy buyer might later come to his senses): "The land is worth four hundred shekels of silver; what is that betwixt me and thee?"

It is easy to see what is on Ephron's mind. But what is Abraham thinking? Abraham weighs out "current money with the merchant"— the pure silver of Ephron's materialism, accepted everywhere in the world of the caravan—letting Ephron think this just another deal. But Abraham swindles the swindler. Ephron has no way of guessing what drives the usually sharp Abraham to make a seemingly bad bargain. The literate reader of this literary text is, however, expected to infer not only Abraham's motives but the motives of the passage itself. As Ephron scratches his head, half chuckling and half wondering what Abraham is up to, the reader should realize that Ephron, like Esau after him, is unknowingly tricked into selling his birthright, and that Abraham is exercising an imaginative grasp on the value of that birthright. The reader himself, in decoding this, practices the litera-cy—the special understanding—necessary to the making of the monotheistic vision. Ephron is like Lot, a businessman selling plots;

Abraham is a poet, a swindler of a higher nature, willing to pay a price to buy the materials of his métier. In making this distinction, the reader becomes an inheritor of these materials.*

Abraham is acquiring his toehold. The idea of the Land he already has, but the land, on which the idea will be imposed and from which the idea will radiate, must be obtained physically, cave by cave, inch by inch. Though Abraham's values rise above those of Lot and Ephron, he knows that his idea depends on land as physical as that which nourishes Lot's and Ephron's goats. As a cave, Sarah's place of burial is worth little; as a token for the whole Land, it is worth the sum. Abraham insists on paying because he wants no doubt to exist about the ownership of this first bit of land, which represents the entirety.

The lands of Canaan are deliberately rendered as a place of plain farms, not a divine Olympus. The ancient Hebrews never imagined that God would enter the world and hand over a mythical land to them (that would be idolatrous); they accepted that the usual kind of land would have to be acquired in the usual way, by purchase and by conquest. In paying a lot of money for a little land, Abraham commits himself to the proposition that though the idea of the Land is priceless, it cannot survive, cannot help transmit the monotheistic vision, unless grounded in real soil, mastered by money and might. The Land cannot be a utopia, a nowhere; the ancient Hebrews needed a somewhere to represent a spiritualized God to themselves.

In fact, the ancient Hebrews went out of their way, especially in the

---

*The story of Abraham's bargain with Ephron should be distinguished from the story of his deal with Abimelech, told two chapters earlier. In Abraham's transaction with Ephron, a complex play of ideas regarding the covenant hovers about the understanding of the mere businessman, while the straightforward transaction with Abimelech contrasts starkly with the covenent. The word *brit* (covenant) is pointedly used to describe Abraham's agreement with Abimelech about a well: "And Abraham reproved Abimelech because of a well of water which Abimelech's servants had violently taken away . . . . And Abraham took sheep and oxen, and gave them unto Abimelech; and both of them made a covenant[*brit*]. And Abraham set seven ewe lambs of the flock by themselves. . . . And he said, For these seven ewe lambs shall thou take my hand, that they may be a witness unto me, that I have digged this well" (Genesis 21). This is the kind of covenant that Lot can understand as a seeker of wells and as the son of Haran who died in Sumeria, the kind of covenant that Ephron thought he made with Abraham.

Book of Joshua, to emphasize the ordinary literalness of the land itself, the ordinary difficulty of getting and controlling territory. They distinguished literal land from the ideas that Land could represent, but they insisted on maintaining both, just as their poets (like ours) insisted on maintaining the play between the literal and metaphorical meanings of words. Unlike the universal Church, which holds that the idea of monotheism no longer requires a land to represent it, the Hebrews repudiated an *ideal* culture in which ideas would stand for themselves, just as their poets (like ours) repudiated a pure meaning that skips the hard acquisition of literacy. The Land of Israel, hedged in and bordered, composed of dirt and idea, is the chief poem of ancient Hebrew culture, and Abraham is Israel's first poet.

Though it is conceivable that another man privileged to be the inventor of monotheism might have let an unrooted dream stand for his idea, this was not the monotheism of Abraham. Perhaps Abraham was preceded by a monotheist whose failure to root idea into place doomed the vision to oblivion. However this might be, we know that Paul, in promulgating Christianity as a catholic religion, detached his version of monotheism from a particular land, just as he disconnected the covenant from its other physical correlative, circumcision: "But he is a Jew, which is one inwardly; and circumcision is that of the heart, in the spirit, and not in the letter" (Romans 2). But this, too, is not the monotheism of Abraham. From a Hebrew perspective, Paul's program fell into exactly the snare that Abraham foresaw; in the absence of a land-tethered metaphor, the single God ran off into the Trinity, among other complications.

It so happened that in the Diaspora the Jews themselves were forced to live with a monotheism that was represented by the Land as a pure idea, but they never found this satisfying. They continued to believe in Abraham's realistic poetics, and they waited to return to a real land. The telling and transmission of the Abrahamic story thus required that the cave of Machpelah be at the butt end of a plowed field, that the story not be told in ethereal terms. Hebrew poets agreed with Robert Frost: poetry and intellectual nationalism need roots, just as tennis needs a net.

Though Sarah's grave became an object of veneration and pilgrimage, this, clearly, was not Abraham's intention, either. The cave is not itself holy, should not itself arouse fanatics and fetishists. Though

Hebrew culture had and has its fanatics, as Israel's critics are quick to notice, Abraham's rational tone is unmistakable. Clearly Abraham meant to forge a connection between a realistic land and a noble idea; he did not intend that bits of soil be venerated per se. His rationalism has persisted throughout the millenia. In any case, the vast majority of Jewish enthusiasts who kiss the dirt in Sarah's cave do no worse than get excited about little plots in a small land. Christendom has demonstrated a more consuming irredentism, and Islam, having wrought holy places on holy rocks from the Atlantic to the Indian Ocean, made Al Kuds (the Holy City, Islam's name for Jerusalem) an indispensable trophy among many others. But Israel in fact founds itself in no empire but in a land that is not ethereal, not sacred, but actual and poetic, plain matter in a small space inspiring thought about the Creator of plain matter.

The poetic vision of Abraham is what the ancient Hebrews wanted to transmit. Often they failed, and literalists and businessmen prevailed. Abraham's manipulation of Lot and Ephron in the name of intellectual monotheism descended into mere manipulation. The prophets answered this failure with more literature, in the form of prophecy, story, and song, with the hope that eventually a literary attitude would sink in. Sometimes the prophets bluntly accused the Hebrews of having perverted imagination, turning it to the weaving of the spider's web. Isaiah charged that

> . . . your lips have spoken lies, your tongue hath muttered perverseness. None calleth for justice, nor any pleadeth for truth: they trust in vanity, and speak lies; they conceive mischief, and bring forth iniquity. They hatch cockatrice' eggs, and weave the spider's web. (Isaiah 59)

At other times the poet's answer to mere shrewdness was to repeat the contrast between Abraham and Lot. The prototypic story along these lines is of course the distinction between Jacob and Esau, Abraham's grandchildren. The older is a dull businessman, and the the younger a shrewd businessman, but he is also something more:

> Esau was a cunning hunter, a man of the field; and Jacob was a plain man, dwelling in tents. And Isaac loved Esau, because he did eat of his venison: but Rebekah loved Jacob. And Jacob sod pottage, and Esau came from the field, and he was faint: And Esau said to Jacob, Feed me I pray thee,

with that same red pottage; for I am faint: therefore was his name called Edom. And Jacob said, Sell me this day thy birthright. And Esau said, Behold, I am at the point to die: and what profit shall this birthright do to me? And Jacob said, Swear to me this day; and he sware unto him: and he sold his birthright unto Jacob. Then Jacob gave Esau bread and pottage of lentils; and he did eat and drink, and rose up, and went his way; thus Esau despised his birthright. (Genesis 25)

In the King James translation, Jacob is described as a "simple" man, which is hardly the intention of the biblical writers. True, the word *tam* sometimes means "simple," but the basic idea is "complete," as in a verse just above our passage, where the word is used to signify that the boys' mother Rebekah is pregnant with a fullness of twins. Jacob is complete in that he possesses a trainable capacity to read the covenant; Esau possesses no such capacity and thus despises his birthright—in truth, he has no idea of what it means. As a hunter and man of the field, as a materialist, he values his birthright in the Land as so much red pottage. The word for "pottage" is *adom*, the root of which gives the Hebrew words for "red," "blood," "Adam," and "Edom." In Hebrew culture the descendants of Esau, the Edomites, would forever be among those who are most ruddy and most bloody, those who are least able to read and to understand, those who are most susceptible, along with the Moabites and the Ammonites, to the charms of Molech.

After Esau there are in the Bible many foolish traders. For example, at the end of the Book of Ruth, the author of this poetic tale juxtaposes two Hebrews, one like Abraham, one like Lot. Lot's intellectual heir is a businessman, protected from infamy by anonymity. He rejects Ruth because she is not a good deal. The other is Boaz, who is able to read in Ruth a fitness to beget Hebrew kings. It is part of the story's literary irony that Ruth, the ancestress of King David, is literally but not intellectually a descendant of Lot.

It is worth telling the story of Ruth here because the Bible draws a formal parallel between her and Abraham. Ruth, a Moabite woman who lived in the time of Israel's Judges some five hundred years after the death of Abraham, married a Hebrew, one of Naomi's two sons. The other son has also married a Moabitess. This marrying out of the fold was a sufficient shame to drive the whole family from Israel into

Moab, where Naomi's husband and her two sons all die, as if in divine retribution for turning away from the Land. But matters are not that simple. For Ruth, it turns out, is to be admired. She becomes famous for her decision to remain with Naomi, adopt her Hebrew ways, and return with her to Israel. The other daughter-on-law remains in Moab.

Without their men and without means of support, Ruth and Naomi survive by taking advantage of the Hebrew law granting to the poor all grain missed by harvesters on their first pass. Naomi sends Ruth to the fields of Boaz, a kinsman noted for his kindliness. Boaz quickly recognizes Ruth's qualities, likening her grasp of monotheism to Abraham's original vision. "Get thee out of thy country, and from thy kindred, and from thy father's house, unto a land that I will shew thee," God said to Abraham, while Boaz says to Ruth, "It hath full been shewed me . . . how thou hast left they father and thy mother and the land of thy nativity, and art come unto a people which thou knewest not heretofore." Both Abraham and Ruth choose the Land over their birthplaces, because it represents the intellectual triumph of monotheism and its poetry over the emptiness of idolatry, and Boaz sees this. By alluding to the founding covenant in his praise of Ruth, Boaz places his wife-to-be pivotally between Abraham and David as the intellectual daughter of the Patriarch and the literary mother of the Poet-King. In so doing Boaz puts himself in the category of those who can read—like Abraham, Ruth, and David.

But Boaz's insight is not sufficient. Left to himself he would not manage to marry Ruth and thereby father the line of David. Preoccupied by business, Boaz sleeps in the field, having forgotten the Land even as he reaps the land's lesser harvest. He himself needs to be manipulated, or he will remain sterile. Ruth, the intellectual daughter of Abraham in every way, possesses the necessary wiles, as does her mother-in-law, whose meaning Ruth quickly grasps. "Wash thyself therefore, and anoint thee, and put thy raiment upon thee, and get thee down to the [threshing] floor," advises Naomi:

> but make not thyself known unto the man, until he shall have done eating and drinking. And it shall be when he lieth down, that thou shalt mark the place where he shall lie, and thou shalt go in, and uncover his feet, and lay thee down; and he will tell thee what thou shalt do. (Ruth 3)

This stratagem becomes more titilating when we recall that Ruth the Moabitess stems from a land notorious in Hebrew culture for sexual depravity. *Moab* means "from father," the tribe having descended from incestuous liaisons between Lot and his three daughters, who on serial nights, as described in Genesis 19, got their father drunk and their wombs seeded, sodden Lot ever unaware. In Numbers 25, the Hebrews slip into "whoredom with the daughters of Moab, And they . . . bowed down to their gods," so the Hebrews learned to be wary of these cousins who tempted them to act on their strongest yet most forbidden impulses. Boaz's own field hands treat Ruth roughly, assuming her to be the usual unchaste Moabite woman, and he has to restrain them. And what does Boaz do when he finds Ruth at the foot of his bed in the middle of a field in the middle of the night? He elevates her seductive behavior: "Blessed be thou of the Lord, my daughter," he says, "For thou hast shewed more kindness . . . inasmuch as thou followedst not young men." This sublimation is a miracle of his insight and hers, in the face of the easy condemnation conventional wisdom would expect. Ruth, superficially like Lot's daughters, even makes sure Boaz has had his wine before she tucks herself in with him, perfumed and oiled! Yet Boaz, manipulated by the right woman, comes to the right conclusion, reading Ruth's sensuality as representing the play of her mind. Ruth comes to her rightful position because Boaz has intellectual reach and because she can push it even further.

Boaz, able to read the Abrahamic vision as it is expressed and manipulated by Ruth, is to be contrasted with a prototypical businessman, who now enters the story as the true descendant of Lot. Naomi discovers that she has inherited a piece of land from her deceased husband, Elimelech. She wishes now to sell the lot. But the rules of ancient Israel require that the purchaser marry Ruth, the widow of Elimelech's son. The prospect of marrying Ruth pleases Boaz, so he is prepared to buy Naomi's field. But he must defer to the businessman, a kinsman who has the first option. Like Abraham, Boaz is not above a little manipulation to make sure he gets what he wants. He helps the businessman misvalue and therefore reject Ruth. To trick the businessman proves easy, for he cannot see what Boaz sees. All Boaz has to do is promote the field to the willing buyer and then, in a change of tone, insinuate that Ruth is no more than a minor blot on the deal:

Then went Boaz up to the gate, and sat him down there: and, behold, the kinsman of whom Boaz spake came by; unto whom he said, Ho, such a one! turn aside, sit down here. . . . And he said unto the kinsman, Naomi, that is come again out of the country of Moab, selleth a parcel of land, which was our brother Elimelech's: And I thought to advertise thee, saying, Buy it before the inhabitants, and before the elders of my people. If thou wilt redeem it, redeem it: but if thou wilt not redeem it, then tell me, that I may know: for there is none to redeem it beside thee; and I am after thee. And he said, I will redeem it. Then said Boaz, What day thou buyest the field of the hand of Naomi, thou must buy it also of Ruth the Moabitess, the wife of the dead, to raise up the name of the dead upon his inheritance. And the kinsman said, I cannot redeem it for myself, lest I mar mine own inheritance: redeem thou my right to thyself; for I cannot redeem it. (Ruth 4)

The businessman clearly thinks a Moabitess would "mar" his inheritance, both as a husband-killer ("the wife of the dead") and by bearing him whores. He cannot see that Ruth possesses the vision of Abraham, that she knows how to read the Land correctly, for he himself lacks this skill. He thinks that land is simply a matter of a good or a bad deal, thus excluding him from the culture that produced the Book of Ruth and from the insight of Ruth, which is the poetry of literary Zionism. By contrast, Boaz does see the value of Ruth (which is *his* value), and his handling of the businessman demonstrates the sublime chicanery that in Hebrew culture is the necessary intellectual prerequisite to monotheism.

The Land is thus inherited by those intellectual descendants of Abraham who understand monotheistic poetry whatever their origin, be it Jacob the second son, or Ruth the loathed Moabitess, or David, a belated son from a large and poor family:

So Boaz took Ruth, and she was his wife: and when he went in unto her, the Lord gave her conception, and she bare a son. . . . And Naomi took the child, and laid it in her bosom, and became nurse unto it. And the women her neighbours gave it a name, saying, There is a son born to Naomi; and they called his name Obed; he is the father of Jesse, the father of David. (Ruth 4)

And those who do not inherit are the intellectual descendants of Lot, be they firstborn like Esau or first-refusing like Boaz's businessman.

We will come later to David, who brought the vision of Ruth to Zion and gave it there a local habitation and a local poetry. Here I want to prepare for the ambiguities of David's glory by noting that Ruth's achievement is itself already shadowed. The Hebrews knew too well that the intellectual life was not easy. Ruth's task, to maintain on a daily basis in her own mind a vision of the universal Creator, required the most outrageous play, as did the task of landing Boaz and thus landing herself. For without having achieved her place on the Land, her intellect would have gone to waste. But Ruth's outrageousness can also lead to much trouble, as we shall see. Though her playful mind, even her scandalous mind, is what is needed as a place for monotheism to root, restraints were also needed. The ancient Hebrews hoped that imagination would root into the Land, where it would be harnessed, given borders. But that is not what happened. In fact imagination often ran wild. Yet the Hebrews stuck with it, because imagination provided the only road to monotheism.

In *The Book of J*, Harold Bloom speaks of the richly literary and therefore scandalous turn of mind of the Yawehist, or J, the putative author of one of the Bible's putative strands. Yet a scandalous tone appears throughout the Bible, including the Book of Ruth, not just in those parts that can be assigned to J. And this tone is present, I believe, not because it slipped through the normative censorship of later redactors, as Bloom seems to believe, but because the Hebrews knew their monotheism to be beholden to literacy—and literacy beholden to the scandal-prone imagination. If one wants an Abraham or a Ruth or a David, one has to create them from material like the story of a Moabite widow who thought like Abraham but behaved like a typical Moabite whore, though she was not one. Literacy is safely tamed in the universities now, but the Hebrews experienced it in the wild (as it still can be), and they let its full fire burn in their minds because it led them to God. They certainly knew godless stories of some power, but they didn't tell those stories, Bloom's claim that J was a secular prose-poet notwithstanding. We are drawn to Ruth not merely because of her secular artistry and intelligence but because she is stunning in the manner of Abraham. The Hebrews would agree with Bloom that God was the literary character J and they invented for themselves; but they also believed they acted in a play that God wrote for them, however darkly. They believed that the poetry complicating Abraham's covenant with God nevertheless brought them closer to the Creator, Himself the quintessential poet.

Chapter 3

Land and Law

But thou shalt have a perfect and just weight, a perfect and just measure shalt thou have: that thy days may be lengthened in the land which the Lord thy God giveth thee.
                              —Deuteronomy 25

Judges and officers shalt thou make thee in all thy gates, which the Lord thy God giveth thee. . . . That which is altogether just shalt thou follow, that thou mayest live, and inherit the land which the Lord thy God giveth thee.
                              —Deuteronomy 16

The people should fight for their law as for their city wall.
                              —Heraclitus, *Fragments*

As told in the Bible, the history of the Hebrews from the time of Jacob to the time of David contains two grand movements. The first is the development in the cauldron of Egypt of a nation capable of receiving the Law at Sinai. The second is the conquest of the Land and the establishment there of a living civilization dedicated to monotheism. Though these two themes have an obvious historical order, they were in fact intertwined. The nature of the Law and the problems of the conquest are woven into all parts of the biblical narrative, into the stories of Jacob and his sons in Egypt, of Moses in Sinai, of Joshua at the conquest of Jericho, of the hellish life under the Judges who followed Joshua, of Saul assuming the kingship over Samuel's objections. But let us maintain a rough historical order and turn here to the theme of Law, focusing specifically on the Hebrew idea of using Law to reinforce the meaning of the Land. It was Law that provided the transition from wandering in the wilderness to a life governed by commandments in the signifying Land.

In order to maintain their interrelated ideas of Land and Law, the ancient Hebrews cultivated two habits of mind. The first was a high form of fiction making, an ability to make and hold a complex idea in the mind, to play a role on an invisible stage in a dramatic relationship with an unseen God. The second was making distinctions, the capacity to distinguish between Abraham's invented monotheism and other created gods. Molech was one. He squatted at center stage, directing sacred prostitutes to urge fathers into the fold, seducing feverish mothers to hurl their babies into his fiery maw. The Hebrews did not regard it blasphemy to think of the Creator as an invention, for they could see that without invention human beings would be unable to grasp God. Nor did the Hebrews regard distinction making as mere hairsplitting; for they could see that without rigorous thought worshipers follow false gods. The Hebrews imagined that God Himself, as poetically described in the very opening lines of the Bible, created the world through high inventiveness and through a series of distinctions, imagining light and distinguishing it sharply from dark, creating earth by dividing it first from sky, then from water.

Fiction making and distinction making infused all aspects of Hebrew civilization. The Land, as we have seen, partakes in a poetic representation of man's relationship to the Creator and, by way of its careful borders, in a distinction between Israel and idolatry. The

Hebrew concept of Law also rests squarely on the pillars of fiction making and distinction making. The Hebrews took the Law as a set of inventions imposed on spontaneous behavior and as a set of distinctions imposed on the gray morass of relationships. Even before the Hebrews enter the Land, while still in Sinai, they are asked to master a matrix of law; distinguishing among cases forms part of the intellectual equipment necessary to the monotheist:

> If an ox gore a man or a woman, that they die: then the ox shall be surely stoned, and his flesh shall not be eaten; but the owner of the ox shall be quit. But if the ox were wont to push with his horn in time past, and it hath been testified to his owner, and he hath not kept him in, but that he hath killed a man or a woman; the ox shall be stoned, and his owner also shall be put to death. (Exodus 21)

The Law, beyond this practicality of distinguishing the innocent owner of a first-time offending ox from the indifferent owner of a chronic gorer, represented to the Hebrews their relationship with God. It thus melded with the Land, the reality of both depending on imagination and discernment. This is illustrated in Deuteronomy 27, where Land and Law are fused at the symbolic moment of crossing into the Land after wandering in the wilderness:

> And it shall be on the day when ye shall pass over Jordan unto the land which the Lord thy God giveth thee, that thou shalt set the up great stones, and . . . write upon them all the words of this law, . . . that thou mayest go in unto the land which the Lord thy God giveth the, a land that floweth with milk and honey.

The milk and honey are fruits of Law, as much as of Land. It was no accident that ancient Zionism wove Land and Law and monotheism into a single tapestry; when Israel lost its capacity for abstract monotheism, that tapestry unraveled, and neither Land nor Law could cohere.

The biblical narrative emphasizes from early on the idea that the Law functions as part of the national poetry. Going back to a period long before the Law was given at Sinai, the redactors insert the story of the origin of a law whose function is primarily poetic. The law concerns the prohibition against eating an animal's thigh veins, a quaintness we can grasp only when we know the story.

Jacob is returning to the Land, his inheritance, from servitude under Laban. He learns that his brother Esau is marching to greet him. Unsure how angry big-boned Esau still is about the swindled birthright, Jacob plots to manipulate Esau one more time. First, he sends a sequence of gifts, timed to soften up the impressionable man. Later, he excuses himself from traveling with Esau on the pretense that he is accompanied by young children. Then Jacob lies about catching up to Esau but stays clear by going in another direction. He even tries to manipulate God Himself in this matter: "O God of my father Abraham, . . . deliver me, I pray thee, from the hand of my brother, from the hand of Esau: for . . . thou saidst I will surely do thee good, and make thy seed as the sand of the sea, which cannot be numbered" (Genesis 32).

The editors of this fable, thinking Jacob's cleverness praiseworthy only insofar as it supported an intellectual culture, made sure to inhibit his imagination. At the very moment that Jacob's name is being changed to Israel, the name that the Land will bear, he is hobbled with a deliberate warning against mere cleverness:

> And Jacob was left alone; and there wrestled a man with him until the breaking of the day. And when he saw that he prevailed not against him, he touched the hollow of his thigh; and the hollow of Jacob's thigh was out of joint, as he wrestled with him. And he said, Let me go, for the day breaketh. And he said, I will not let thee go, except thou bless me. And he said unto him, What is thy name? And he said, Jacob. And he said, Thy name shall be called no more Jacob, but Israel: for as a prince has thou power with God and with men, and hast prevailed. . . . And Jacob called the name of the place Penuel: for I have seen God face to face, and my life is preserved. And as he passed over Penuel the sun rose upon him and he halted upon his thigh. Therefore the children of Israel eat not of the sinew which shrank, which is upon the hollow of the thigh, unto this day. (Genesis 32)

In the midst of his further toying with Esau, Jacob dreams, and after the dream he is made to limp; he "halted upon his thigh." What does this mean? Clearly he is being told to slow down, to channel his quicksilver mind into an enterprise that requires less nimbleness and more meditation. When he was called Jacob, the father of the House of Israel was a mere manipulator; now that he is named Israel he must rise to poetry. Something more than mere craftiness is needed, and this something more, rather surprisingly, is represented by a law. "Unto this day," Jews discard the hindquarters of cattle not because the law forbidding the consumption of thigh veins usefully regulates daily life but because it reminds them of Jacob's thigh. The law evokes the halting of Jacob's dream, and in so doing both celebrates Jacob's mind's-eye grasp of divinity "face to face" and submits this "power with God" to an angel's shackle. The Hebrew legislators in emphasizing beef veins were reminding themselves that a mind capable of high monotheism had to be disciplined to rise above the low urge to manipulate Esau. Because Jacob's descendants must be disciplined to rise from cleverness to monotheism, they are commanded to observe the law of veins. Thus Law, beyond the mundane function of regulating diet, took its place within the Land as part of a signifying civilization capable of transmitting monotheism.

The very survival of the Land and its civilization depended on the survival of the Law and its power to signify:

> Ye shall make you no idols nor graven image, neither rear you up a standing image, neither shall ye set up any image of stone in your land, to bow down unto it: for I am the Lord your God. Ye shall keep my sabbaths, and reverence my sanctuary: I am the Lord. If ye walk in my statutes, and keep my commandments, and do them; Then I will give you rain in due season, and the land shall yield her increase, and the trees of the field shall yield their fruit. And your threshing shall reach unto the vintage, and the vintage shall reach unto the sowing time: and ye shall eat your bread to the full, and dwell in your land safely. And I will give peace in the land and ye shall lie down, and none shall make you afraid: and I will rid evil beasts out of the land, neither shall the sword go through your land. . . . And if ye shall despise my statutes, or if your soul abhor my judgments, so that ye will not do all my commandments . . . I will even appoint over you terror, consumption, and the burning ague that shall consume the eyes, and cause sorrow of heart. . . . They that hate you shall reign over you; and ye shall flee when none pursueth you. (Leviticus 26)

The modern reader may mistake this for hellfire. But the emphasis is not on terror but on creating both individual and national health of mind. Keeping the monotheistic vision and the statutes representing it promotes a unity of culture, a communal strength on the Land, so that "none shall make you afraid"; but flouting the laws of the Land disintegrates the community and abandons its citizens to the paranoia of the isolated mind, which "shall flee when none pursueth."

While obedience wards off the dissolution of the Land, the Law promises even more. "Ye shall therefore be holy because I am holy," says Leviticus 12, going on to distinguish dietary laws: "To make a difference between the clean and the unclean, and between the beast that may be eaten and the beast that may not be eaten" (to "make a difference"—*le-havdil*—is what God did at the beginning). Leviticus 20, again iterating that word *le-havdil*, specifically links dietary laws with the power of both Law and Land to represent a sanctified relationship with the distinction-making Creator: "Ye shall therefore keep all my statutes, and all my judgments, and do them: that the land, whither I bring you to dwell therein, spue you not out. . . . You shall therefore put difference between clean beasts and unclean . . . for I the Lord am holy, and have severed you from other people, that ye should be mine."

This monotheism the Hebrews lived with was a new concept, and they needed the Law and the Land to remind them of its abstractions. God may have given the Hebrews the Law at Sinai, just as he gave monotheism to Abraham in Haran, but the Hebrews knew that they had to create both for themselves in their own minds and use the Land to remind themselves to do so. Now we think we can dispense with connecting laws to a specific land, but the Hebrews doubted this was possible in the long run. The second half of the Fifth Commandment, for instance, is now dropped, though this could not have been the case with the Hebrews, who found that abstractions waft away unless they are rooted: "Honour thy father and thy mother: that thy days may be long upon the land which the Lord thy God giveth thee." The interrelated ideas of monotheism, Land, and Law were all the creations of the same poetry-making civilization, all works of art that in turn stimulated the minds of the next generation to remake what had once been God's direct gifts. In a sense, God's gifts of monotheism, Law, and Land were not abiding; the gift of mind however was, as long as Hebrews in every generation renewed their intellectual civilization.

Many of the ancient Hebrew laws pertained to the Land itself. Some of these may seem quaint and arbitrary. But the quaintness becomes poetry if it is read, as in the following sequence:

Thou shalt not sow thy vineyard with divers seeds: lest the fruit of thy seed which thou has sown, and the fruit of thy vineyard, be defiled. Thou shalt not plow with an ox and an ass together. Thou shalt not wear a garment of divers sorts, as of woollen and linen together. Thou shalt make thee fringes upon the four quarters of thy vesture, wherewith thou coverest thyself. (Deuteronomy 22)

The practice of growing apples and oranges in separate orchards is not for the purpose of promoting horticultural efficiency but of sharpening the distinction between God and Molech and between Israel and idolatrous lands. The late rabbis, having lost much of their culture's poetics early in the common era, puzzled over this law of mixed trees, concluding that the righteous Hebrew would observe it blindly, despite the scoffing of neighboring nations, because the Almighty wanted it observed for His own reasons. But the law is not so mysterious; it is part of Hebrew poetry and rooted in the Land. There is a meaning to it: keeping unmixed orchards can remind one not to mix in the mind God with gods. The same can be said for the avoidance of mixed plow teams and mixed cloth. Distinction making must be practiced at every turn if one is to succeed in distinguishing God from Molech. Thus the Hebrews instituted the ceremony of *Havdalah* ("distinction making") to mark the conclusion of the Sabbath and to separate it from the workweek, and they distinguished between dairy and meat dishes, refraining from mixing the two at any one meal.

So must fiction making be made part of daily practice, as in the law of fringes (which pertains to the *talit*, or fringed prayer shawl). The fringes themselves and the law governing them are meant to evoke a poetry of memories:

And it shall be unto you for a fringe, that ye may look upon it, and remember all the commandments of the Lord, and do them; and that ye seek not after your own heart and your own eyes, after which ye use to go a whoring: That ye may remember, and do all my commandments, and be holy unto your God. I am the Lord your God, which brought you out of the land of Egypt. (Numbers 15)

The Hebrew fringes were 613 in number, representing all the 613 commandments recorded in the Books of Moses, a mind-expanding poem; and the Hebrews were expected to *read* their fringes.

At all times, the Law, in its poetry, turns the Hebrew back to the Land, and from thence to God, as in the laws of first fruits:

> And it shall be, when thou are come in unto the land which the Lord thy God giveth thee for an inheritance, and possessest it, and dwellest therein; That thou shalt take of the first of all the fruit of the earth, which thou shalt bring of thy land that the Lord thy God giveth thee, and shalt put it in a basket, and shalt go unto the place which the Lord thy God shall choose to place his name there. And thou shalt go unto the priest that shall be in those days, and say unto him, I profess this day unto the Lord thy God, that I am come unto the country which the Lord sware unto our fathers for to give us. (Deuteronomy 26)

The poetic laws concerning first fruits obviously recall the intellectual value of the Land. According to the law, the citizens took their first fruits to the priests. But they were not mere taxpayers who did what they did under penalty of law. Rather they used the occasion as a ritual to remind themselves of the God who gave them a fruitful and signifying Land: "I profess this day unto the Lord . . . that I am come unto the country which the Lord sware unto our fathers for to give us."

The Land also figured in laws that in our own culture are without connection to land. We make unrooted laws forbidding citizens from taking the law into their own hands; the Hebrews gave due process a local habitation in a monotheistic nation:

> When the Lord thy God hath cut off the nations, whose land the Lord thy God giveth thee, and thou succeedest them, and dwelleth in their cities, and in their houses; Thou shalt separate three cities for thee in the midst of thy land . . . that every slayer may flee thither. And this is the case of the slayer, which shall flee thither that he may live: Whoso killeth his neighbour ignorantly, whom he hated not in time past; As when a man goeth into the wood with his neighbour to hew wood, and his hand fetcheth a stroke with the ax to cut down the tree, and the head slippeth from the helve, and lighteth upon his neighbour, that he die; he shall flee unto one of those cities, and live: Lest the avenger of the blood pursue the slayer, while his heart is hot, and . . . slay him; whereas he was not worthy of death, inasmuch he hated him not in time past. (Deuteronomy 19)

> And he shall dwell in that city, until he stand before the congregation for judgment. (Joshua 20)

The distinction between first-degree murder and accidental homicide is not rendered as mere abstraction but given a physical home: a "separate" city of refuge, in which the accidental killer can find safety until he is tried. Even if the killing proves intentional, the murderer is entitled to due process "before the congregation"; this principle, too, is grounded in the creation of the cities of refuge. Here poetry binds the Law to the Land: the felicitously phrased vignette of the man who kills accidentally when his ax's "head slippeth from the helve" is at once a legal case and a poetic fiction that establishes due process in a monotheist's Land. In other lands the blur of idolatry paralleled the instability of borders and the blot of lawlessness, while in Zion ideas of Land and Law maintained a stable nation and a just culture, at least according to the Hebrew ideal.

The ancient Hebrew laws pertaining to agriculture and to the cities of refuge obviously connect Law and Land as ideas central to intellectual monotheism. But it is, perhaps, the laws of the Sabbath that best illuminate the plane on which Law and Land meet. Like the Land, the Sabbath requires both invention and distinction. It is rooted not in nature but in imagination, and it requires for its maintenance an artificial distinction from other days. It is imposed on the seamless year as the Land is marked on the borderless earth. Because ideas of the Land and the Sabbath shared the same intellectual ground, the two ideas fused. The Sabbath, originally a reminder of the creation and of the discernment it required, grew to represent liberation from Egypt for a more intellectually free life in the Land, as noted in Deuteronomy 5: "And remember that thou wast a servant in the land of Egypt, and that the Lord thy God brought thee out thence through a mighty hand and by a stretched out arm: therefore the Lord thy God commanded thee to keep the sabbath day."

Leviticus 25 reinforces the intellectual pairing of Sabbath and Land by placing both under the governance of similar laws:

> And the Lord spake unto Moses in mount Sinai, saying, Speak unto the children of Israel, and say unto them, When ye come into the land which I give you, then shall the land keep a sabbath unto the Lord. Six years thou shalt prune thy vineyard, and gather in the fruit thereof; But in the seventh year shall be a sabbath of rest unto the land, a sabbath for the Lord: thou shalt neither sow thy field, nor prune thy vineyard. That which groweth of

its own accord of thy harvest thou shalt not reap, neither gather the grapes of thy vine undressed: for it is a year of rest unto the land.

This fugue of laws governing the week's Sabbath and the Land's sabbatical offers the earthly pleasures of living in a law-abiding community. And it offers something more, the possibility of living in a Land that is alive with the creative force of God Himself, requiring rest in the manner of God, who rested on the seventh day of creation.

For the ancient Hebrews, failure of mind stemmed from failure of fiction making and distinction making, and these failures led to the simultaneous loss of the Sabbath, the Law, and the Land, which in turn led to the loss of the intellectual power to imagine God. The Land, the Law, and the Sabbath were thus to be protected, distinguished from that which was not the Land, not the Law, not the Sabbath. *Iruvin*, an entire tractate of the *Talmud*, is devoted to borders, distinctions of every kind, both practical and theoretical. Even the study of these matters had to be distinguished from that which was not study. Just as one should not mix cloth or orchards or plough teams, one should not mix the study of Law with other pleasures.

In a passage from the *Mishnah Avot*, Rabbi Jacob warns about trying to study Law while taking a walk through a compelling landscape: "He who walks by the way and studies and breaks off his study and says 'How beautiful is this tree, how beautiful is this fallow' Scripture counts it to him as if he were guilty against himself." This passage has often served the libel that the ancient rabbis were joyless. But as R. Travers Herford notes (it is his translation of *Pirke Aboth* [Schocken, 1962] I am using), the rabbis never forbade pleasure in the creation, even providing a benediction for the apprehension of beauty. What Rabbi Jacob is warning against is the blurring of Law with other pleasures. A spring hike is fine in itself, but he "who walks by the way" should not be studying, and vice versa. Thus the "Scripture" that Rabbi Jacob has in mind is probably the verses on mixed cloth, orchards, and plough teams. For Rabbi Jacob and his predecessors, distinction making penetrated every aspect of life, preventing the loss of the Land's civilization.

Fearful of this loss, the ancient Hebrews pushed their culture of law and discernment as far as they could, always trying to hold in mind the Law's resonance and never creating a culture of mere minutiae.

Though empty legalism filled lesser minds in Israel, as in all nations of literacy, the ancient Hebrews at their best never deserved Christendom's insult of pedantry. The *Talmud* everywhere makes intellectual distinctions but eschews hairsplitting. Mere pedants were thrown out of houses of study, as was Rabbi Yermiah during an exchange recorded in the tractate *Baba Batra*; he postulated a quibbling problem about the ownership of a pigeon that pecked precisely and improbably halfway between two cotes. By posing this trivial question, Rabbi Yermiah had undermined the fundamentals of distinction making, and he was expelled.

That Hebrew Law partook of the serious business of poetry even colors the Hebrew remaking of the Near Eastern myth of the first man. Adam and Eve fit into ancient Hebrew culture not as bearers of Christianity's primal sin, but as examples of what was primal sin to the ancient Hebrews—the dissolution of the intellectual capacity for the Law's poetry: "And the Lord God commanded the man, saying, Of every tree of the garden thou mayest freely eat: But of the tree of the Knowledge of good and evil, thou shalt not eat of it: for in the day that thou eatest thereof thou shalt surely die" (Genesis 2).

Characteristically the Bible's redactors present a deep paradox here. Adam must distinguish one tree from all the rest, to refrain from eating its fruit. But it is the fruit of the very tree that promises the ability to distinguish between "good and evil." If Adam lacks this ability at the outset, how can he observe the Law? This paradox, like others in the Bible, is probably not meant to be resolved, but its import is clear. Distinctions are possible without perfect understanding, and flouting divine distinctions leads to disaster—possibly to the loss of Land (Eden, in this case). This holds even if the failure to maintain distinctions arises from the hope of improving understanding. In the Hebrew culture, understanding is highly valued, but not for itself; if it is sought for itself it becomes another idol.

Unable to imagine the serpent's guile and unable to distinguish forbidden from permitted, Adam and Eve find themselves lawless and landless, exiled from the paradise of landed significance:

> And the woman said unto the serpent, We may eat of the fruit of the trees of the garden: But of the fruit of the tree which is in the midst of the garden, God hath said, Ye shall not eat of it, neither shall ye touch it, lest ye

die. And the serpent said unto the woman, Ye shall not surely die: For God doth know that in the day ye eat thereof, then your eyes shall be opened, and ye shall be as gods, knowing good and evil. And when the woman saw that the tree was good for food, and that it was pleasant to the eyes, and a tree to be desired to make one wise, she took of the fruit thereof, and did eat, and gave also unto her husband with her; and he did eat. . . . And unto Adam [God] said, Because thou has hearkened unto the voice of thy wife, and hast eaten of the tree, of which I commanded thee, saying, Thou shalt not eat of it: cursed is the ground for thy sake. (Genesis 3)

The Garden of Eden, where trees stood for commitment to a godly life of distinction making, now became a desert of failed law and poetry. Eden thus foreshadows Zion, where Molech and other serpents beckoned minds away from the right uses of Law and Land. Eventually Zion was lost as was Eden.

But the children of Zion, as they sat in exile, would reimagine Eden and thus distinguish themselves from Adam, thereby restoring the Land's Law and its fruits. Ezekiel, for instance, writing in the worst of times as part of the generation carried into Babylon, imagines a return to an ideal Zion, where the king himself bows to the Law: "The prince shall not take of the people's inheritance by oppression, to thrust them out of their possession; but he shall give his sons inheritance out of his own possession: that my people be not scattered every man from his possession" (Ezekiel 46).

The words "possession" and "scattered" work on large and small scales, indicating that national survival depends on the observance of justice, by king and subject alike, especially in matters of land. A king who evicts a farmer capriciously violates the Law's poetry, ruins the Land, prepares his own exile. But the opposite is also true. The prince who cultivates distinctions maintains the farmer in his homestead and the nation in its homeland, thereby creating Ezekiel's paradise. When the prince distinguishes between what is his to give and what belongs to others, says Ezekiel (36), "This land that was desolate is become like the garden of Eden."

Insofar as Ezekiel's idealized Zion is a Land of Law, it is a place of rationality, as Abraham intended, founding his nation not in a mystical dreamland but in the hard-rock fields of Ephron. The Law, when it was observed, reinforced the rationality of the Land, which in turn represented the reasonableness of monotheism. It is easy, of course, to find a fanatical Jew in every period of Israel's history, but fanaticism never has been Israel's way; Israel's fanatics have always been small in number. Monotheism is essentially a rational idea, a dismissal of superstition, a proclamation of the underlying unity of the creation, over which conflicting river deities can have no power. "From Moses' day onwards, and throughout their history, rationalism was a central element in Jewish belief," writes Paul Johnson in *A History of the Jews* (Harper and Row, 1987):

> In a sense, it is *the* central element, for monotheism is itself a rationalization. If supernatural, unearthly power exists, how can it be, as it were, radiated from woods and springs, rivers and rocks? . . . And if God lives, how can his power be arbitrarily and unequally divided into a pantheon of deities? The idea of a limited god is a contradiction. Once the process of reason is applied to divinity, the idea of a sole, onmipotent and personal God, who being infinitely superior to man in power, and therefore virtue, is consistently guided in his actions by systematic ethical principles, follows as a matter of course. . . . Ethical monotheism began the process whereby the world-picture of antiquity was destroyed. (pp. 38–39)

The ancient Hebrews pointedly contrasted their rationality with the bizarre idolatry of their neighbors, which featured the irrationality of child-sacrifice. As the Hebrews saw it, this idolatrous practice not only overthrew reason but destroyed the stability of law and government. To contrast with their idea that Law and Land had to be cultivated as symbols of a rational society, the Hebrews told themselves this story about a battle with the Moabites, set in the time when Israel had split into two kingdoms. "And when the king of Moab saw that the battle was too sore for him, . . . he took his eldest son that should have reigned in his stead, and offered him for a burnt-offering upon the wall. And there was great indignation against Israel" (2 Kings 3).

The rival Hebrew kings often quarreled, but on this occasion in the mid–ninth century B.C.E., perhaps seventy-five years after the death of Solomon, Jehoshaphat King of Judah and Jehoram King of Israel manage to keep the peace long enough to drive the Moabites back to their own walled city. In retreat, the Moabite King Mesha grows desperate. He simultaneously expresses a mad faith that child-sacrifice might save the day and destroys his city's hope of future governance;

the "eldest son" who is sacrificed on the city wall is he who "should have reigned." In Mesha, the Hebrews would have recognized an inverted Moshe (Moses), a ruler who metes out a lethal law instead of rational Torah. For the Hebrews, Moses' Torah was a Tree of Life precisely because it made sense, and idolatry lead to death because it was madness, as in Proverbs 13: "The law of the wise is a fountain of life, to depart from the snares of death." In Mesha the Hebrews would have seen also an inverted Abraham, one who lacks the rationalist's aversion to infanticide. The Hebrews were appalled by Mesha, and they "departed from him, and returned to their own land."

It is the essentially reasonable nature of the Zionist enterprise that will make it easy for contemporary Arabs to establish peace with Israel. The Land and the Law demand preservation of life, forbid the irrational sacrifice of sons on the walls of armed cities at war. A reciprocated rationalism, an Arab condemnation of the murder of Jews to match an Israeli condemnation of the murder of Moslems, will lead ineluctably to peace. A border will be drawn, and it will help represent the rationality of Law on both sides. Or perhaps this kind of border will not be drawn. Calls of fanaticism will be hurled back and forth. Those Arabs who stood on rooftops and cheered as unprovoked Iraqi missiles hurtled into Israeli cities will press their case that Jews are still more fanatical. Whether or not they succeed, Israel, will reassume its lawful defense of the Land.

Chapter 4

Land and Loot

I see
The imminent death of twenty thousand men,
That for a fantasy and trick of fame
Go to their graves like beds, fight for a plot
Whereon the numbers cannot try the cause,
Which is not tomb enough and continent
To hide the slain.
                              —*Hamlet* IV

The worst readers are those who proceed like plundering soldiers:
they pick up a few things they use, soil and confuse the rest, and
blaspheme the whole.
           —Friedrich Nietzsche, *Mixed Opinions and Maxims*

THE ANCIENT HEBREWS ASSIGNED ALL THEIR WORST IMPULSES TO THEIR neighbors. Since the neighbors were their cousins—the children of Lot; or the children of Abraham's first son, Ishmael; or the children of Isaac's first son, Esau—there was no denying that these impulses remained in the family and were always present in the Hebrew breast. In separating himself from Lot, Abraham achieved nothing permanent. His descendants would stoop again and again to the level of Lot and worse. Lot merely did not understand the possibility of using the Land to represent the covenant; the Hebrews themselves often degraded the Land even when they did understand.

Hebrew degradation of their own Land occurs in parallel with the conquest of the Land, which often became a mere looting. This sorry history, like the history of the Law's failure, is woven into the narrative from beginning to end. Adam and Eve can be seen as looters of Eden who degraded the purpose of their paradise and were exiled, like the Hebrews themselves. The children of Abraham took Adam and Eve as a warning, but most of the time that failed to help. In fact, the story of the conquest is, in the Bible's rendering, more notable for its lapses than its successes.

The redactors of the Bible laced through their narrative a brooding tale of the conquest as they looked back on it from their Babylonian exile. They surveyed the entire period of Hebrew settlement of the Land, from Abraham to the first exile of 586 B.C.E., when the Hebrews were themselves conquered. The redactors knew that Abraham's direct descendants never inherited the Land and that the generation after Abraham's great-grandson Joseph wound up as slaves in Egypt. They knew from their sources, whose many inconsistencies they harmonized, that even after the Exodus in 1250 B.C.E. the Hebrews were too "stiffnecked," too cantankerous and unwise, to be allowed in the Land. Illiterate, they had to wander in the desert for forty years, apparently requiring at least that long to master the prerequisite intellectual skills for life on the Land, including the patience to submit to the Law. Even when Joshua finally crossed the Jordan into Canaan around 1210 B.C.E., the Hebrew skills were still flickering, making the conquest sluggish. In fact there never was a true conquest, only a few scattered military successes and a waxing and waning influence. In the two hundred years after Joshua, during the period of the Judges, large portions of the Land slipped in and out of Hebrew control. Where the

71

Hebrews did rule they often marred their heritage rather than express it; it was a mean-spirited time, as the redactors reconstructed it.

Late in the eleventh century B.C.E., the Hebrews abandoned their attempt to control themselves as individuals. They demanded a king. Samuel, the last Judge, was indignant, accusing the people of forsaking God. He reminded them that every Hebrew must make an individual effort to recreate the covenant, as Abraham did; to install a king was intellectual and spiritual treason, a lazy handing over of intellectual work. In this regard, the redactors preserved two traditions: one showing a positive view of the Hebrew kings as models of intellectual monotheists who provided the nation with worthy models, and one showing that Samuel was probably right. Saul ruled until the year 1000 B.C.E., David to 962, Solomon to 922, all of them, in one way or another, fulfilling and then sullying the covenant's promise. We will deal with Saul in this chapter, with David and Solomon later. All of their stories were left deliberately ambiguous by the redactors, whose literary approach takes in both the ideals and the betrayal of ancient Zionism.

Like all nations, ancient Israel had to be imposed on a borderless area, taken from previous residents. But unlike other wars of establishment, the conquest of the Land was not meant to be an occasion for military glory or national gloating but for self-warning. The redactors were not squeamish about warfare, but, worried that their civilization would only produce warriors, they chose to preserve a set of cautionary tales of men whose minds extended no further than the tips of their swords. Running through the Bible is a string of stories whose common theme is the ancient Hebrew temptation to reduce the Land from a poetic emblem of monotheistic culture to an idol that could be possessed. In story after story the Hebrews reminded themselves to take a higher view; the reminders were necessary.

If it was shortsighted to chop up the Land into the unenlightening plots of Lot, Ephron, and Boaz's prototypical businessman, it was unforgivable to plunder the Land as loot at the very moment its conquest was supposed to represent Hebrew culture in general and monotheism in particular. Three stories of ignoble conquest, whose canonization was embarrasing but necessary, are worth bringing together here for their exposure of the Hebrew temptation to reduce the Land to loot. These three events are spread across the history of ancient Israel, from the time of the patriarchs to the time of the kingdom. In all three instances, the story, remains essentially the same.

The first episode is related in Genesis 34, which tells of Simeon and Levi's vengeance on the town of Shechem in Samaria and on its king's son, also named Shechem. Already the conquest of the Land is intimated. Abraham has become wealthy, and his son Jacob has returned from Assyria with even greater wealth—with wives and thirteen children, twelve sons and a daughter. This extended family is making its influence felt in the lands of Canaan. The sons of Jacob know of the covenant, know that they will eventually possess the Land, and we can imagine that they swagger. The Canaanites, unaware that a single land rather than tribal domains is at stake, unaware of their impending fate, are beginning to notice the Hebrew achievement.

Jacob's daughter Dinah "went out to see the daughters of the land. And when Shechem the son of Hamor the Hivite, prince of the country, saw her, he took her, and lay with her, and defiled her." But Dinah the Hebrew seems to have brought out qualities in Shechem beyond his lust. Something quivers in him besides his loins, and he reaches out for the Hebrew idea, clumsily but sincerely:

> And his soul clave unto Dinah the daughter of Jacob and he loved the damsel, and spake kindly unto the damsel. . . . And Shechem said unto her father and unto her brethren. Let me find grace in your eyes, and what ye shall say unto me I will give. Ask me never so much dowry and gift, and I will give according as ye shall say unto me: but give me the damsel to wife.

Shechem's newfound gentleness includes his willingness to join the Hebrews in their covenant with God. True, to his own people he promotes a prospective merger with the Hebrews as a good business oportunity, but he does not miss the more abstract meanings of the Hebrew enterprise. However, the Hebrews, on this occasion, are moving in the opposite direction, choosing to degrade the covenant to an instrument of vengeance and plunder. It is Simeon's and Levi's plan to pretend brotherhood with the citizens of Shechem, to persuade them to circumcise themselves, then attack them when they are most sore. Where their father Jacob elevated trickery and playacting to the imaginative grasp of monotheism, the degenerate Simeon and Levi see only that imagination is a useful source of deceit; in their minds, even circumcision and the covenant for which it stands can be made the stuff of ruse, just as the Land can be made booty:

> And the sons of Jacob answered Shechem and Hamor his father deceitfully. . . . And they said unto them, We cannot do this thing, to give our sister to one that is uncircumcised; for that were a reproach unto us: But in this will we consent unto you: If ye will be as we be, that every male of you be circumcised; Then will we give our daughters unto you, and we will take your daughters to us, and we will dwell with you, and we will become one people. . . . And their words pleased Hamor, and Shechem Hamor's son. And the young man deferred not to do the thing, because he had delight in Jacob's daughter: and he was more honourable than all the house of his father.
>
> And Hamor and Shechem his son came unto the gate of their city, and communed with the men of their city, saying, These men are peaceable with us; therefore let them dwell in the land, and trade therein; for the land, behold, it is large enough for them; let us take their daughters to us for the wives, and let us give them our daughters. Only herein will the men consent unto us for to dwell with us, to be one people, if every male among us be circumcised, as they are circumcised. Shall not their cattle and their substance and every beast of theirs be ours? only let us consent unto them, and they will dwell with us. And unto Hamor and unto Shechem his son hearkened all that went out of the gate of the city; and every male was circumcised, all that went out of the gate of his city.
>
> And it came to pass on the third day, when they were sore, that two of the sons of Jacob, Simeon and Levi, Dinah's brethren, took each man his sword, and came upon the city boldly, and slew all the males. . . . They took their sheep, and their oxen, and their asses, and that which was in the city, and that which was in the field, And all their wealth, and all their little ones, and their wives took they captive, and spoiled even all that was in the house. And Jacob said to Simeon and Levi, Ye have troubled me to make me to stink among the inhabitants of the land, among the Canaanites and the Perizzites. (Genesis 34)

By reproving Simeon and Levi for making him "stink," Jacob means that his family is vulnerable to attack now that he is known for perfidy, but the ancient editors expected their readers to catch Jacob's implication that to convert circumcision itself into deceit and deceit into booty represents a stinking corruption of the Hebrew mind. The

Hebrews valued a clever mind capable of deceit only because the liar's fiction-making capacity can be trained up to monotheism; but mere deceit defiles the mind, renders circumcision foul, and the Land putrid. To his dying day, Jacob never forgave Simeon and Levi, blasting them for crudity even on his deathbed: "Instruments of cruelty are in their habitations. . . . I will divide them in Jacob and scatter them in Israel." The insensitive brothers seem oblivious to Jacob's reproach, defending themselves lamely with a dogged literalness: "And they said, Should he deal with our sister as with an harlot?" Content to have run off with the booty of Shechem's sheep, they have defiled themselves much more than Shechem defiled Dinah.

Jacob is so deeply disappointed in Simeon and Levi precisely because he was exactly like them when he was young. He has risen above his mere cleverness, but he can see that these two sons never will; besides, he does not like being reminded of his own mean-spirited trickery. We should hold in mind the story of Jacob's stealing Esau's blessing, for it is the prototype of all the stories of looting we are discussing. The blessing that Jacob steals is the blessing of the covenant, the key to possession of the Land. To the young Jacob, getting the blessing is a game, arranged by his mother. Rebekah has overheard Isaac asking Esau to fetch him venison, "That I may eat, that my soul may bless thee before I die." While Esau obeys his father, she immediately puts into play a counterplot favoring Jacob, the son who will eventually understand what to do with the blessing, even if he is yet unknowing:

And his mother made savoury meat, such as his father loved. And Rebekah took goodly raiment of her eldest son Esau, which were with her in the house, and put them upon Jacob her younger son: And she put the skins of the kids of the goats upon his hands, and upon the smooth of his neck: And she gave the savoury meat and bread, which she had prepared, into the hand of her son Jacob. And he came unto his father, and said, My father: and he said, Here am I; who art thou, my son? And Jacob said unto his father, I am Esau thy firstborn; I have done according as thou badest me: arise, I pray thee, sit and eat of my venison, that thy soul may bless me. And Isaac said unto his son, How is it that thou hast found it so quickly, my son? and he said, Because the Lord thy God brought it to me. And Isaac said unto Jacob, Come near, I pray thee, that I may feel thee, my son, whether thou be my very son Esau or not. And Jacob went near unto Isaac his father; and he felt him, and said, The voice is Jacob's voice, but the hands are the hands of Esau. And he discerned him not, because his hands were hairy, as his brother Esau's hands: so he blessed him. And he said, Art thou my very son Esau: And he said, I am. And he said, Bring it near to me, and I will eat of my son's venison, that my soul may bless thee. And he brought it near to him, and he did eat: and he brought him wine, and he drank. And his father Isaac said unto him, Come near now, and kiss me, my son. And he came near, and kissed him: and he smelled the smell of his raiment, and blessed him, and said, See, the smell of my son is the smell of a field which the Lord hath blessed. Therefore God give thee of the dew of heaven, and the fatness of the earth, and plenty of corn and wine. (Genesis 27)

By rabbinic tradition Isaac was confused from the time of his near sacrifice at the hands of *his* father. Now, he recognizes Jacob's voice, and he is dimly aware that something is amiss, asking again and again which son is before him, but he cannot "discern" the ruse and misreads the costume of goatskins. Isaac's literal blindness has a moral dimension as well. He thinks that Esau is the son who deserves the blessing not only because he is the elder but because he smells like a field—apparently, the blessing of the Land belongs in his view to someone who smells like land. This literalism provided painful comedy for the Hebrews, as did Isaac's pitiful preoccupation with the literal food and drink provided by the hunter Esau. Isaac, it seems, devotes little interest to Abraham's food for thought.

Jacob, easily tutored by his mother in the skills of deceit and in the pluck to succeed, would recognize that his father had the wrong idea about the covenant. But that does not ennoble Jacob's bald-faced lies. If Isaac thinks of the blessing as literally "the fatness of the earth," that is his blindness; but if Jacob thinks the blessing he steals is only a ticket to "plenty of corn and wine," then he too has a lesson to learn. And indeed the lesson does come, as we have seen, at Penuel, where Jacob's name is changed to Israel and he is sent away limping, warned that his task is higher then the continuing manipulation of Esau. Eventually Jacob came to understand that successful deception was not the main goal of his existence; but the shame of his beginning made him particularly sensitive to Simeon's and Levi's descent from covenant to clever looting. It became a goal of Jacob—and of Hebrew education—to lift the House of Jacob above his own youthful trickery and above the chicanery of Simeon and Levi, especially in matters concerning the Land.

This brings us to our second story of loot. That the Hebrews might rise above Simeon's and Levi's failed understanding, Achan won a place in the Book of Joshua. Achan serves in the infantry that storms Jericho. He has heard Joshua's warning that the Land is not a "thing," that this is no common war of plunder, that the soldiers in riveting their minds on higher meanings will take no booty. "And ye, in any wise keep yourselves from the accursed thing, lest ye take of the accursed thing, and make the camp of Israel a curse, and trouble it." But Achan cannot resist; he sneaks spoil back to his tent. After this, the war goes badly for the Hebrews. God has to intervene to explain why He has withdrawn his support from what has become a merely martial enterprise. The materialism of Achan must be repudiated, for he has struck a blow at the spiritual core of Hebrew life. The editors of the story thus arrange matters to emphasize that in a literary culture Achan, seemingly a likable young man who lapses momentarily, must be treated harshly:

> And the Lord said unto Joshua, Get thee up; wherefore liest thou thus upon thy face? Israel hath sinned, and they have also transgressed my covenant which I commanded them: for they have even taken of the accursed thing, and have also stolen, and dissembled also, and they have put it even among their own stuff. Therefore the children of Israel could not stand before their enemies, but turned their backs before their enemies, because they were accursed: neither will I be with you any more, except ye destroy the accursed from among you. . . . In the morning therefore ye shall be brought according to your tribes . . . and the household which the Lord shall take shall come man by man. And it shall be, that he that is taken with the accursed thing shall be burnt with fire, he and all that he hath: because he hath transgressed the covenant of the Lord, and because he hath wrought folly in Israel. (Joshua 7)

When Achan "dissembled," he degraded that capacity of mind which might see the monotheistic vision and remember the abstract purpose of the conquest. His is not the sublime dissembling of Jacob.

He cheats to gain a thing, not a birthright. His "folly" thus goes deeper than what is usually implied by this word; it cannot be tolerated if intellectual monotheism is to survive. In the assembly of the people, Joshua quickly ferrets out the guilty man, addressing Achan tenderly, recognizing him as a repentant young man who has stumbled into being made an example; nevertheless Joshua will not flinch from the heaviest punishment:

> And Joshua said unto Achan, My son, give, I pray thee, glory to the Lord God of Israel, and make confession unto him; and tell me now what thou hast done; hide it not from me. And Achan answered Joshua, and said, Indeed I have sinned against the Lord God of Israel, and thus and thus have I done: When I saw among the spoils a goodly Babylonian garment, and two hundred shekels of silver, and a wedge of gold of fifty shekels weight, then I coveted them, and took them; and, behold, they are hid in the earth in the midst of my tent, and the silver under it. . . . And Joshua, and all Israel with him, took Achan the son of Zerah, and the silver, and the garment, and the wedge of gold, and his sons, and his daughters, and his oxen, and his asses, and his sheep, and his tent, and all that he had: and they brought them unto the valley of Achor. And Joshua said, Why hast thou troubled us? the Lord shall trouble thee this day. And all Israel stoned him with stones, and burned them with fire, after they had stoned them with stones. (Joshua 7)

Israel has won a hackneyed castigation for its supposedly harsh law as well as criticism for its plundering colonialism in the very valley where Achan was stoned, just north of Jericho. Clearly, *both* criticisms cannot obtain in the story of Achan. In fact neither are appropriate, now or in the past. The harshness of this law was rarely enforced, because it was not to be taken literally. Rather, the harshness stood for a set of attitudes, among them contempt for the materialism of plunder. The Hebrews used the Law in the same way they used the Land, to represent to themselves the values of their civilization. The story of Achan's cruel death along with the stoning of his family is, after all, a story, set in a literary context with literary objectives.

Lest the Hebrews, like Achan, slip into a seemingly innocent, mindless trivialization of their culture, his story was retold with a king as its protagonist—the very first king of Israel, Saul from the tribe of Benjamin. The stories of King Saul seem to come from two, conflicting traditions that the redactors deliberately set against each other. In one set of stories, Saul is a compelling youth who wins God's blessing and Samuel's esteem, a tall and powerful warrior who rescues Israel from the Philistines and sets the right tone for the nation. The Philistines, invaders from the shore of the Mediterranean around Gaza, had been applying the superior technology of chariots to advance on the hill country of Judea, the heartland of Israel, where foot soldiers fought with old-fashioned arms; but Saul forces the Philistines to retreat. In the opposing set of stories, Saul is the fulfillment of Samuel's warning that the Hebrews will be ruined if they forsake their intellectual obligations by submitting themselves to a king. In a story from this latter set Saul is memorialized as a mere looter, not unlike Achan.

We should have Samuel's warnings in front of us before we proceed to Saul the looter. God tells Samuel that He reads from the people's demand for a king the old idolatrous impulse, the old failure to make in the mind a vision of the creator:

> Hearken unto the voice of the people in all that they say unto thee: for they have not rejected thee, but they have rejected me, that I should not reign over them. According to all the works which they have done since the day that I brought them up out of Egypt even unto this day, wherewith they have forsaken me, and served other gods, so do they also unto thee. Now therefore hearken unto their voice: howbeit yet protest solemnly unto them and shew them the manner of the king that shall reign over them. And Samuel told all the words of the Lord unto the people that asked of him a king. And he said, This will be the manner of the king that shall reign over you: He will take your sons, and appoint them for himself, for his chariots, and to be his horsemen; and some shall run before his chariots. . . . And he will take your daughters to be confectionaries, and to be cooks, and to be bakers. And he will take your fields, and your vineyards, and your oliveyards, even the best of them, and give them to his servants. (1 Samuel 8)

In Samuel's view, and in God's, the request for a king is blasphemy, at least according to this branch of the Hebrew tradition regarding kinship. And of course the punishment for forsaking God is the usual loss of the Land, here rendered in the image of the king seizing the lands of heretofore independent farmers, and the loss of the future through the loss of one's children. In the usual version of the Hebrew betrayal, the children are sacrificed to strange gods, according to the viciousness of local idolatry. The wrinkle here is that the dread king will simply confiscate the sons and the daughters to work on his estates. Already there is the implication that the king will reduce the entire nation to his private booty.

Saul actually thrives for a while, as the positive stories of kingship are given brief sway. When the Ammonites from the high mountains to the east of the Jordan attack the Hebrew border city of Jabesh, itself just east of the Jordan, Saul rises with thundering charisma and gentle magnanimity, forgiving those who previously doubted his worth and have now become the object of the people's wrath:

> And they told him the tidings of the men of Jabesh. And the Spirit of God came upon Saul when he heard those tidings, and his anger was kindled greatly. And he took a yoke of oxen, and hewed them in pieces, and sent them throughout all the coasts of Israel by the hands of messengers, saying, Whosoever cometh not forth after Saul and after Samuel, so shall it be done unto his oxen. And the fear of the Lord fell on the people, and they came out with one consent. . . . And it was so on the morrow that Saul put the people in three companies; and they came into the midst of the host in the morning watch, and slew the Ammonites until the heat of the day: and it came to pass, that they which remained were scattered, so that two of them were not left together. And the people said unto Samuel, Who is he that said, Shall Saul reign over us? bring the men, that we may put them to death. And Saul said, There shall not a man be put to death this day: for to-day the Lord hath wrought salvation in Israel. (1 Samuel 11)

But this alignment of God and Samuel behind Saul does not last. The intellectual failure of the Hebrews must yet again be brought to the fore. Saul must fall, mainly because he is an emblem of the people, who have already fallen in choosing him. He was successful in defending Israel at its border with the Ammonites in Jabesh, but then he himself steps across a border.

The beginning of Saul's downfall is the taking of booty from Amalek, that nation which, unprovoked, had earlier attacked Israel out of pure spite, laying "wait for him in the way, when he came up from Egypt." The story of Saul's fall into literalism is told in 1 Samuel

15. Saul is asked to obliterate the ancient adversary without identifying with its rapacity; he is to take no spoil. "But Saul and the people spared . . . the best of the sheep, and of the oxen, and of the fatlings, and the lambs, and all that was good, and would not utterly destroy them: but every thing that was vile and refuse, that they destroyed utterly." In the scene in which Samuel confronts Saul with his lapse, we are offered a contrast between the nimble-minded Samuel's literacy (which includes wry humor) and the pathetic literalness of the King (which includes self-serving, shifting falsehoods):

> And Samuel came to Saul: and Saul said unto him, Blessed be thou of the Lord: I have performed the commandment of the Lord. And Samuel said, What meaneth then this bleating of the sheep in mine ears, and the lowing of oxen which I hear? . . . And Saul said unto Samuel, Yea, I have obeyed the voice of the Lord, and have gone the way which the Lord sent me, and have brought Agag the king of Amalek, and have utterly destroyed the Amalekites. But the people took of the spoil, sheep and oxen which should have been utterly destroyed, to sacrifice unto the Lord thy God in Gilgal. And Samuel said, Hath the Lord as great delight in burnt offerings and sacrifices, as in obeying the voice of the Lord? Behold, to obey is better than sacrifice, and to hearken than the fat of rams. For rebellion is as the sin of witchcraft, and stubbornness is as iniquity and idolatry. Because thou hast rejected the word of the Lord, he hath also rejected thee from being king. And Saul said unto Samuel, I have sinned: for I have transgressed the commandment of the Lord, and thy words: because I feared the people and obeyed their voice. Now therefore, I pray thee, pardon my sin, and turn again with me, that I may worship the Lord.

But it is too late for Saul. Like Achan, he must be made an example. Because his lies turn and turn, because he cannot maintain the attack on the Amalekites on a high plane, because he distracts himself with a literalist's distinction between "good" and "vile" booty rather than focusing on the distinction between brute force and spiritual dominion in the Land, Saul earns the opprobrium of Samuel and of his literary followers, who regarded Saul's cheap lying as typical of the idolatrous mind. Indeed, Samuel bluntly accuses Saul of "idolatry," of literalism, of idolatrous admiration for the "fat of rams"; he holds up to Saul his own punning literary sophistication, as he mocks Saul with an onomatopoetic baahing, "*Mehhhhh kol ha-tson*—whaaaaat meaneth then this bleating." Samuel's intellectual scorn for Saul's literalism thus becomes the chief point of the story.

While King Saul is not stoned like Achan, he suffers the intellectual equivalent: his mind is taken from him. The redactors of the Bible render Saul's psychiatric illness with considerable insight and compassion; they understand that Saul's paranoia, his delusional lashing out at David, and his mad counsel with witches are not the result of wilful moral failure but mark instead a mental deterioration. In a modern way, they understand that Saul is not in control of himself, that his overly concrete thinking reflects mental disease. But despite their sensitivity to his plight, they hold him up as an example of the consequences of the literalism that reduces the Land to loot, and they bemoan his acquired inability to read the Land's meaning as a warning to the nation. For the deterioration of Saul's mind is in fact a mirror of the failed minds of the Hebrews.

Perhaps his later psychiatric illness had nothing to do with the degradation of his values as they are portrayed here, but the ancient Hebrews clearly regarded Saul's mental deterioration as a marker (and perhaps as a punishment) for his literalism. The redactors are careful to note Saul's paranoid behavior, recording even the small detail of his need to keep his back against a protecting wall, as in 1 Samuel 20: "And the king sat upon his seat, as at other times, even upon a seat by the wall," and they attend closely to the expression of his delusional suspiciousness:

> That all of you have conspired against me, and there is none that sheweth me that my son hath made a league with the son of Jesse, and there is none of you that is sorry for me, or sheweth unto me that my son hath stirred up my servant against me, to lie in wait, as at this day. (1 Samuel 22)

The redactors also record what is probably a psychotic misinterpretation of David's harp playing; Saul thinks his harpist makes a menacing gesture:

> And the evil spirit from the Lord was upon Saul, as he sat in his house with his javelin in his hand: and David played with his hand. And Saul sought to smite David even to the wall with the javelin; but he slipped

away out of Saul's presence, and he smote the javelin into the wall: and David fled, and escaped that night. (1 Samuel 19).

And the redactors note Saul's skulking off to a witch to share his magical thinking, showing his pathetic hopes to conjure with her the demise of his imagined enemy Samuel: "And Saul disguised himself, and put on other raiment, and he went, and two men with him, and they came to the woman by night: and he said, I pray thee, divine unto me by the familiar spirit, and bring me him up, whom I shall name unto thee" (1 Samuel 28). But these astute observations of psychopathology are meant to subserve the general theme of the danger of reducing the Land to a thing, the danger of literalism. That the paranoid personality cannot avoid concrete thinking was duly noted but not forgiven. Intellectual failure might be explained as psychopathology, but it could not thereby earn forgiveness or toleration. Saul wins no more forgiveness than did Simeon and Levi from Jacob, than did Achan from Joshua.

It is fitting that Saul give way to David, the poet-king who, despite lapses of his own, establishes the Land as both place and idea, who sets its capital in Zion as Jerusalem the City of Peace, who bequeaths to the world a nationalism that rises at least in theory but often in practice above booty, jingoism, and conquering sword. What has kept Israel at home in a tiny land is the Land's enlarging poetry, in which a universal culture has all the room it needs. In Psalm 147, David weaves a pictorial tapestry of a well-cultivated land, bordered like a sonnet, planted with significance and with poetry, governed by statute, and driven by monotheism:

Praise the Lord, O Jerusalem; praise thy God, O Zion. . . . He maketh peace in thy borders, and filleth thee with the finest of the wheat. He sendeth forth his commandment upon earth: his word runneth very swiftly. He giveth snow like wool: he scattereth the hoar frost like ashes. He casteth forth his ice like morsels: who can stand before his cold? He sendeth out his word, and melteth them: he causeth his wind to blow, and the waters flow. He showeth his word unto Jacob, his statutes and his judgments unto Israel. He hath not dealt so with any nation: and as for his judgments they have not known them.

David's poetic sensibility thus weaves land and culture into a unity under God, above booty, above craven nationalism. The Creator of the universe commands the wind and the waters, yet He can be concentrated in the little space of a fit mind, just as His cosmic power over "cold" can be focused locally, as small as an ice storm, even smaller, "like wool." And the converse is also true in David's grand vision: little Zion, if its intellect is intact, opens out to the universe, from wool and wheat to the grandeur of God's word running swiftly through vastness. A mind like David's, trained by monotheistic poetry to create intellectual nationalism, can also establish the Law, which as we have seen is itself intimately connected to the Land and to literary monotheism. For the God who rooted Abraham in the Land "showeth . . . his statutes and his judgments unto Israel."

Chapter 5

History and Hell

Human history becomes more and more a race between education and catastrophe.

—H. G. Wells, *The Outline of History*

Put me in remembrance.

—Isaiah 43

THE HEBREWS, IN ADDITION TO ACQUIRING THE FICTION- AND DISTINC-
tion-making capacities needed to grasp monotheism, found themselves able to grasp history, which also requires invention and
discernment. History, like the unseen God, has no birth but in invention, no existence but in the mind, no significance or validation unless
enshrined in an intellectual culture. The Hebrew writers transformed
the business ledgers and court records of their neighbors into a study
of developing ideas, converting chronicle into monotheistic history the
way mere earth was made into the Land. Like the Greeks, they recognized that they could have no history until they could trace the status
of their civilization in events. In recording "historical events" they
were sophisticated in distinguishing between approximate truth and
outright falsehood. Yet they knew they would choose the history dic-
tated by their values. Their concept of history thus required an
antecedent idea involving national purpose. For the Hebrews, the prerequisite idea was intellectual Zionism, a source of our own intellectual historicism.

As soon as Abraham grasps the God-given concept of using place to
signify value, monotheism takes on a history, perhaps creates history,
for the Hebrew narrators complicate the covenant between Abraham
and God with a historical context and with the curriculum vitae of the
patriarch. We are told that Abraham was seventy-five when God first
promised to make a great nation from his seed. Before this he has no
chronology, no history; after the covenant, however, we are told how
old Abraham is at every step in his career. His chronology, in fact, creates both the history of monotheism and history in general, and his
history persisted into the story of Hebrew civilization. History stopped
for the Hebrews when the civilization was destroyed in the Land by
the Romans in 135 C.E. They lost interest in it, stopped writing it,
stopped using their former history as history. Instead they converted it
to myth.

From Abraham on, the Hebrew sense of history sprang from the
idea of living in a signifying Land. Then it was turned back on the
Land to record the story of the Land's significance. Thus the capacity
for history both marked the adequacy of intellectual life in the Land
and helped transmit the idea of the Land. When the Hebrews
remembered their history, the rest of their cerebral skills remained
intact. The converse was also true. When the people forgot their his-

tory, they also forgot everything else of value, including poetry, Law, and the unseen God. As history melted out of the mind, God disappeared (there was no mind to hold Him), and then the Land dissolved—one part to be absorbed by the Ammonites, another by the Midianites. When the intellectual life and the sense of history returned, the Land reassembled in the mind as well as on the ground, like a repressed memory.

To prevent the disintegration of both mind and Land, the transmission of an unbroken history and an unfractured historicism became an obligation of Hebrew education. But the determining force of history is difficult to transmit. Despite its creation of one of the great national histories, Hebrew culture constantly forgot itself, thus allowing the Land to crumble into meaningless parts. This was especially true during the two centuries before the rule of Israel's kings, when judges did the best they could to manage the Hebrews' chronic forgetting; during the two centuries before the exile to Babylonia, when prophets desperately tried to restore the national memory; and during the period following the return from Babylonia under the leadership of Ezra and Nehemiah. After only fifty years in Babylonia those who returned were astonished to find they had virtually forgotten the very existence of the Torah, let alone its contents. They wept for shame when the Law had to be read out loud and translated to them, for their Hebrew, too, had degenerated. This last group of forgetters now spoke Aramaic, the lingua franca of the ancient Middle East, and they discovered they had grown deaf to the music of the Land's language.

The Book of Judges portrays the period before the rule of King Saul during which the Hebrews continually lost their history:

> And Joshua the son of Nun, the servant of the Lord, died, being an hundred and ten years old. . . . And also all that generation were gathered unto their fathers: and there arose another generation after them, which knew not the Lord, nor yet the works which he had done for Israel. And the children of Israel did evil in the sight of the Lord, and served Baalim: And they forsook the Lord God of their fathers, which brought them out of the land of Egypt, and followed other gods, of the gods of the people that were round about them, and bowed themselves unto them, and provoked the Lord. . . . and he delivered them into the hands of the spoilers that spoiled them. (Judges 2)

The story of Jephthah in Chapter 11 of Judges anatomizes the forgetting that destroys a nation. Set in a time of whoring after other people's idols, his story begins by introducing Jephthah as a "son of an harlot." When his half-brothers throw him out of the family home because he is a bastard and a roughneck, Jephthah retreats to the outskirts of the Land across the Jordan to a lawless place ironically named Tob, or Good, where he gathers "vain men," a gang in an anti-Land.

But it is to the highwayman Jephthah that the Hebrews must turn in order to repel the Ammonites, who recognize that the forgetful and now mindless Hebrews are easy prey. Suddenly the Ammonites have discovered a historical claim to a part of Israel, and they mean to annex what they say is theirs. Nothing stands between them and success, unless Jephthah can be persuaded to take up arms on the Hebrew side. Jephthah convinces his desperate fellow Hebrews to make him dictator should he succeed. It must have been painful to record this fall from Joshua to Jephthah, even more painful to present Jephthah as a master of history. Nevertheless, to make an ironic point, the editors of Judges have Jephthah give a lesson in history to Ammon's king. Jephthah reminds Ammon that the lands in question were taken from the Amorites and never belonged to the Ammonites; after summarizing Israel's long relationship to the area between the Arnon and Jabok rivers, dating back to the time "when Israel came up from Egypt," Jephthah stresses the fact that neither the Ammonites nor their kin the Moabites had ever claimed this territory:

> And the Lord God of Israel delivered Sihon and all his people into the hand of Israel, and they smote them: so Israel possessed all the land of the Amorites, the inhabitants of that country. . . . And now art thou any thing better than Balak the son of Zippor, king of Moab? did he ever strive against Israel, or did he ever fight against them, While Israel dwelt in Heshbon and her towns, and in Aroer and her towns, and in all the cities that be along by the coasts of Arnon, three hundred years? why therefore did ye not recover them within that time?

The historical argument, of course, fails with the land-grabbing Ammonites, who go to war with Jephthah. But Jephthah is not comfortable about fighting under the gossamer banner of history; he is too much the materialist to rely on something so abstract. In fact, he cannot proceed on the basis of history because he does not understand it. Therefore, he makes a devilish bargain:

> And Jephthah vowed a vow unto the Lord, and said, If thou shalt without fail deliver the children of Ammon into mine hands, then it shall be, that whatsoever cometh forth of the doors of my house to meet me, when I return in peace from the children of Ammon, shall surely be the Lord's, and I will offer it up for a burnt offering.

The vow backfires as it always does in myths with this motif, but with a Hebrew twist. Jephthah triumphs and returns home, only to find that his daughter is the first to greet him. Indeed, the wording of the vow almost guarantees that he will sacrifice his daughter, who as he must know is devoted to him and therefore likely to be the first to come forth:

> And it came to pass, when he saw her, that he rent his clothes, and said, Alas, my daughter! thou hast brought me very low, and thou art one of them that trouble me: for I have opened my mouth unto the Lord, and I cannot go back. . . . And she said unto her father, Let this thing be done for me: let me alone two months, that I may go up and down upon the mountains, and bewail my virginity, I and my fellows. And he said, Go. And he sent her away for two months: and she went with her companions, and bewailed her virginity upon the mountains. And it came to pass at the end of two months, that she returned unto her father, who did with her according to his vow which he had vowed: and she knew no man. And it was a custom in Israel, That the daughters of Israel went yearly to lament the daughter of Jephthah the Gileadite four days in a year.

Jephthah's literalness irked rabbinical commentators, who were troubled, especially, by his misplaced sense of a binding obligation. Why didn't the man take advantage of the laws commanding the annulment of vain vows? But Jephthah cannot see that his vow is vain or that it conflicts with the meaning of Hebrew history, which tells of Abraham's unbinding his son and abandoning the vow to sacrifice him. Jephthah's name means "he will open," but this, too, is intended ironically. He is really another Lot, whose name, we recall, means "enclosed," and that is the real meaning of Jephthah's name, too. He will never open his mind, not to the past, not to the future. Ignorance of history condemns him to repeat the old idolatry of child sacrifice.

The specifically Hebrew meaning of Jephthah's vain vow is that it seals for him a fate that an educated Hebrew would recognize as a hell composed of various versions of lapsed history: he has to make an unsuccessful historical argument to the uncomprehending Ammonites, suffer from the absence of his own understanding of history, and mourn the loss of his posterity when his personal history is shattered. For the ancient Hebrews, the simplest definition of hell was a place where parents inevitably sacrifice their own children.

Jephthah's story is told not only to mock the man but to urge a wiser use of history. Though the lament for Jephthah's daughter may charm, the reader is meant to recognize it as an unreflective, pagan-like ritual creating a monument to child-sacrifice, an uncritical substitute for the history of Isaac's reprieve from the knife. Jephthah creates a new holiday, trite days of maidens wandering the land that substitute for Israel's traditional holy days, which all root into the history of the Land. Passover, Weeks, and Tabernacles celebrate central cultural history, the birth of the nation and the giving of the Law on Sinai, and also include in their ceremonies the fruits of the Land. Thus Jephthah reduced holy day to holiday, history to folklore. This degradation of history was in effect its own punishment. "The anger of the Lord was hot against Israel," both as a rebuke from outside and as a self-affliction of the failed mind.

The problem was forgetting. The solution was remembering, to recall "the way which their fathers walked," both in the sense of retracing in the mind the physical journey from wilderness to civilization in the Land, and in the sense of observing the customs and the statutes that provided a way of life for their forefathers. The Hebrews did everything they could to institutionalize memory. They bound bits of Scripture to their doorposts, to their hands, and to their very foreheads in phylacteries; they created a special holy day that they named New Year's or Day of Remembrance (though it was in the middle of the calendar); they wove the telling of history into the cycle of *all* the holy days; they commanded the diligent teaching of history to their children "when thou walkest by the way, when thou liest down, and when thou risest up . . . that thou mayest go in and possess the good land which the Lord sware unto your fathers" (Deuteronomy 6).

Nevertheless they kept forgetting. But the Land was there as the reminder of last recourse, and for fourteen hundred years, from the conquest of Jericho to the Bar Kochba rebellion in 135 C.E., the Hebrews remembered to remember, pulling themselves back again and again from intellectual failure to a rigorous national life, capable of writing history, reading history, and transmitting history. For Hebrews, poetry creates the monotheistic vision, which law distinguishes from other invented gods. History, in turn, transmits the culture of intellectual monotheism from generation to generation, so long as the Land persists as a reminder to remember.

At its best, the entire Hebrew culture resonated with history. Into the new intellectual history the Hebrews reshaped even old legends. For example, an early fragment about Lamech is infused with the idea that a man lacking the capacity for monotheism would also lack the capacity for history, and vice versa: "And Lamech said unto his wives, Adah and Zillah, Hear my voice; ye wives of Lamech, hearken unto my speech: for I have slain a man to my wounding, and a young man to my hurt. If Cain shall be avenged seven-fold, truly Lamech seventy and sevenfold" (Genesis 4).

Lamech brags to his wives that in vengeance or self-defense he killed a young man who had wounded him, if only trivially. The rabbis assume that the purpose of this passage is to memorialize Lamech as the inventor of weapons, but what the text emphasizes is Lamech's perversion of historical thinking. Lamech uses Cain's history to absolve his own violence, reasoning that if God spared the cold-blooded Cain then surely He sanctions self-defense. But in his bravado Lamech forgets the part of Cain's story forbidding vengeance. The function of the mark of Cain was to remind mortals that only God can take vengeance. It is part of the Bible's constant needling of the intellectually slipshod Hebrews that the first person in the Bible allowed to quote history is also the first to abuse it. Like Jephthah, Lamech is unfit to live in the Land. He descends directly from Cain, the wanderer.

The correct use of history is illustrated by Isaiah. In a deeply poetic passage aimed at comforting the Hebrew nation as it mourns in Babylonian exile after its most recent period of forgetting, the Prophet has God himself draw on the history of Noah, giving the idea of history its ultimate provenance:

> Enlarge the place of thy tent, And let them stretch forth the curtains of thy habitations, spare not; Lengthen thy cord, and strengthen thy stakes. . . .

In a little wrath I hid My face from thee for a moment; but with everlasting kindness will I have mercy on thee, saith the Lord thy Redeemer. For this is as the waters of Noah unto Me: for as I have sworn that the waters of Noah should no more go over the earth, so have I sworn that I would not be wroth with thee, nor rebuke thee. For the mountains shall depart, and the hills be removed; but my kindness shall not depart from thee, neither shall the covenant of my peace be removed. (Isaiah 54)

Weaving together the main threads of Hebrew civilization even as he imagines that civilization recomposing itself, Isaiah can again assume an audience capable of catching the allusion to the promise of the Land (that "tent" with its "cords" and "stakes" in which the poetry-making culture of Zion resides). As the nation recovers its intellectual powers, Isaiah can draw on a sensibility capable of reimagining the God of history. Isaiah's God evokes Noah, offering the rainbow and its promise as an antidote to Jephthah's monstrous child-sacrifice— bathing the Land in the compassion it represents.

Only mind and poetry can elevate the chronicle of brutish events to the kind of history imagined by Isaiah's God. And only the awareness of this kind of history can maintain mind and poetry on a level sufficient to grasp the civilization of monotheism. Thus Isaiah's note is echoed throughout ancient Hebrew culture, especially in the psalms attributed to David where historical memory rises up as the preserver of Zion. For David and other Hebrew psalmists, history roots in the Hebrew mind and in the Hebrew Land, and not reliably elsewhere: "How shall we sing the Lord's song in a strange land? If I forget thee, O Jerusalem, let my right hand forget her cunning. If I do not remember thee, let my tongue cleave to the roof of my mouth." The emphasis here is on Jerusalem as a signifying place and on *remember*. Monotheism begets poetry and law, and these beget history, which transmits monotheism—as long as Hebrews remember what Jerusalem and the Land signify.

As the redactors looked over the materials that they brought with them into exile in Babylonia, they singled out David as the figure who placed monotheistic civilization on the stage of world history. Abraham made Hebrew history possible by introducing monotheism and giving his descendants an idea to trace; but he himself was a private person, not eager to let his neighbors know what he was thinking.

Moses set the national history in motion, but he also was introspective, a stutterer who needed his brother Aaron to speak for him. And Moses never escaped the wilderness, never stood before the world at large. David, by contrast, not only understood and galvanized monotheistic history but acted in it as a self-conscious mover on the world's stage. Thus Abraham and Moses come down to us as mythical figures, almost as composite characters who represent genius too large for any one mind, while David reaches out to us from his historical period, a charismatic but life-sized man rooted in his day—"like unto the name of the great men that are in the earth." In this he resembles England's King Henry the Eighth, while Abraham and Moses are like King Arthur.

The living and compelling reality of King David recommended itself to the redactors in Babylonia not only because David's achievements were worthy but because the redactors hoped to realize in historical time, yet again, a nation ruled as Israel once was by David. They were not concerned chiefly with a salvational state governed by a messiah in eternity. David's reign was idealized, but not to the extent that it became utopian. In exile, the redactors wanted to return to working out the fate of the Hebrew nation in the Land, within the historical fabric, as David had done. And so they celebrated David, king of Israel at the time of its maximum expansion, even when they understood that the materialism of David's empire threatened the older idea of the Land far more than did Saul's stark kingdom.

We will come later to the dark ambiguities of David's mastery of Zion, to the hell even he created. Here, let us record the historical moment in which David consolidates his power in Jerusalem after he has already reigned seven years in Hebron. From this account, we will learn something of the approach of the master historian in David's court, whose breathtaking Books of Samuel were given their final form by the redactors in Babylonia.

> David was thirty years old when he began to reign, and he reigned forty years. In Hebron he reigned seven years and six months: and in Jerusalem he reigned thirty and three years over all Israel and Judah. And the king and his men went to Jerusalem unto the Jebusites, the inhabitants of the land: which spake unto David, [taunting him,] saying, Except thou take away the blind and the lame, thou shalt not come in hither: thinking David

cannot come in hither [for even the blind and the lame can defend our city from the motley likes of David]. Nevertheless David took the strong hold of Zion: the same is the city of David. And David said on that day, Whososever getteth up to the gutter [i.e., gets through the underground water system to surprise the city], and smiteth the Jebusites, and the [so-called] lame and the blind, that are hated of David's soul, he shall be chief and captain. Wherefore they said, The blind and the lame shall not come into the house [i.e., it became proverbial, and people mockingly said, "the blind and the lame are on guard, and that is supposed to keep David out"]. So David dwelt in the fort, and called it the city of David. . . . And David went on, and grew great, and the Lord God of hosts was with him. . . . And David took him more concubines and wives out of Jerusalem, after he was come from Hebron: and there were yet sons and daughters born to David. (2 Samuel 5)

I have had to supplement the text, which in the Hebrew is poetical-ly compact but readable, because the King James translation is unin-telligible as it stands. Our passage begins in the standard tone of straightforward chronicles, telling us David's age and the length of his reign. But then something new happens. This matchless writer turns chronicle into history by layering into events the excitable character of David, who returns tit for tat with the scoffing Jebusites. Implied between the lines, David is saying "If they are going to make fun of me by telling me that the blind and the lame could repel me, then I will be even harsher than I might have been; I will slaughter the hon-orable soldiers of Zion's stockade as if they were hateful, just as a bully would butcher the genuinely blind and lame." Apparently David was so witty that his violent humor from that day became proverbial; Because this ability to generate humorous sayings also reflected the new king's character, the historian wove the saying into his narrative fabric, which is subtle and of many colors, though the tones are always muted.

We also learn from this passage, as if in passing, of David's ability to motivate men by rewarding ingenuity and bravery. All through his career he promoted able men, and this made him loved. Here he offers captainships as if in careless magnanimity, though it seems clear that the carelessness is calculated beforehand to please his troops, who always loved his seeming spontaneity and high spirits. Similarly, he seems spontaneous in his plan to invade the city of Zion through its waterworks, but that must have been planned in advance, too. With a light touch, David even makes it seem as if his troops have themselves stumbled on the stratagem of the waterworks. So, from a few poetic lines of history, we learn that David is hotheaded yet cunning, witty and inventive, generous and calculating, of bold and exuberant initiative yet capable of small-minded vindictiveness.

We also learn of the hellish future that David is already sowing with his violence and sensuality. David inspires his people, yet the redactors knew he could also disappoint. At this moment of his conquest of Jerusalem, Zion is hardly more to him than a fort, chosen apparently because it was more secure than Hebron. In leaving Hebron, he has left the home of Abraham, who established the right use of the Land; he has also left the site of the patriarchal burying ground, which can hardly be a promising sign. And surely the purpose of displacing the Jebusites cannot be the joking proverb that David's soldiers spread over the Land, nor can the objective be all the concubines and wives that David took "out of Jerusalem." The implication is that David— the very David who establishes Zion as a cultural symbol—is blind here to the meaning of the enterprise. In a sense *he* is one of the Jebusites' blind men—at least he makes himself blind when convenient, and perhaps that is why the blind and lame "are hated of David's soul." The highly intelligent David probably can guess at the interfamilial warfare his multiple wives and their quarrelsome royal children will instigate, but facing that would be inconvenient for his passions; to be reminded of this blindness would be hateful to him.

Something even darker is implied in the description of the conquest of Zion. The proverb mocking the Jebusites for saying David "shall not come into the house" has ironic overtones that Hebrew readers would recognize. *Bayit*, or "house," is also the Hebrew word for "temple," which David was not given to build, not given to enter. He was kept out of *the* house, as Moses was kept out of the Land. Perhaps he was kept out because of his licentiousness, with those concubines and worse, which in the end made more problems for him than his cleverness could solve. He was kept out to remind the Hebrews that neither David's perversion of exuberance nor the intrigues of his contentious children and their ambitious mothers was the purpose of ancient Zionism.

The story of God's witholding from David the privilege of building the Temple is told delicately soon after the description of Jerusalem's conquest. God Himself brings up the problem with the High Priest Nathan, setting it in its appropriate historical context:

> Go and tell my servant David, Thus saith the Lord, Shalt thou build me an house for me to dwell in? Whereas I have not dwelt in any house since the time that I brought up the children of Israel out of Egypt, even to this day, but have walked in a tent and in a tabernacle. . . . Now therefore so shalt thou say unto my servant David, Thus saith the Lord of hosts, I took thee from the sheepcote, from following the sheep, to be ruler over my people, over Israel. And I was with thee whithersoever thou wentest, and have cut off all thine enemies out of thy sight and have made thee a great name, like unto the name of the great men that are in the earth. Moreover I will appoint a place for my people Israel, and will plant them, that they may dwell in a place of their own, and move no more; neither shall the children of wickedness afflict them any more, as beforetime, . . . since the time that I commanded judges to be over my people Israel[;] and [I] have caused thee to rest from all thine enemies. Also the Lord telleth thee that he will make thee an house. And when thy days be fulfilled, and thou shalt sleep with thy fathers, I will set up thy seed after thee, which shall proceed out of thy bowels, and I will establish his kingdom. He shall build an house for my name, and I will establish the throne of his kingdom for ever. (2 Samuel 7)

God tells Nathan—by implication the King is too besotted with concubines for God to speak to him directly—to braid together for David three histories that should be interrelated in his mind already. First is the history of Israel coming out of Egypt and through the dreadful period of the Judges to rest in its own house. Following that is the personal history of David coming out of a sheepcote to overcome Goliath and Saul and other enemies before achieving rest in his own palace. Finally there is the history of God coming to rest in the prepared Land, in His Temple at Jerusalem. As always, these histories are meant metaphorically; there is no suggestion that God is going to dwell in the Temple literally, only that His presence will be felt by those who can recall that it was He who wished to "plant" them in the Land and He who wished to make personal and national history sing to each other of monotheism. David is just the person in Hebrew history who can best grasp how these personal, national, and divine histories must intertwine and support one another, or be lost altogether. Yet he is told that he is not going to build the Temple, not going to come into the house. This will be left for his son Solomon.

Why must David be diminished with this withholding, with this ambiguity in his personal history? David cannot be allowed to build the Temple because he is willing to toss aside his profound understanding and bring down around himself the hell of failed history, including lost children. We will see something of this in the next chapters. But against the image of David, the swashbuckling brigand who treated the conquest of Zion as a joke, we must celebrate the countervailing images. The historian of 2 Samuel, as well as the redactors who followed him, could count on their readers supplying—even to the story of the conquest of the Jebusite stronghold—the Davidic richness of later Zion. The Hebrews knew that David would make Zion a radiant symbol of what the nation as a whole could be. They knew that he could do this precisely because he possessed the old cleverness of Jacob. As the author of 2 Samuel knew what he was doing when he composed his sonnet-like history of the conquest of Jerusalem, so David knew what he was doing when he brought Zion into history by establishing his capital there. As we shall see, the jokester of the Jebusite fort understood what Zion might be.

Chapter 6

David in Zion

Therefore they shall come and sing in the height of Zion, and shall flow together to the goodness of the Lord, for wheat, and for wine, and for oil, and for the young of the flock and of the herd: and their soul shall be as a watered garden

—Jeremiah 31

Only those who know the supremacy of the intellectual life—the life which has a seed of ennobling thought and purpose within it— can understand the grief of one who falls from that serene activity into the absorbing soul-wasting struggle with worldly annoyances.

—George Eliot, *Middlemarch*

DAVID'S CONSOLIDATION OF POWER WAS BREATHTAKING. HE CRUSHED the Philistines, moving freely through their great cities of Gath and Ashkelon. Never again did they trouble Israel. Slowly they dropped out of history, though they gave Palestine its name in the centuries after the Hebrews themselves were decimated and the name of Israel had grown loathsome (the Greeks thought the Jews boorish, while the Romans thought them ungovernable).

In quick order David unified the lands of the Hebrew tribes, and then he doubled the nation's size by marching north and east to Damascus and beyond, to the very banks of the Euphrates. The Moabites and the Edomites in the rugged country east of the Jordan fell to his machine. Every settled place to the verge of the great southern deserts of Sinai and Arabia submitted to David. In the northwest David made peace with the Phoenicians, who remained strong and independent, content to dominate the Mediterranean while David ruled the hinterlands. And David ruled with an extortionist's hand:

> Then David put garrisons in Syria of Damascus: and the Syrians became servants to David, and brought gifts. And the Lord preserved David whithersoever he went. And David took the shields of gold that were on the servants of Hadadezer, and brought them to Jerusalem. And from Betah, and from Berothai, cities of Hadadezer, king David took exceeding much brass. . . . Then Toi sent Joram his son unto king David. . . . And Joram brought with him vessels of silver, and vessels of gold, and vessels of brass: Which also king David did dedicate unto the Lord, with the silver and gold the he had dedicated of all the nations which he subdued; Of Syria, and of Moab, and of the children of Ammon, and of the Phillistines, and of Amalek, and of the spoil of Hadadezer, son of Rehob, king of Zobah. And David gat him a name. (2 Samuel 8)

These payments of tribute are told in a deadpan style. Though much of what David conquered was acknowledged by the Hebrews themselves as not theirs, nationalistic pride and private astonishment silenced criticism, at least for a while. It was hard to disapprove of David's exuberance, especially since the vast wealth that now flowed into the Land was used to create institutions of high culture. We learn that the tribute being paid into the new national coffers funded new national bureaucracies. Where King Saul appointed only one official, his cousin Abner, the military chief, David had in mind a much

101

grander state. King Saul's palace in Gibeah-of-Benjamin was a simple fort (it has been excavated in modern times), again not what David had in mind. David transformed the rustic ways of the old tribes, and he got away with it because he never let his problematic materialism destroy his purpose to make Zion sing. The historian of 2 Samuel eventually satirizes David for his mindless lumping together of conquests—Moab and Ammon made into fiefs alongside Amalek and the Philistines (the latter two God himself had cursed, while the former two God expressly protected from Hebrew acquisitiveness)—but here the author quietly celebrates David because of the institutions he established with the money he extorted and then "dedicated unto the Lord."

Chapter 8 of 2 Samuel ends with a thumbnail summary of David's new bureaucracy:

> And David reigned over all Israel; and David executed judgment and justice unto all his people. And Joab the son of Zeruiah was over the host: and Jehoshaphat the son of Ahilud was recorder; and Zadok the son of Ahitub, and Ahimelech the son of Abiathar, were the priests; and Seraiah was the scribe; And Benaiah the son of Jehoiada was over both the Cherethites and the Pelethites; and David's sons were chief rulers.

These posts may sound quaint to moderns, but in their day they were thought of as just the opposite, as innovative and impressive. David "executed judgment and justice" not by sitting under a tall tree in the manner of Deborah and other early Hebrew judges but by establishing courts, over which he seems to have presided personally, although only in a formal sense. With much to oversee, he did not spend his days in the courtroom. The recorder was the "remembrancer," a secretary of state who most likely managed the extensive correspondence with the provinces, where business was brisk and complex. The scribe was probably in charge of the extensive libraries, a person of great importance in this literate society. There would have been no literacy then and no Bible today if there had not been complex institutions to safeguard the nation's intellectual work. Priests had to be trained in buildings with support services; ascetics posing in the desert would not do, European painting of biblical scenes notwithstanding. The busy capital required its own police force, and this was the work of the the Chereti and the Peleti, remnant tribes of Philistines.

With his newfound wealth, David established the capital of Israel in Jerusalem on Mount Zion, building extensive courts to administer the law, colleges to train priests, and libraries to store the poetry and history that was accumulating. This was all for a purpose. David called the real and idealized city after one of its hills, planning to make it radiate the culture of intellectual monotheism. For David, Zion was the fulfillment of Abraham's imagination, a state of mind as much as a place, an attitude that rooted in particular, dramatic soil. On and around Mount Zion, from whence vistas were deep, David founded institutions to cultivate that state of mind. He was particularly interested in the poetic sensibility, on which all of ancient Hebrew culture rested. He wrote poetry, and he collected poetry. That psalms written long after his death were attributed to him represents not so much an overextension of royal patronage as an acknowledgment of the source of Israel's formal literary culture.

It was because of his understanding of ancient Zionism that David was forgiven for making the Land into a minature empire—not an empire of a size that would impress Babylonia or Assyria, let alone Greece or Rome, not really different in scale from the Canaan that Abraham walked—but conceptually more crude than the Land. His poetry made all that loot and all those buildings represent something higher:

> According to thy name, O God, so is thy praise unto the ends of the earth: thy right hand is full of righteousness. Let mount Zion rejoice, let the daughters of Judah be glad, because of thy judgments. Walk about Zion, and go round about her: tell the towers thereof. Mark ye well her bulwarks, consider her palaces; that ye may tell it to the generation following. For this God is our God for ever and ever. (Psalm 48)

> The mighty God, even the Lord, hath spoken, and called the earth from the rising of the sun unto the going down thereof. Out of Zion, the perfection of beauty, God hath shined. (Psalm 50)

David was forgiven his vast materialism also because of his understanding of the law, so closely allied with poetry in the culture of monotheism. Under his reign the national laws, scattered in various forms of Mosaic and pre-Mosaic tradition, achieved structure and perspective. David's scholars did the early work of editing and canonizing the Bible, which weaves law and poetry, education and parable, into a single fabric. David himself captures the union of poetry and law under monotheism in Psalm 78:

> Give ear, O my people, to my law: incline your ears to the words of my mouth. I will open my mouth in a parable: I will utter dark sayings of old: Which we have heard and known, and our fathers have told us. We will not hide them from their children, showing to the generation to come the praises of the Lord, and his strength, and his wonderful works that he hath done. For he established a testimony in Jacob, and appointed a law in Israel, which he commanded our fathers, that they should make them known to their children.

In addition, David was forgiven because he founded a school of history that preserved the nation's oral tradition, those old stories of the patriarchs that illustrate the themes of the national culture. And David also enshrined a poetic view of history in the psalms, one not far from our own, in which the Hebrews are directed to seek in God's merciful memory a model to replace their lapsing ability to remember; again Psalm 78:

> And they remembered that God was their rock, and the high God their redeemer. Nevertheless they did flatter him with their mouths, and they lied unto him with their tongues. For their heart was not right with him, neither were they stedfast in his covenant. But he, being full of compassion, forgave their iniquity, and destroyed them not: yea, many a time turned he his anger away, and did not stir up all his wrath. For he remembered that they were but flesh; a wind that passeth away, and cometh not again. How oft did they provoke him in the wilderness, and grieve him in the desert! Yea, they turned back and tempted God, and limited the Holy One of Israel. They remembered not his hand, nor the day when he delivered them from the enemy. How he had wrought his signs in Egypt, and his wonders in the field of Zoan.

God "remembered" that the Hebrews were but flesh, and then the Hebrews "remembered that God was their rock." For remembering the possibility of this reciprocity, David was himself forgiven a licentiousness that "tempted God," spared to set Zion against "wilderness."

A cynical view of David would insist that if he understood the possibility of a reciprocal relationship with God it was as a manipulative scoundrel, his religiosity a mere cover for his rapacity. Furthermore, a cynic would regard David's decision not to build the Temple as another manifestation of his cunning, not as God's fussy preference for leaving the Temple for Solomon. Did not David refuse to build the Temple because he foresaw that Temple priests would grow too powerful, as they eventually did, creating a kind of hereditary papacy? Did he not scribble all those poems, or pay somebody to write them for him, to mask his realpolitik with poesy? This is not, however, the view of the historian of 2 Samuel, who shadows his portrait of David with dark ambiguity but not with cynicism. David's poetry is presented as truly redemptive.

For example, David's famous lamentation on the death of Saul and Jonathan shows David rising with noble sensibility above the ruffian's world of warfare and women. It convinces us, even as it convinced the historian of 2 Samuel and millenia of his readers, that David, even at the beginning of his ascendency, was as genuine in his enlarged outlook as he was in his readiness to seize the main chance created by the throne's vacancy. Saul and Jonathan have both fallen on Mount Gilboa, in the wars with the Philistines:

> Ye mountains of Gilboa, let there be no dew, neither let there be rain, upon you, nor fields of offerings: for there the shield of the mighty is vilely cast away, the shield of Saul, as though he had not been anointed with oil. . . . Saul and Jonathan were lovely and pleasant in their lives, and in their death they were not divided: they were swifter than eagles, they were stronger than lions. Ye daughters of Israel, weep over Saul, who clothed you in scarlet, with other delights, who put on ornaments of gold upon your apparel. How are the mighty fallen in the midst of the battle! O Jonathan, thou wast slain in thine high places. I am distressed for thee, my brother Jonathan: very pleasant hast thou been unto me: thy love to me was wonderful, passing the love of women. How are the mighty fallen, and the weapons of war perished! (2 Samuel 1)

When David values Jonathan's love beyond the love of women, he says a great deal. The partial list of his wives and children in 1 Chronicles 3 is lengthy even without the "sons of the concubines." Yet we believe David here when he says that women were not his highest love. We believe him when he implies that war was not his highest value either, as he pictures Saul's loveliness outliving his shield, which moulders in a field, "the weapons of war perished." We believe him, too, when he values "high places," where Israel builds altars to God and governs herself with Jonathan's wisdom and decency. In marking these high places as Jonathan's ("thine"), David modestly refrains from claiming them for himself, and he implicitly elevates Jonathan's monotheism over the rites of *other* high places, devoted as they were to idolatry and the supreme value of "weapons of war."

We believe David's sincerity when he invokes the feeling citizens of the Land as "ye daughters of Israel"—by which he means monotheists, not potential concubines. We believe in his submission to the Land itself as he begs for the withholding of rain from Gilboa—not because he wants crops there to fail but because he honors the Land as an abiding mourner of those who might have sustained its civilization. Implicitly, David raises the value of the Land over the passing glory of war, over the passing delight of women, even over the passing dignity of royalty, among whom he must modestly count himself as one of the "mighty" doomed to fall eventually. Finally, we believe David because his poetry moves us.

Thus the worldly historian of 2 Samuel can note David's flaws and still offer him as a master poet of monotheism. It comes as some disappointment to discover that David only held to his own achievement intermittently, that he himself frequently "remembered not." But David is one of the great heroes of the ancient Hebrews not because he was always wise but because he always understood the precise relationship between his intellectual failure and his intellectual goals. Unlike most of his fellow citizens, he knew when he was forgetting monotheistic civilization; he never so lapsed that he failed to recognize his regression. It may not seem a high compliment, but the ancient Hebrews thought that David possessed as good a mind as one could hope for in a human being. If all Israel maintained even the faltering standard of David, all might yet be well. Perhaps this is most clear in the story of David's cunning conquest of Bathsheba.

The story, told in 2 Samuel 11 and 12, is deliberately set in the context of the Land's defense. Ammon is again making claims on Israel. David, weary of the old battles, weary of applying his mind unremittingly to monotheistic culture and its protection, chooses to stay home while others fight, allowing his high creativity to wander into seemingly pleasant diversions. His old problem of womanizing reasserts itself, and his manipulative talents run amok, freed by this unaccustomed leisure:

> And it came to pass, after the year was expired, at the time when kings go forth to battle, that David sent Joab, and his servants with him, and all Israel; and they destroyed the children of Ammon, and besieged Rabbah. But David tarried still at Jerusalem. And it came to pass in an eveningtide, that David arose from off his bed, and walked upon the roof of the king's house: and from the roof he saw a woman washing herself; and the woman was very beautiful to look upon. And David sent and enquired after the woman. And one said, Is not this Bathsheba, the daughter of Eliam, the wife of Uriah the Hittite? And David sent messengers, and took her; and she came in unto him, and he lay with her; for she was puri-fied from her uncleanness: and she returned unto her house. And the woman conceived, and sent and told David, and said, I am with child.

The warping of David's intelligence is almost comical. The royal peeping Tom inquires into Bathsheba's state of menstruation, assuring himself that she has observed the laws of purification, while he himself prepares to violate the laws against adultery. Soon, the misuse of his mind degenerates into the old trickery of Simeon and Levi and of undeveloped Jacob himself. For David now has the problem of cover-ing an embarrassing pregnancy. Feigning the need for a report from the front, he summons Uriah, assuming the man will want to sleep with his wife and thus provide a plausible explanation for how Bathsheba conceived while her husband was in the trenches; David even provides a hearty, pre-coital dinner:

> And David said to Uriah, Go down to thy house, and wash thy feet. And Uriah departed out of the king's house, and there followed him a mess of meat from the king. But Uriah slept at the door of the king's house, with all the servants of his lord, and went not down to his house. And when they had told David, saying, Uriah went not down unto his house, David said unto Uriah, Camest thou not from thy journey? why then didst thou not go down unto thine house? And Uriah said unto David, The ark, and Israel, and Judah abide in tents; and my lord Joab, and the servants of my lord, are encamped in the open fields; shall I then go into mine house, to eat and to drink, and to lie with my wife? as thou livest, and as thy soul liveth, I will not do this thing.

Ironically, Uriah the Hittite stands above the King of Israel in his devotion to high purpose. The whole culture of ancient Israel, as represented by the ark of law, is on the line, and Uriah means not to trifle. He will not lie with his wife while Israel is at war. Was David stung by Uriah, who is making more of a reproach than he realizes? Not quite yet. David is in the cunning mode and is to sink even lower. He next tries another stratagem; perhaps if the overly solemn Uriah gets drunk the man will yet sleep with his wife:

> And David said to Uriah, Tarry here to-day also, and to-morrow I will let thee depart. So Uriah abode in Jerusalem that day, and the morrow. And when David had called him he did eat and drink before him; and he made him drunk: and at even he went out to lie on his bed with the servants of his lord, but went not down to his house.

The humor gets darker. The wily David, failing to manipulate Uriah, must now figure out how to kill him clandestinely. He does this by having Uriah himself bear a letter to Joab demanding that Uriah be placed and abandoned in a lethal battle. Cunning begets cunning. With the death of Uriah successfully carried out, Joab, who has recently committed serious tactical errors in the field, uses his knowledge of David's scandal as blackmail to protect himself from an anticipated tongue-lashing:

> Then Joab sent and told David all the things concerning the wars; And charged the messenger, saying, When thou has made an end of telling the matters of the war unto the King, And if so be that the King's wrath arise, and he say unto thee, Wherefore approached ye so nigh unto the city when ye did fight; knew ye not that they would shoot from the wall? Who smote Abimelech the son of Jerubbesheth? did not a woman cast a piece of a millstone upon him from the wall, that he died in Thebez? why went ye nigh the wall? then say thou, Thy servant Uriah the Hittite is dead also.

The ploy works. About to chastise the messenger for the needless loss of life in poorly planned battles, David is fed the death of Uriah and stroked into purring, "Thus shalt thou say unto Joab, Let not this thing displease thee, for the sword devoureth one as well as another." David is thus shielded from exposure and Joab is protected from the King's wrath. Meanwhile the civilization of Israel itself is in peril of disintegrating into mere cleverness.

But rescue is still possible. Eventually David reawakens his literary sensibility, his ability to read himself. He gets help from Nathan the High Priest, but the emphasis is on David's own introspection, as when he accepts the application of Nathan's parable:

> There were two men in one city; the one rich, and the other poor. The rich man had exceeding many flock and herds: But the poor man had nothing, save one little ewe lamb, which he had bought and nourished up: and it grew up together with him, and with his children; it did eat of his own meat, and drank of his own cup, and lay in his bosom, and was unto him as a daughter. And there came a traveler unto the rich man, and he spared to take of his own flock and of his own herd, to dress for the wayfaring man that was come unto him; but took the poor man's lamb, and dressed it for the man that was come to him. And David's anger was greatly kindled against the man; and he said to Nathan, As the Lord liveth, the man that hath done this thing shall surely die . . . because he had no pity. And Nathan said to David, Thou art the man. . . . And David said unto Nathan, I have sinned against the Lord. And Nathan said unto David, The Lord also hath put away thy sin; thou shalt not die. (2 Samuel 12)

All the while Nathan is telling his parable, he is watching David for a response. What is at issue is David's ability to read, to apply the intellectual skills of monotheistic culture. Nathan knows that David, usually quite adroit in this regard, has been nodding of late. As Nathan tells his parable, he has to adjust for David's present obtuseness, adding details that David would usually find superfluous. Thus, apparently seeing that David has failed to catch his drift, Nathan becomes more pointed, personifying the ewe ("drank of his own cup, and lay in his bosom") so that David will realize he is not talking about sheep. Even so, David takes the story literally. He wants to punish the malefactor, thinking him thief and poacher. But at least he rightly reads the rich man's lack of "pity." This is all the opening Nathan needs. When he says bluntly, "Thou art the man," David immediately recovers his celebrated literary consciousness, knowing that the ewe is Bathsheba. "I have sinned against the Lord," says the King.

Afterwards, to confirm that David has returned to himself, we are given a glimpse of his usual astute reading. The sickly baby produced by David's illicit union with Bathsheba has died and the King's servants whisper among themselves, fearful of giving the King the bad news. "But when David saw that his servants whispered, David perceived that the child was dead: therefore David said unto his servants, Is the child dead? And they said, He is dead." David has instantly pierced the meaning of his servants' whisperings, although he rendered himself deaf to evidence of his earlier, roaring injustices (no doubt there was whispering then too, which he ignored). This is the literate David, the David who is valued, the David who in his better moments can sustain monotheistic civilization.

Many pious readers of this passage wonder at God's (and hence the ancient Hebrew culture's) easy forgiveness of David's heinous acts. How can such an immoral man be tolerated? The death of the sinless baby seems a thin, symbolic punishment, misplaced and hardly sufficient. But the point, I think, is not David's morality. It is his intellect, which, because it is self-correcting, must be celebrated, despite its lapses. It is only in a mind susceptible to poetry, such as David's, that a moral culture can be planted. The Hebrews believed that as long as intellect grasps God and recognizes its own relative debasement, there is a hope of civilization. One spares David his life because there are, apparently, no better human lives with which to work, no better way of establishing pity in the Land.

The story of David's murder of Uriah concludes with the destruction of Ammon, that baby-burning, Molech-worshiping enemy of Zion; with David's marriage to Bathsheba; and with the birth of Solomon. Freed momentarily from the harassment of idolatry, David is able to preserve for Solomon and for a new generation the recognition that "out of Zion, the perfection of beauty, God hath shined." David goes on to reinvigorate the Land through the right training of mind:

> Remove from me the way of lying: and grant me thy law graciously. I have chosen the way of truth; thy judgments have I laid before me. I have stuck unto thy testimonies: O Lord, put me not to shame. I will run the way of thy commandments, when thou shalt enlarge my heart. (Psalm 119)

That David wishes to give up lying for psalmistry, cunning for an enlarged heart filled with monotheistic culture, is all to the good. Nevertheless, the writers of the Bible must acknowledge that the protection of the Land and the maintenance of monotheistic culture depends upon the impulse to lie, which must be trained to higher purposes. Thus the destruction of Ammon and the securing of peace for

Zion concludes with a political charade, a reminder that the monotheist who begins with lying must ascend:

> And Joab fought against Rabbah of the children of Ammon, and took the royal city. And Joab sent messengers to David, and said, I have fought against Rabbah, and have taken the city of waters. Now therefore gather the rest of the people together, and encamp against the city, and take it: lest I take the city, and it be called after my name. And David gathered all the people together, and went to Rabbah, and fought against it, and took it. And he took their king's crown from off his head, the weight whereof was a talent of gold with the precious stones: and it was set on David's head. And he brought forth the spoil of the city in great abundance. . . . So David and all the people returned unto Jerusalem. (2 Samuel 12)

There is no attempt to dress up David's glory here. It is quite clear that David depends on Joab's softening up the quarry before he swoops in for the kill. There is even the suggestion that David is borrowing another king's idol-worshipping glory when he sets Ammon's crown on his own head, mistaking weight of gold for weight of character. But military heroism is not what is most valued here. Rather, David's capacity to mimic the role of a military hero signals the capacity for a higher mimicry, especially the imaginative establishment of Zion, "the perfection of beauty" out of which "God hath shined." In the end, it is not important that David masquerades as a great conquerer but that he "and all the people returned unto Jerusalem," the actual and metaphoric capital of Zion.

Chapter 7

Brickkiln and Winepress

If I ascend up into heaven, thou art there; if I make my bed in hell, behold, thou art there.

—Psalm 139

Blood is the god of war's rich livery.

—Christopher Marlowe, *Tamburlaine*

THE STORY OF BATHSHEBA AND OF NATHAN'S PARABLE DOES NOT QUITE conclude with David borrowing the glory of the vanquished king of Ammon but with a darker verse. "And he brought forth the spoil of the city in great abundance. And he brought forth the people that were therein, and put them under saws, and under harrows of iron, and under axes of iron, and made them pass through the brickkiln: and thus did he unto all the cities of the children of Ammon. So David and all the people returned unto Jerusalem" (2 Samuel 12).

What are we to make of David's harshness? The chilling execution of a captive population is made all the more horrible by the twisted pressing into service of peacetime tools and by the matter-of-fact tone which ushers civilians into the fiery brickkiln. The makers of the Bible would have, of course, no way of hearing terrible echoes from twentieth century ovens, but the brickkiln is awful enough without echoes. The conquest and defense of the Land was an ugly business, but surely it need not have been this ugly. If the ancient Hebrews took pains to warn themselves against becoming mere warriors, what did they think about the part of their lives that was nevertheless taken up with the most nasty kind of warfare?

I am afraid that the makers of the Bible recognized ugly warfare as an inescapable habit of their times; a nation could be secured in no other way. And there was God's command to uproot baby-burning idolators, such as those in Ammon. But the ugliness lingers, and it must be confronted. There are hints that ancient Hebrew readers were expected to bring intellect and a literary sensibility to the problem of slaughtering human beings. There is no suggestion that those recounting David's conquest of Ammon mean to celebrate the victory. Rather, the opposite is implied.

First, as we have noted, David's violence is preceded by stories revealing his darker passions and suggesting that he goes to Ammon as a wildly driven man. He was caught at murder and lost a son as a consequence. Like a schoolboy, he endured a lecture by Nathan. Blackmailed by a general who learned of his sins, he then suffered the condescension of this general, who allows him in his indolence to take false credit for the fall of Ammon. Thus, the writers of the Bible present Ammon's demise not as a desirable feature of David's Zionism, but as a consequence of the King's boredom, his wandering exuberance, and his pitiful need to vent his own mortification.

Further, the ancient Hebrews who knew history would recognize other ironies in connection with David's "triumph" in Ammon. David had no reason for going there in the first place. Moses himself had reminded the children of Israel of their obligation to distinguish themselves from other people and to resist seizing lands belonging to surrounding tribes, including Ammon:

> Thou art to pass over through, Ar, the coast of Moab, this day: And when thou comest nigh over against the children of Ammon, distress them not, nor meddle with them: for I will not give thee of the land of the children of Ammon any possession; because I have given it unto the children of Lot for a possession. (Deuteronomy 2)

Perhaps David's brutality, not different in kind from the cruelty of kings in other lands but different in the analysis it was expected to provoke, derives in part from his need to drown in blood his sickening fear that he is far from the Land and its purposes, at sea in "the city of waters," adrift in Rabbah, far from the Zionist enterprise. Thus the Bible's editors, in their dry conclusion that "David and all the people returned unto Jerusalem," slyly suggest that David and his followers, having strayed from the city of peace, are in need of repentance, which is the other meaning of the Hebrew word for *return*.*

The Bible's treatment of David in Rabbat-Ammon provides the beginnings of our own intellectual repudiation of war. Though our culture has not progressed much in this respect since biblical times, that we take any critical view of war at all owes much to the Bible's poetic challenge to mindless militarism. Shakespeare's critical presentation

---

*The masterly writer of 2 Samuel implies a progressive deepening of David's sins, from adultery with Bathsheba to the murder of Uriah to the undermining of his civilization's purpose. David's enraged slaughter of civilians at Rabbat-Ammon, a place in which, by God's own instruction, he should not have set foot, is in this view the worst of all of David's transgressions, precisely because it sinks from personal to national corruption. *Avayra goreret avayra* (Sin leads to deeper sinning) says Simeon ben Azai in Chapter IV of *Pirke Avoth*, in the same way fulfilling an "easy commandment" leads to the shouldering of a more difficult one. Yet the rabbis, when they came to list David's transgressions, ignored the satire of the writer of 2 Samuel and explained away the travesty of Rabbat-Ammon. The rabbis' judgment in this matter is accepted as final; nevertheless, the literary manner of the telling of David's exploits in Rabbat-Ammon suggest otherwise (see *Shabbat* 56a).

of Henry V's invasion of France, for example, which is couched in a thin pretext, stems from a long tradition going back to David. The hint that David's violence is the spawn of vicious guilt makes possible Shakespeare's similar thought about Hal, who wanders through the English camp on the eve of the battle of Agincourt lecturing his soldiers on the problems that "spotless" kings bear in employing "guilty" soldiers. It is, of course, Hal himself who is feeling guilty for turning his soldiers from contemplation of his own stolen crown in order to usurp another crown in France. He prays, "O Lord,/O, not today, think not upon the fault/My father made in compassing the crown!"

But prayer is not really Hal's mode; he is most eloquent at channeling guilt into violence. Here he is threatening the Governor of Harfleur:

> *. . . why in a moment look to see*
> *The blind and bloody soldier with foul hand*
> *Defile the locks of your shrill-shrieking daughters;*
> *Your fathers taken by the silver beards,*
> *And their most reverend heads dashed to the walls;*
> *Your naked infants spitted upon pikes,*
> *While the mad mothers with their howls confused*
> *Do break the clouds . . .*

Partly because he has access to an ancient literary heritage, Shakespeare, like the writers of the Bible, knows that men may march into foreign territory principally to vent steaming guilt.

We should also note that the writer of 2 Samuel is careful to signal that David's cruelty is a tendency of his character, not a one-time occurrence. We have seen David's violent reaction to the Jebusites, "hated of David's soul." And his marching of the Ammonites through saws and harrows recalls the earlier subjugation of the Moabites that set the military tone for his reign: "And he smote Moab, and measured them with a line, casting them down to the ground; even with two lines measured he to put to death, and with one full line to keep alive. And so the Moabites became David's servants, and brought gifts" (2 Samuel 8).

Again the tools of peace are usurped. The image is shocking. The Moabites are measured by the rope-length, without bothering to count them as individuals. Those measuring two rope-lengths are slaughtered, one rope-length are made servants. The ones saved bring "gifts," a euphemism for the ransom on their measured lives. In Hebrew poetry, the measuring rope or line, probably taken over from Egyptian architecture, is rich with associations. Behind David's measuring out the Moabites, a contrasting use of the line shines forth— God's measuring out the universe: "Then the Lord answered Job. . . . Where wast thou when I laid the foundations of the earth? declare, if thou hast understanding. Who hath laid the measures thereof, if thou knowest? or who hath stretched the line upon it" (Job 38)?

In parallel with David's abuse of the measuring line in Moab stands the idolator's abuse of carpentry:

> They that make a graven image are all of them vanity. . . . The carpenter stretcheth out his rule; he marketh it out with a line; he fitteth it with planes, and he marketh it out with the compass, and maketh it after the figure of a man. . . . Yea, he maketh a god, and worshippeth it. (Isaiah 44)

The Hebrew reader would acknowledge that David was one who had "understanding" of God the Creator, yet they could see he was also one who could lapse into a violence that made him indistinguishable in Ammon from the native idolators there.

Despite his presumed literary perspective, the ancient Hebrew would not regard David's destruction of Ammon as entirely misdirected. Indeed, the ancient reader would have been tempted to applaud. It was true that Ammon belonged to the children of Lot and that David did not have the right to attack it. But Lot, we remember, was a literalist, interested in things. His descendants were idolators. They sacrificed their own first-born babies to Molech. And over the centuries the Ammonites applauded every misfortune in Israel, including the exile into Babylonia:

> Thus saith the Lord God; Because thou saidst, Aha, against my sanctuary, when it was profaned; and against the land of Israel, when it was desolate; and against the house of Judah, when they went into captivity; Behold, therefore . . . I will make Rabbah a stable for camels, and the Ammonites a couching place for flocks: and ye shall know that I am the Lord. (Ezekiel 25)

Thus it is in the cultural air of ancient Israel to tolerate hostility toward Moab and Ammon. We saw this in Boaz's protection of Ruth the Moabitess from the unpleasantness of his field hands. In this context,

Hebrew readers would be tempted to forgive David his cruelty in Ammon, home of child-sacrifice and hatred of Israel. Thus the writer of 2 Samuel leaves David's warfare in its full ambiguity, with emphasis on the need to distinguish between rightful defense of the Land and use of the Land as an excuse to bully. It is easy to bully those who can be accused of child-sacrifice.

Though we live in an age during which the dominant religion on earth celebrates a God who sacrificed His only begotten Son, modern readers have difficulty understanding the attraction of child-sacrifice. Nevertheless, the ancient Hebrews found the Ammonite custom of burning children strangely attractive. Starting from God's original injunction, they had to warn themselves against the barbaric practice repeatedly, even before they came to the Land:

> When the Lord thy God shall cut off the nations from before thee, . . . take heed to thyself that thou be not snared by following them. . . . For every abomination to the Lord, which he hateth, have they done unto their gods; for even their sons and their daughters they have burnt in the fire to their gods. (Deuteronomy 12)

Sadly, this warning often failed, and the Hebrews lapsed into the old temptation to appease the local gods of fertility and accidental death. They sacrificed their babies, hoping to win salvation for themselves and for their crops and animals, thus provoking Jeremiah and Ezekiel to chastise those who did so:

> And they have built the high places of Tophet, which is in the valley of the son of Hinnom, to burn their sons and their daughters in the fire; which I commanded them not, neither came it into my heart. (Jeremiah 7)

> With their idols have they committed adultery, and have also caused their sons, whom they bare unto me, to pass for them through the fire, to devour them. (Ezekiel 23)

The Hebrew temptation to protect their frail lives by burning their babies was connected in their minds to their other mortal temptation, which was bringing God directly into the world as a local protector. Child-sacrifice and incarnation were two parts of the same desperate urge to clutch at palpable straws and abandon the mind's-eye grasp of the Creator who resides *outside* the vastness of the universe. From the point of view of the ancient Hebrews, Christianity, with its incarnation and sacrifice of the only begotten son, is the return of the Hebrew repressed.

Thus David's burning of the Ammonites in their own brickkiln might seem poetic justice to readers eager to extirpate Molech's maw from their own fiery imaginations. But details in the story of the brick-kiln warn Hebrew readers not to exculpate themselves by burning others. There is a close resemblance between the Hebrew words for brickkiln (*malben*) and for the idol-oven in which Ammonite babies were incinerated (*malkam*); this resemblance is closer in Hebrew, where "k" hardly differs in shape from "b"—the similarity is so close that it causes a textual problem here, where it is unclear if "k" or "b" is meant. Further, the Hebrews would note the similarity between *malkam* and *melech* ("king") and between *melech* and *Molech*, which also means "king." In noting this punning on *king, Molech, brickkiln*, and *idol-oven*, Hebrew readers would recognize that distinctions are being demanded. They would recognize that King David achieves no glory for Zion by purging himself in a desperate usurpation of the Ammonite kiln. Rather he makes of himself a *King Molech, his kiln a baby-oven.*

All this and more hovers over the Bible's deadpan description of the conquest of Ammon, darkening David's celebration. Hebrews thought it no loss that they held this conquest for only a short period, and they never thought it part of the Land. But the impulse to fire up the brickkiln was omnipresent; bloodthirstiness thrived. Pyromania was everpresent, even in the conquest of the Land, which was suppos-edly carried out at the behest of God:

> For Joshua drew not his hand back, wherewith he stretched out the spear, until he had utterly destroyed all the inhabitants of Ai. . . . And Joshua burnt Ai, and made it an heap for ever, even a desolation unto this day. And the king of Ai he hanged on a tree until eventide: and as soon as the sun was down, Joshua commanded that they should take his carcass down from the tree, and cast it at the entering of the gate of the city, and raise thereon a great heap of stones, that remaineth unto this day. (Joshua 8)

The gory details are underscored, not because the Hebrews were proud of them but because they knew they had to keep a check on their bloodlust. The "great heap of stones" over Ai and its king is as much a monument to the problematic human love of sword and fire as it is to Joshua's victory.

There are modern readers who think the Bible a primitive book that takes pleasure in retelling ancient massacres. But this is a simplistic view. Other ancient peoples may have taken unthinking pleasure in turning their enemies into rubble, but the Hebrews submitted their bloodlust to poetry. Since their bloodlust rivaled that of their neighbors, much poetry was required. Thus David's bloodlust was met not only by David's own capacity for poetry but by the poetry of the nation.

For example, Isaiah, the Hebrews' poet laureate, tempted his readers to make their God into a warrior only to reprimand them for their indulgence of violence. In one of the most astonishing passages in the Bible, Isaiah appears to envision an anthropomorphic God, imagining Him as an armed warrior on earth, drenched in the very blood decreed a sacrament of life. Isaiah sets his scene during the Assyrian onslaught in the late eighth century B.C.E., when a nervous watchman, staring fearfully to the east from the ramparts of Jerusalem, thinks he sees a divine soldier approaching Jerusalem. The mortal challenges the God he sees and receives an answer:

> Who is this that cometh from Edom, with dyed garments from Bozrah? this that is glorious in his apparel, traveling in the greatness of his strength? I that speak in righteousness, mighty to save. Wherefore art thou red in thine apparel, and thy garments like him that treadeth in the winevat? I have trodden the winepress alone; and of the people there was none with me: for I will tread them in mine anger, and trample them in my fury; and their blood shall be sprinkled upon my garments, and I will stain all my raiment. For the day of vengeance is in mine heart, and the year of my redeemed is come. And I looked, and there was none to help; and I wondered that there was none to uphold: therefore mine own arm brought salvation unto me; and my fury, it upheld me. And I will tread down the people im mine anger, and make them drunk in my fury, and I will bring down their strength to the earth. (Isaiah 63)

Can the watchman's vision of this *miles gloriosus* catch a likeness of the God of the Hebrews?

The passage, however, expects sophistication of its readers. First, Isaiah distances the vision of the Bloody Warrior by placing it in the mind of a sleepless, anxious watchman, who from the walls of besieged Jerusalem imagines a conversation he might have with Israel's rescuer, should He appear. Then, one notes, literary understatement further distances the bloodbath that the watchman is wishing on his enemies; we see no mangled corpses, only the winepress and a stained cloak. Further, the interlocutor's God does not advertise his incarnation as much as He chastises the Hebrews for failing to join Him in the repudiation of bloody idolatry: "And I looked, and there was none to help, and I wondered that there was none to uphold."

Daringly, the passage admits and controls the very impulses Isaiah spent his life combatting—the yearning for incarnation, for blood, and for the intellectual simplicity that repeatedly brought Israel to the verge of annihilation. In a hypothetical future, after God Himself has begun the retransformation of a backsliding Israel, Isaiah foresees the "treading" of Edom not as a military victory but as a pressing out of Edomite idolatry and violence from the grape of Hebrew life. This is a bad vintage in the Warrior's vat, yielding no sweet wine, and it has been harvested not in Bozrah but locally, in Israel, the only habitation of idolatry of real concern to the Hebrews.

The Edomites, we recall, descended from Esau, the red-faced, bloody hunter who sold his birthright for a mess of red pottage. He traded the inheritance of monotheism not because he despised it but because, without the imagination to hold it in his mind, he could not read it or value it. The ruddy Edomites, living in caves in red mountains, did on occasion harass the ancient Hebrews, but these cousins of the House of Israel, living on the physical and spiritual border of the Land, mainly functioned metaphorically. They represented the hunger of the Hebrew mind for the rejected, familial temptation to make idols and to fight only for more blood. During Isaiah's time the Edomites were a minor threat to the Hebrews—the more powerful armies descended from Assyria, further to the north and east. But Isaiah sets his scene in Edom because the enemy he wants to see defeated is not Assyria but one as close as cousins, as close as Edomite bloodlust and literalism, as close as the Hebrews' own undermining of monotheism, which made possible the advent of local idolatry. (Thus Jephthah's land of Tob is set in the territory of the Edomites, to which his Hebrew mind often drifted.)

Isaiah's plan is not to bring God literally into the world—that would reduce the vatmaker to his vat, the winemaker to his wine. He is bringing mind and metaphor to bear on the persistent wish to have God in the world and to live by war alone. Isaiah wants the House of David to see that God is neither in the winevat nor on the battlefield but in the minds of monotheists whose battles are mainly intellectual. At the bottom of Isaiah's vat, there is *no* literal battlefield and *no* literal warrior and *no* literal blood. There is not even literal wine. To the watchman the wine may be blood, and a superficial reader may see here the notion of a bloodthirsty god, but Isaiah's poetry insists that in the last analysis the wine in the vat is Hebrew bloodlust. If a victorious Israel is to sip wine in a truly defended Jerusalem, it has to master the interdependent arts of metaphor and monotheism, bringing mind to bear on intellectual battles while keeping God and man out of war. Failure to do so leads to idolatry, to the death of mind and nation, as the Warrior goes on alone.

The only fury admired is moral fury. In Isaiah's passage, the Warrior, abandoned by Israel, goes on alone in a poetic rage, whose center is far from the battlefield and the brickkiln. The winevat that matters is moral consciousness: "And I will tread down the people in mine anger, and make them drunk in my fury." The anger of Isaiah's Warrior demands that brute force be channeled into mind power, and thus the Warrior encourages the Hebrews to make prowess sublime. It was essential that their culture teach Hebrews to read the brickkiln and the winepress so that they might see that monotheism depends on David's brain, not David's brawn.

So what did the ancient Hebrews think of David's ugly warfare? They thought it ugly. They thought that though war seemed unavoidable, poetry might transmute it into a vigor of mind able to beat swords into ploughshares, thus reversing David's conversion of harrows into instruments of torture:

> . . . for out of Zion shall go forth the law, and the word of the Lord from Jerusalem. And he shall judge among the nations, and shall rebuke many people: and they shall beat their swords into plowshares, and their spears into pruning hooks: nation shall not lift up sword against nation, neither shall they learn war any more. (Isaiah 2)

Because David's own poetry provided the tradition in which Isaiah worked, David was in the end forgiven his assault on Rabbat-Ammon.

The writer of 2 Samuel lets David's poetry have the final word. He moves David's boastful song about his early victories to the end of the book, and then he allows it to elide into a deeply poetic psalm on the ideal ruler who grounds himself in the fear of God rather than the fear of men. "Thy gentleness hath made me great," sings David in the war song of 2 Samuel 22. Soon he seems to forget God's gentleness as he celebrates his violent victories: "Thou hast also given me the necks of mine enemies, that I might destroy them that hate me." This shout of triumph, however, gives way to something closer to Isaiah's pacifism, David's last poem:

> Now these be the last words of David. . . . The spirit of the Lord spake by me, and his word was in my tongue. The God of Israel said, . . . He that ruleth over men must be just, ruling in fear of God . . . as the light of the morning, when the sun riseth, even a morning without clouds; as the tender grass springing out of the earth by clear shining after rain. (2 Samuel 23)

However brutal David was, his poetry insists that in the end he be judged by the standard of the God-fearing ruler who springs forth like the tender grass rather than by the standard of the warrior who pounces on the necks of enemies.

Thus the Hebrews helped invent the idealist's critique of war even while they themselves were caught in its trenches. Could they witness the present, they would have sympathy for their embattled descendants who strive for peace even while enemies taunt them into the old and common brutality. The ancient Hebrews would not be surprised to find Israel still struggling with her enemies, still subject to external terror and to unleashed internal nastiness, despite new stirrings of peace. Nor would they be surprised by the generally vicious tenor of the modern world, not very different from their own.

Perhaps they would be startled to learn that modern intellectuals, who have inherited their antiwar sentiments from Isaiah, brand modern Israel a purveyor of violence. On the other hand, as we shall see, the ancient Hebrews were well acquainted with irrational hatred of Zionism, and Israel's present situation might come as no surprise. In any case, Israel will continue to torment itself with its own poetic consciousness—continuing to forbid war on Rabbat-Ammon even while the world recalls with tolerance the war of Rabbat-Ammon on

Jerusalem, continuing to press for the poetry that converts swords into ploughshares, and continuing to suffer the accusations of those who find comfort in imagining Israel to be not the inventor of pacifist poetry but of brutality itself. All this, as Isaiah's watchman demonstrates, is part of the defense of the Land.

Chapter 8

Ritual in the Land

Ye shall not offer unto the Lord that which [has its testicles] bruised, or crushed, or broken, or cut; neither shall ye make any offering thereof in your land.
—Leviticus 22

It is superstition to put one's hope in formalities; but it is pride to be unwilling to submit to them.
—Pascal, *Pensées*

THE SPECTER OF BLOODLUST HAUNTS THE BIBLE—IT IS A BLOODY BOOK. The Hebrews believed their enemies really wanted to destroy them and that they themselves should reciprocate in kind, and they feared that like the mortified David, they would pursue war for war's sake. To weave into daily life a warning against the madness of blood, the Hebrews added to the poets' cry a profusion of rituals designed to deflect rage. One of these involved a complex set of animal sacrifices, so that when the Second Temple stood in Jerusalem a river of animal blood streamed from the priests' many knives, requiring a fast-flowing system of underground aquaducts to disperse the clotting tide. Similarly, the Hebrew dietary laws, which prohibited the eating of blood, dampened bloodlust, as did laws of purification, including rites dealing with the blood of childbirth and menstruation.

Many of these rituals accompanied the cycle of the seasons, with citizens obligated to go up to Jerusalem to offer sacrifices during the spring festival of Passover, the summer festival of Weeks, and the fall festival of Tabernacles. These holidays all radiated with historical significance as well, but the seasonal sacrifices were reminders that the fruits and riches of the Land would engender bloody feuds unless bloodletting was held in check by the priestly ritual. The soundness of life in the Land depended on these rituals of timely sacrifice and discerning diet:

> It shall be a perpetual statute for your generations throughout all your dwellings, that ye eat neither fat nor blood. (Leviticus 3)

> And ye shall not walk in the manners of the nation, which I cast out before you. . . . But I have said unto you, Ye shall inherit their land, and I will give it unto you to possess it, a land that floweth with milk and honey: I am the Lord your God, which have separated you from other people. Ye shall therefore put difference between clean beasts and unclean, and between unclean fowls and clean. . . . And ye shall be holy unto me: for I the Lord am holy, and have severed you from other people, that ye should be mine. (Leviticus 20)

And the failure to observe ritual led to exile:

> Thou hast not brought me the small cattle of thy burnt-offerings; neither hast thou honored me with thy sacrifices. . . . Therefore I have profaned

the princes of the sanctuary, and have given Jacob to the curse, and Israel to reproaches. (Isaiah 43)

The beginnings of Hebrew ritual, like the beginnings of Hebrew civilization, are with Abraham, who builds a simple altar to God when he first arrives in the Land before going on to Egypt. Upon his return from Egypt, the ritual he conducts soon reaches the Hebrew standard of poetic theater. We recall how Abraham divided the carcasses of sacrificial animals into "pieces," according to God's prescription; how God uses this occasion and its "horror of great darkness" to visit upon Abraham a vision of the coming slavery in Egypt, how Abraham accepts with quiet dignity the burden of Hebrew poetry and its complications:

> And it came to pass, that when the sun went down, and it was dark, behold a smoking furnace, and a burning lamp that passed between those pieces. In the same day the Lord made a covenant with Abram, saying, Unto thy seed have I given this land. (Genesis 15)

The redactors of the Bible thus make it clear that part of what defines the founding father's intellectual skills is his ability to read the eerie poetry of Hebrew ritual. This kind of ritual reaches its most sublime form when God demands that Abraham sacrifice Isaac:

> God did tempt Abraham, and said unto him, Abraham: and he said, Behold, here I am. And he said, Take now thy son, thine only son, whom thou lovest, even Isaac, and get thee into the land of Moriah; and offer him there for a burnt offering upon one of the mountains which I will tell thee of. And Abraham rose up early in the morning, and saddled his ass, and took two of his young men with him, and Isaac his son, and clave the wood for the burnt offering, and rose up, and went unto the place of which God had told him. Then on the third day Abraham lifted up his eyes, and saw the place afar off. And Abraham said unto his young men, Abide ye here with the ass; and I and the lad will go yonder and worship, and come again to you. And Abraham took the wood of the burnt offering, and laid it upon Isaac his son; and he took the fire in his hand, and a knife; and they went both of them together. . . . And they came to the place which God had told him of; and Abraham built an altar there; and laid the wood in order, and bound Isaac his son, and laid him on the altar upon the wood. And Abraham stretched forth his hand, and took the

knife to slay his son. And the angel of the Lord called unto him out of heaven, and said Abraham, Abraham: and he said, Here am I. And he said, Lay not thine hand upon the lad, neither do thou any thing unto him: for now I know that thou fearest God, seeing thou hast not withheld thy son, thine only son from me. (Genesis 22)

The binding of Isaac begins like other stories of child-sacrifice but ends as a ritual that mocks forever in Hebrew culture the notion that God demands innocent blood. Abraham brings to this ritual his Hebrew mind and his poetry and discernment. Nor is he above a lie. In fact he tells a falsehood on the way to the planned killing that transforms the act into poetic ritual. On approaching Moriah, which tradition identifies with the future home of ritual on the Temple Mount, Abraham realizes he is crossing a forbidden border. In a pretense that colors what is to follow, he tells his servants to go no farther, with the implication that nobody should go farther. Then he adds what then seems an untruth: "Abide ye here with the ass, and I and the lad will go yonder; and we will worship, and come back to you."

At this point he plans to come back *without* Isaac. But when he says both he and Isaac will return (the Hebrew is emphatically *we*), his lie reveals the psychological truth that he does not want to kill Isaac, wants to return with him. The lie, in fact, reveals the truth of the ritual of which it is a part, that the father will not kill the son, will not cross the line that Abraham draws even before he ascends Moriah and that his seed will forever distinguish. In telling a lie and in drawing a line beyond which his servants may not pass, Abraham conducts a ritual that forever sets a father's love and the high form of Hebrew lying above child murder.

Hebrew ritual penetrated much deeper into the life of the people than does modern religious cermony; it created a living theater of thought that addressed among other issues the problem of bloodlust. For example, just as Isaiah diverts the fobidden wish for a bloodied god into the transforming realm of poetry, so Aaron the High Priest is commanded to submit forbidden blood to poetic ritual:

Then shalt thou kill the ram, and take of his blood, and put it upon the tip of the right ear of Aaron, and upon the tip of the right ear of his sons, and upon the thumb of their right hand, and upon the great toe of their right foot, and sprinkle the blood upon the altar round about. And thou shalt take of the blood that is upon the altar, and of the anointing oil, and sprinkle it upon Aaron, and upon his garments, and upon his sons, and upon the garments of his sons with him: and he shall be hallowed, and his garments with him. (Exodus 29)

How can one be hallowed by this primitive flicking and daubing of blood? Why should blood splashed from a ram onto Aaron's right ear partake in the service of God? The Hebrews refrained from eating blood to remind themselves of the sanctity of life; here they are asked to splash blood about an altar, seemingly converting a place of monotheistic worship into a slaughterhouse. To the modern reader, this seems strange, even repugnant. But clearly bits of blood were for the Hebrews like words in a poem, governed by context.

In Aaron's poem, conducted on the very mount to which Abraham brought the doomed Isaac, the blood daubed upon harkening ear, prehensile thumb, and advancing foot commit the priest and his audience to heed, grasp, and follow the idea that the blood of life is sacrosanct. The bloody garments clothe the priest in metaphors which remind the worshipper that it is precisely monotheism and the capacity for metaphor that prevent human life from descending into bloody violence. Aaron's congregants banned red beef from the dinner table as part of a ritual respecting the blood of pulsating life. Oddly, they also watched it splashed on the altar in order to meditate further on blood, the sustainer of life. Though the modern sensibility may mock the "primitivism" of ancient Hebrew ritual, there was nothing primitive about the urge to quench the appetite for blood with a poetic meal of blood-theater.

The commandment to observe this and other rituals is specifically tied to harmonious life in the Land and to liberation from Egypt, the land famous in Hebrew thought for the bloodbath in which Pharoah first submerged the Hebrews and in which his own firstborn and his own people eventually drowned. Hovering in the wings of Aaron's altar-stage is Pharoah's irrational bloodthirsty wish for the death of Hebrew babies and his consequent suffering from the plague of blood. Also in the background is Israel's choice to become a nation of God, capable of understanding Aaron's ritual because they are free from bloody Egypt:

And I will sanctify the tabernacle of the congregation, and the altar: I will sanctify also both Aaron and his sons, to minister to me in the priest's office. And I will dwell among the children of Israel, and will be their God. And they shall know that I am the Lord their God, that brought them forth out of the land of Egypt, that I may dwell among them. (Exodus 29)

The rituals of the Passover holiday commemorate in detail the distinction between the bloodbath that had to be visited on "the land of Egypt" and the symbolic sacrifices that will give peace and meaning to life in the Land. On their last night in Egypt, the Hebrews were instructed to collect the blood of ritually slaughtered lambs, one for every house, and to mark their doorposts with this blood so that they might be spared when God passed through Egypt killing all the first-born—from cattle to the sons in Pharaoh's house. The sacrifice of the lambs was reenacted every subsequent year, as Moses instructed even on the eve of the Exodus:

> And it shall come to pass, when ye be come to the land which the Lord will give you, according as he hath promised, that ye shall keep this service. And it shall come to pass, when your children shall say unto you, What mean ye by this service? That ye shall say, It is the sacrifice of the Lord's passover, who passed over the houses of the children of Israel in Egypt, when he smote the Egyptians, and delivered our houses. (Exodus 12)

Of course, the rituals of Passover also include dietary prescriptions. These represent historical aspects of the holiday and also disciplined the Hebrews in ways they were learning to recognize—when they attended. The Hebrews had to flee Egypt on such short notice they had no time to let their bread rise. When the Hebrews were enjoined to eat no leavened bread during Passover, they were asked not merely to recall the historical basis of the custom but to elevate their commemoration to the level of a national poem:

> And it shall be when the Lord shall bring thee into the land of the Canaanites . . . which he sware unto thy fathers to give thee, a land flowing with milk and honey, that thou shalt keep this service. . . . Unleavened bread shall be eaten seven days; and there shall no leavened bread be seen with thee, neither shall there be leaven seen with thee in all thy quarters. And thou shalt shew thy son in that day, saying, This is done because of that which the Lord did unto me when I came forth out of Egypt. And it shall be for a sign unto thee upon thine hand, and for a memorial between thine eyes, that the Lord's law may be in thy mouth: for with a strong hand

hath the Lord brought thee out of Egypt. Thou shalt therefore keep this ordinance in his season from year to year. (Exodus 13)

Notice that the Hebrews, as is their custom, sharpen the distinction between leavened and unleavened bread by forbidding the presence of leavening during Passover. They did not think of unleavened bread in the way we regard a Thanksgiving turkey, as a lightly symbolic food whose presence does not exclude any other food. For unleavened bread to carry its Hebrew freight, it had to be isolated, made dramatic in its radical distinction from its opposite. Notice, too, that the rituals of Passover, because they are sharp and specific, can be made to reverberate with other specific Hebrew rituals, such as the daily donning of phylacteries (*tefillin*). The custom of wearing these leather boxes on the arm and "between thine eyes" grew out of this very passage, making concrete and ritualistic that which may have once been pure metaphor. *Tefillin* contain the passage cited above as well as others asking the Hebrews to participate in rituals that keep bloodlust at bay—the law in their mouth, and the covenant between their eyes.

Sensitivity to the purposes of Hebrew national poetry allows us to read the specification of the animals to be used in ritual sacrifice: "Ye shall not offer unto the Lord that which [has its testicles] bruised, or crushed, or broken, or cut; neither shall ye make any offering thereof in your land." In Hebrew, the words for this bruising and crushing refer to testicles, an allusion missed by the King James translators. The animals must be intact not simply because defects would be repugnant to God; the animals should be undamaged because they are to participate in a national ritual of purification that confines slaughter to the Temple and rejects cruelty altogether. Because the injunction to avoid animals with damaged genitals is given and then repeated in the context of "your land," the rabbis understood the verse in the largest, national sense, as a general ban on cruelty to animals and as a law against human castration. In Egypt, certain classes of nobility were castrated as part of their dedication to temple service. (Potiphar may have been emasculated, as his office is described by a Hebrew word, *saris*, whose root refers to castration; Thomas Mann followed this hint in his stories of Joseph.) From the lower classes, eunuchs were provided as necessary. In Moab, animals and humans were carved to meet the needs of frenzied rituals. But in Israel, ritual was meant to lead in the opposite direction, to the stately dramatization of the dignity of life. It is the larger idea of the state, the Land, that gives the selection of animals for ritual slaughter its stateliness and its morality.

The motive to channel bloodlust into national poetry, as illustrated by the regular cycle of animal sacrifice, was typical of Hebrew ritual in the Land. This kind of ritual spread from the Temple into the daily lives of the people. For instance, the ritual of bitter waters, which also appears "primitive" on first glance, is in fact a sophisticated attempt to abort, on the domestic front, the potential bloody consequences of a husband incensed with jealousy. The description of the ritual begins with the acknowledgment that husbands may rage on either rational or irrational grounds:

> Speak unto the children of Israel, and say unto them, If any man's wife go aside, and commit a trespass against him, And a man lie with her carnally, and it be hid from the eyes of her husband, and be kept close, and she be defiled, and there be no witness against her, neither she be taken with the manner; And the spirit of jealousy come upon him, and he be jealous of his wife, and she be defiled: or if the spirit of jealousy of his wife, and she be not defiled: Then shall the man bring his wife unto the priest. (Numbers 5)

This understanding that "the spirit of jealousy" may afflict the husband of a chaste wife grows out of the Hebrew interest in the vagaries of the fiction-making mind. Long before Shakespeare created Othello and Browning created the monstrous Duke who speaks "My Last Duchess," the makers of the Bible knew that the power to fabricate, so useful in the making of monotheism, could get out of control. They knew that a wife might lie or tell the truth with equal conviction. They also knew that a delusional husband might murder an innocent wife; even a husband with rational grounds for suspicion was likely to shed blood irrationally.

A ritual thus seemed necessary to distinguish, at least poetically, between a wife's truth and lie, between a husband's delusion and rightful sense of injury. The Hebrews hoped that a mind-centered ritual that encouraged "remembrance" and "memorial," that emphasized fiction making and distinction making, would minimize crimes of passion:

Then shall the man bring his wife unto the priest, and he shall bring her offering for her, the tenth part of an ephah of barley meal; he shall pour no oil upon it, nor put frankincense theron; for it is an offering of jealousy, an offering of memorial, of binging iniquity to remembrance. (Numbers 5)

The Hebrew word for "remembrance" is much larger in scope than its English equivalent. It is perhaps best translated as "mindfulness," both here and elsewhere in Hebrew culture. For example, New Year's Day is called in Hebrew the Day of Remembrance, meaning not merely the day on which one remembers the past year but the day on which God and man take rigorous stock. In any case, the idea behind bringing a suspected wife to the priest was to submit passion to mind and memory:

And the priest shall set the woman before the Lord, and uncover the woman's head, and put the offering of memorial in her hands, which is the jealousy offering: and the priest shall have in his hand the bitter water that causeth the curse: And the priest shall charge her by an oath, and say unto the woman, If no man have lain with thee, and if thou hast not gone aside to uncleanness with another instead of thy husband, be thou free from this bitter water that causeth the curse: But if thou hast gone aside to another instead of thy husband, and if thou be defiled, and some man have lain with thee beside thine husband: Then . . . the Lord make thee a curse and an oath among thy people, when the Lord doth make thy thigh to rot, and thy belly to swell; And this water that causeth the curse shall go into thy bowels, to make thy belly to swell, and thy thigh to rot: And the woman shall say, Amen, amen. And the priest shall write these curses in a book, and he shall blot them out with the bitter water. (Numbers 5)

Thus the ritual moves rage and jealousy into the realm of disciplined theater, and from there into "a book," and finally into symbolic oblivion. That is the hope, which is enacted in a drama that underpins our more modern strategies of sublimation. Of course ancient Hebrew society had not yet managed to expunge the sexism of submitting only women to a largely symbolic risk of genital rot ("thigh" is a euphemism), but it did have the virtue of noting that men may be crazed, and that men and women alike must either submit to poetic and discerning ritual or be swept into a chaos of lies, delusions, and vengeance.

Even at their worst, the Hebrews remembered ritual and poetry, so that now and again they might banish bloodlust and cultivate the Land's mindfulness. To keep mindfulness alive, the Hebrews often reminded themselves of those who abused or did not understand the rituals of Hebrew civilization, thus making a desert of the Land.

Perhaps the most famous abuser of poetic ritual was Samson, a man who first trivialized and then threw away his inheritance. His story is told in Judges 13–15. It is a time of near chaos. The Philistines are tormenting the Hebrews, who are weak and have forgotten much about the daily rituals that once invigorated national life. Samson is to be yet another "Judge" in a long string of undistinguished leaders; like the others he falls short. But God, it seems, has made a special effort to get Samson off to a good start even while he is still in utero. God sends an angel to his mother to have the yet unborn boy consecrated to God as a Nazirite, a priestly being who does not cut his hair, does not drink, and is particularly careful in his ritual observances. Samson, of course, betrays his Nazirite vows. But the point is made that his physical strength, like Israel's, depends directly upon observance of ritual.

Samson's problems actually begin with his father, Manoah, who may be the most stupid man in the Bible, with the least literacy, least poetry, least understanding of ritual. Manoah naps at home, letting his wife work for him in the fields; it turns out that he lets her do all the intellectual work of the family, too. When an angel announces to Samson's mother that she will bear a son consecrated to ritual and to God's service ("For lo, thou shalt conceive, and bear a son; and no razor shall come on his head: for the child shall be a Nazirite unto God from the womb: and he shall begin to deliver Israel out of the hand of the Philistines"), she immediately recognizes that she is indeed speaking with an angel. Manoah, however, despite his wife's description of the messenger ("his countenance was like the countenance of an angel of God, very terrible"), has no insight into the angel's immaterial nature. In a scene notable for its dry humor, he tries to learn the angel's human name and to give the ethereal being food.

Manoah also has to be instructed by his wife on the right reading of the angel's message, which he understands belatedly; it is no wonder that the angel speaks mainly to Samson's mother, leaving the illiterate Manoah to trot behind:

And Manoah said unto the angel of the Lord, I pray thee, let us detain thee, until we shall have made ready a kid for thee. And the angel of the Lord said unto Manoah, Though thou detain me, I will not eat of thy bread: and if thou wilt offer a burnt offering thou must offer it unto the Lord. For Manoah knew not that he was an angel of the Lord. And Manoah said unto the angel of the Lord, What is thy name, that when thy sayings come to pass we may do thee honor? And the angel of the Lord said unto him, Why askest thou thus after my name, seeing it is secret? So Manoah took a kid with a meat offering, and offered it upon a rock unto the Lord: and the angel did wonderously; and Manoah and his wife looked on. For it came to pass, when the flame went up toward heaven from off the altar, that the angel of the Lord ascended in the flame of the altar. . . . Then Manoah knew that he was a angel of the Lord. And Manoah said unto his wife, We shall surely die, because we have seen God. But the wife said unto him, If the Lord were pleased to kill us, he would not have received a burnt-offering and a meat-offering at our hands, neither would he have shewed us all these things, nor would as at this time have told us such things as these.

For Manoah, ritual is nothing but a magic show. He finally believes he has seen an angel when he has ocular proof of celestial fire, but he still does not know the meaning of what he has seen. The emphasis on Manoah's gawking at miracle is not meant to be validated by the Hebrew reader, who is expected to eschew this sort of circus. The whole passage is meant as a contrast between two ways of regarding ritual: Samson's mother reasons clearly that the consecration of her unborn son to a life of ritual is not to be feared but welcomed for its enhancement of his potential grasp of God, while Manoah can only fret that the ritual he has witnessed threatens him with instant death and that he must soon sacrifice a kid to somebody, if only he could guess to whom.

Manoah's doltish sense of the ritual he witnesses augurs poorly for his son. It is true that Samson inherits his mother's sense of poetry and her ability to read ritual, but he also inherits something of his father's coarseness. In the end Samson follows his father and throws away his culture of poetic ritual. He becomes a kind of Esau. But first he finds it necessary to degrade ritual into riddles and practical jokes. It is well known that trivializing of his mission leads to Delilah's ability to wheedle from him the secret of his Nazirite strength. Less often remembered is the similar story told of his first romance, during which Samson uses poetic ritual to serve brutality rather than control it. Not surprisingly, this story begins with Samson's eyeing a Philistine woman, a version of Israel whoring after foreign gods:

> And Samson went down to Timnath, and he saw a woman in Timnath of the daughters of the Philistines. And he came up, and told his father and his mother, and said, I have seen a woman in Timnath of the daughters of the Philistines: now therefore get her for me to wife. Then his father and his mother said unto him, Is there never a woman among the daughters of thy brethren, or among all my people, that thou goest to take a wife of the uncircumcised Philistines. And Samson said unto his father, Get her for me; for she pleaseth me well.

Holy Samson's crudity may shock, but we must remember that he is living in the crude age of Jephthah and Manoah, whom he is addressing. The vulgarity gets worse, as Samson, a Nazirite who must refrain from violence even to the point of not applying a razor to his head, slays a lion with his bare hands. The editorial comment is that Samson was thus moved by "the Spirit of the Lord," but this is meant ironically. The slaying of the lion is such a shameful act that he must hide it from his parents, like a schoolboy, just as he must later hide that he eats from the lion's carcass, an act forbidden to all Hebrews, Nazirite or not, as prescribed in Leviticus 11 ("And whatsoever goeth upon his paws . . . are unclean unto you: whoso toucheth their carcase shall be unclean"):

> Then went Samson down, and his father and his mother, to Timnath, and came to the vineyards of Timnath: and, behold, a young lion roared against him. And the Spirit of the Lord came mightily upon him, and he rent him as he would have rent a kid, and he had nothing in his hand: but he told not his father or his mother what he had done. And he went down, and talked with the woman; and she pleased Samson well. And after a time he returned to take her, and turned aside to see the carcase of the lion: and, behold, there was a swarm of bees and honey in the carcase of the lion. And he took thereof in his hands and went on eating, and came to his father and mother, and he gave them, and they did eat: but he told not them that he had taken the honey out of the carcase of the lion.

Samson's passing of the forbidden food to his parents alludes to Eve's passing the apple to Adam. Having now made a joke of Hebrew dietary laws, Samson proceeds to degrade poetry. Challenging the local louts, whom he invites to a party for his fiancée, he fabricates a riddle out of his taste of honey:

> And Samson said unto them, I will now put forth a riddle unto you: if ye can certainly declare it me within the seven days of the feast, and find it out, then I will give you thirty sheets and thirty change of garments. . . . And he said unto them, Out of the eater came forth meat, and out of the strong came forth sweetness. And they could not in three days expound the riddle. And it came to pass on the seventh day, that they said unto Samson's wife, Entice thy husband, that he may declare unto us the riddle, lest we burn thee and thy father's house with fire. . . . And Samson's wife wept before him, and said, Thou dost but hate me, and lovest me not: thou has put forth a riddle unto the children of my people, and hast not told it me. . . . And she wept before him the seven days, while their feast lasted: and it came to pass on the seventh day, that he told her, because she lay sore upon him: and she told the riddle to the children of her people. And the men of the city said unto him on the seventh day before the sun went down, What is sweeter than honey? and what is stronger than a lion?

One recognizes the gift of poetry in Samson's riddle and in his speech. But in his hands ritual descends to the level of his fiancée's charades and the louts' strong-arm tactics. Soon Samson himself has decended to mere violence, which again is partially masked by the ironic evocation of "the Spirit of the Lord":

> And he said unto them, If ye had not plowed with my heifer, ye had not found out my riddle. And the Spirit of the Lord came upon him, and he went down to Ashkelon, and slew thirty men of them, and took their spoil. . . . And his anger was kindled, and he went up to his father's house.

We observe Samson's intelligence in his ability to read instantly that he has been tricked by his colluding wife and friends, and we again admire his poetic diction, but we also see that he has become a mere lout, spoiling Philistine cities not out of any desire to strengthen intellectual monotheism but out of an urge to get even. That Samson goes back to his father's house is supposed to suggest a possibility of a return to his abandoned life of Nazirite ritual, but in fact Samson, the son of Manoah, goes on to Delilah, degrading once again the skills that were meant to lift the Hebrews above the kindling of anger and the taking of spoil.

Delilah, of course, learns Samson's Nazirite secret and has him shorn. He immediately loses his physical strength, but this is no more than the objective correlative to his moral strength, which he has already lost. The Philistines pluck out his eyes. He winds up in Gaza, where "he did grind in the prison house," far from Zion, harnessed to a wheel, going round and round, a toy of the Philistines ("Call for Samson, that he may make us sport"), thus completing an anti-ritual of intellectual blindness and trifling.

While he is still in captivity Samson's hair grows back. The Philistines summon him to their temple to entertain them with mere feats of strength, now without any ritual significance at all. That he uses one such occasion to bring down the Philistine Temple of Dagon and bury himself under its rubble constitutes an anti-ritual summing his career of noisy heroics.

At their best, the Hebrews did not emulate Samson, did not throw away their intellectual skills, did not degrade poetry into riddle, did not kill every lion that roared. Instead they maintained a culture of measured ritual, and they attained, at moments, the wisdom of Solomon, making the Land flourish, as we note in this description from the *Mishna* of the ritual of dedicating the first fruits, summarized in Martin Buber's *On Zion* (Schocken Books, 1973):

> . . . the Mishna (Bikkurim III) sounds as though the intention was to pre-serve something lost and past for the memory of future generations. We hear how the people from the surrounding country come to Jerusalem with the first-fruits, those living close at hand with fresh fruits, those far away with dried. In the early morning the procession enters the city, head-ed by pipers, then the sacrificial bull with gilded horns, and behind it the men, bearing baskets filled with fruits and garlanded with grapes, each according to his wealth, golden baskets, silver baskets and baskets woven from stripped willow-twigs. The artisans of Jerusalem come out to meet them, greeting those from each place in turn: "Brothers, men from the place of such and such a name, may you come in peace!" But when they stood by the temple hill the king himself took his basket on his shoulders

and entered in with them. In the forecourt the Levites sang the verse from the Psalms: "I will exalt thee, YHVH, for thou hast drawn me up." . . . Thus we appreciate the full meaning of the passage on the offering of the first-fruits, the unique document of a unique relationship between a people and a land. (p. 10)

Chapter 9

The Wisdom of Solomon

Imagination—It is that deceitful part in man, that mistress of error and falsity, the more deceptive that she is not always so; for she would be an infallible rule of truth, if she were an infallible rule of falsehood.

—Pascal, *Pensées*

The proverbs of Solomon the son of David, king of Israel; To know wisdom and instruction; to perceive the words of understanding.

—Proverbs 1

A garden inclosed is my sister, my spouse; a spring shut up, a fountain sealed. Thy plants are an orchard of pomegranates, with pleasant fruits; campshire, with spikenard, Spikenard and saffron; calamus and cinnamon, with all trees of frankincense; myrrh and aloes, with all the chief spices: A fountain of gardens, a well of living waters.

—Song of Solomon 4

SOLOMON, DAVID'S SON, INHERITED HIS FATHER'S SMALL EMPIRE AND ALL his great trappings of state. The alliance with Hiram, prince of Tyre and king of all the Phoenician lands, was still intact, fruitful for both the master of the sea and the master of the hinterlands. Solomon, like David before him, kept the coast-marauding Philistines in thrall, which gave Hiram a free hand at sea. Hiram, in turn, provided Solomon with shipping outlets to markets in the Mediterranean, and the two of them financed joint ventures to the Far East, trading in metals and jewels, in myrrh and frankincense through Solomon's port at Etzion-Geber, on the northernmost reach of the Red Sea near modern Eilat. Some of their fleets required three years to make a round trip to the far coasts of Africa and India. The Queen of Sheba, mistress of spices and gold but without the means to ship her riches from her Arabian nation along the Red Sea, sought in Solomon a partner who could bridge the continents; by legend, he provided her an heir as well.

With wealth from the world's every known quarter flowing into the kingly coffers, Solomon undertook an ambitious program of building, including new cities, new trade centers, new quarters for visiting merchants whose every want was considered, including the provision of pagan shrines. After all, idolators could not be expected to do in Israel as the House of Israel did. These shrines angered the conservative priesthood and the pious commonfolk, who took little interest in international trade, even though it was the source of the nation's material prosperity. Solomon partly silenced the murmurs by constructing the famous First Temple, which would stand as a center of hallowed sacrifices for almost four hundred years before the Babylonians leveled it and carried its riches back to the east, from whence they had originally come via trade.

All in all, Solomon's reign was peaceful, a time of plenty, a bustling yet humdrum time, with the machinery of business clicking smoothly. Alliances were maintained and new ones created, mainly by marriage. We are told of thousands of horses and hundreds of wives, most of them obtained through astute political maneuvers. Even the old land of slime and slavery, the hated land of Egypt, was brought in this manner into Solomon's new world order. So businesslike was Solomon's state that a daughter of Pharaoh could be brought to Jerusalem as a royal bride without this fact—of great historical resonance—earning more than a footnote on Solomon's need to live in David's old house while completing work on his own, grander palace and on the Temple: "And Solomon made affinity with Pharaoh king of Egypt; and took Pharaoh's daughter, and brought her into the city of David, until he had made an end of building his own house, and the house of the Lord, and the wall of Jerusalem round about" (1 Kings 3).

But the redactors of the Bible do not really think this mundane history the purpose of their craft. For them, Solomon's grandeur lay not in his material triumphs but in his mind, and they take great pains not to emphasize the economic history of Solomon's reign (this has to be teased out) but the moral history. They wish to show that Solomon inherited from his father more than a set of business arrangements, that Solomon was endowed with David's imaginative faculty and put it to work in the way the Hebrews most admired, thus allowing the Land to flourish under his wise rule. In the background, they sketch Solomon's economic activities, mainly because these eventually undermined his wisdom and bankrupted the Land. The lavish expenditures on palaces, temples, and courts led directly, as we shall see, to quarrels between the North and South of the Land, and in the end to the division of the nation into two rival kingdoms.

The writers of the Bible value Solomon's imagination, his poetry, his grasp of the covenant, and his historical place in protecting it. They expected their readers to take with some misgivings Solomon's incidental marriage to a daughter of the Pharaoh, just as they expected their readers to value his understanding of Egypt's place in Hebrew history, as in this deeply poetic meditation, publicly spoken on the occasion of dedicating the Temple:

> I am risen up in the room of David my father, and sit on the throne of Israel, as the Lord promised, and have built an house for the name of the Lord God of Israel. And I have set there a place for the ark, wherein is the covenant of the Lord, which he made with our fathers, when he brought them out of the land of Egypt. . . . And Solomon stood before the altar of the Lord in the presence of all the congregation of Israel, and spread forth his hands toward heaven; And he said, Lord God of Israel, there is no God like thee, in heaven above, or on earth beneath, who keepest covenant and mercy with thy servants that walk before thee with all their heart. . . . But will God indeed dwell on the earth? behold, the heaven and

heaven of heavens cannot contain thee; how much less this house that I have builded? Yet have thou respect unto the prayer of thy servant, and to his supplication, O Lord my God. . . . Then hear thou in heaven, and forgive the sin of thy servants, and of thy people Israel, that thou teach them the good way wherein they should walk, and give rain upon thy land, which thou hast given to thy people for an inheritance. . . . That thine eyes may be open unto the supplication of thy servant, and unto the supplication of thy people Israel, to hearken unto them in all that they call for unto thee. For thou didst separate them from among all the people of the earth, to be thine inheritance, as thou spakest by the hand of Moses thy servant, when thou broughtest our fathers out of Egypt, O Lord God. (1 Kings 8)

The writers of the Bible admire Solomon because of this poetry and because of this understanding. Solomon knows that God does not dwell on earth, not in heaven either, nor in the heaven of heavens, but in men's hearts, insofar as they can hold Him there. According to Solomon's wisdom, prayer and supplication might help to remind the people of the God who must live in imagination and so might the Temple, but prayer and the Temple are reminders only, not direct manifestations of God. Solomon calls on his people to cultivate the poetry of prayer, and the poets of the Bible love him for it.

The ancient Hebrews wished to emphasize two underpinnings of Solomon's wisdom, two pillars that supported his intellectual life. Before there could be consciousness of human history, before there could be monotheism, before there could arise the idea of using an invented Land to represent revelation and covenant, before the artificiality of law could be accepted, before the Sabbath could be imposed on nature, before David could rise from opportunism to poetry, before Zionism could thrive and Solomon be wise, two powers had to be present in the readied mind.

The first is the power to dream, to imagine, to invent, to hold in the mind a picture without physical correlative. One cannot be a monotheist unless one can retain an abstract idea of a distant God who receives no corroboration from burbling springs or from the rising moon. But the power to imagine and invent is by itself, as we have seen, an unruly beast. One invents all sorts of nonsense, as did the Egyptians with their divine cats and mummies, or the Hebrews with their golden calf. Thus, in the view of the Hebrew makers of the Bible, imagination must be tempered by the power of analysis, by distinction making, the second pillar of the adequate monotheist's mind.

To envision the invented Creator (He can have no other existence in the creation but in the creative mind) and to distinguish Him from other invented gods was the the task of the ancient Hebrews. They educated themselves to this task in every way they could, seeking to deepen imagination and to sharpen discernment. Just as they practiced the art of story telling to cultivate imagination, so they practiced the discipline of distinction making (mocked by the uninitiated as mere rabbinical hairsplitting) to guard their minds against nonsense. Their culture of law and literacy was the training ground of monotheism, and their monotheism was the proof of the value of their culture. That monotheism gave birth to Hebrew culture and was in turn nourished by Hebrew law and poetry, inspiring a unity of civilzation, at least intermittently. (For moderns, who have inherited Hebrew monotheism and Hebrew culture as separable parts of Western tradition, this unity is no longer useful.)

Solomon, like his father, understood that the dreaming mind and the distinction-making mind sustain the Land. This is best seen in the famous story of Solomon and the two harlots who claim maternity of one baby. The story has two parts; the first part emphasizes the relationship of imagination to monotheism, while the second focuses on the connected theme of distinction making. The story, told in 1 Kings 3, is set at the beginning of Solomon's reign. Solomon begins with a dream, in which he manifests the monotheist's capacity to envision the invisible: "In Gibeon the Lord appeared to Solomon in a dream by night: and God said, Ask what I shall give thee." This Aladdin-like motif, already old in literary culture, is turned to Hebrew purposes; Solomon will ask not only for the power of imagination, which he already possesses, as evidenced by his dream, but for the other power necessary to the monotheist, the ability to discern: "I am but a little child: I know not how to go out or come in. . . . Give therefore thy servant an understanding heart to judge thy people, that I may discern between good and bad: for who is able to judge this thy so great a people?"

Note that Solomon is not quite asking for the same power of discerning good from evil that Adam and Eve sought. The primal parents wanted understanding for its own sake, not so that they could be God's servants—as Solomon wishes—but to be like God. Thus, God is pleased with Solomon. Or rather, the ancient redactors validate that which is valuable in their culture:

> And God said unto him, Because thou has asked this thing, and hast not asked for thyself long life; neither hast asked riches for thyself, nor hast asked life of thine enemies; but hast asked for thyself understanding to discern judgment; Behold, I have done according to thy words: lo, I have given thee a wise and an understanding heart; so that there was none like thee before thee, neither after thee shall any arise like unto thee.

This part of the story concludes by God's linking Solomon's imaginative capacity to the covenantal requirement that the Law be observed in the Land:

> And if thou wilt walk in my ways, to keep my statutes and my commandments, as thy father David did walk, then I will lengthen thy days. And Solomon awoke; and behold it was a dream. And he came to Jerusalem, and stood before the ark of the covenant of the Lord, and offered up burnt offerings, and made a feast to all his servants.

Intuitively, Solomon moves from dream to Law to Jerusalem, the capital of the Land, making an intellectual's feast in Zion. Or, perhaps, it is the tellers of the story who make the feast.

The second part of the story, that dealing with the two harlots, mainly illustrates Solomon's discernment, but it also reveals a penetrating imagination. To determine who is the true mother and who the false, Solomon must make fine distinctions. But to do so, he must first invent a play to make events work themselves into his control. This part of the story proceeds on two planes, one involving the conundrum posed to Solomon, the other aimed at the reader, who is asked to solve a riddle slightly different from that pierced by the King. There are two harlots; neither is named, thus setting the reader's challenge. The plaintiff and the defendant argue before Solomon on the day after his dream. "And Solomon awoke; and behold it was a dream. . . . Then came there two women, that were harlots, unto the King, and stood before him."

The plaintiff's claim seems straightforward:

> O my lord, I and this woman dwell in one house, and I was delivered of a child with her in the house. And it came to pass the third day after that I

was delivered, that this woman was delivered also: and we were together; there was no stranger with us in the house, save we two in the house. And this woman's child died in the night; because she overlaid it. And she arose at midnight, and took my son from beside me, while thine handmaid slept, and laid it in her bosom, and laid her dead child in my bosom. And when I rose in the morning to give my child suck, behold, it was dead; but when I had considered it in the morning, behold, it was not my son, which I did bear. (1 Kings 3)

The defendant puts forward a brief defense. "Nay; but the living is my son, and the dead is thy son." She does not have much to say, or perhaps she is interrupted by her more loquacious neighbor, who rebuts, "No; but the dead is thy son, and the living is my son."

Solomon, knowing he can call no witnesses to help ("there was no stranger with us in the house"), has to rely on an imaginative approach to make the right distinction; he offers a pseudo-distinction, which is also a primitive sacrifice—the division of a living baby:

Then said the King, The one saith, This is my son that liveth, and thy son is dead; and the other saith, Nay; but thy son is the dead, and my son is the living. And the king said, Bring me a sword. And they brought a sword before the king. And the king said, Divide the living child in two, and give half to the one, and half to the other. Then spake the woman whose the living child was unto the king, for her bowels yearned upon her son, and she said, O my lord, give her the living child, and in no wise slay it. But the other said, Let it be neither mine nor thine, but divide it. Then the king answered and said, Give her the living child, and in no wise slay it: she is the mother thereof. (1 Kings 3)

Now this is very clever, a wise and valid distinction, resting on an imaginative dramatization of maternal instinct. The story, however, is not preserved and retold merely to prove that Solomon is smart but to urge the people of Israel to cultivate the power of dream and of discernment so that they too might share the dream of the covenant and distinguish it from folly and idolatry, thus securing the Land. In fact the passage asks the reader to practice imaginative discernment on the spot.

The reader is meant to wonder which of the unnamed women got the baby. Which was she who asked the King to spare the child?

Which is the liar? Solomon knows, but does the reader? Was it the plaintiff who was awarded the baby? Following Congreve, one might speculate: "Guilt is ever at a loss, and confusion waits upon it; when innocence and bold truth are always ready for expression" (*The Double Dealer*). From this persective one might hear true maternity in the noisy plaintiff's story, and most readers, it seems, assume it is she who is telling the truth. But in fact the passage leaves in question the plaintiff's veracity. She could have been a clever liar, like others in the Bible who debase the Hebrew gift of invention—like Simeon and Levi, like Jacob himself, who masqueraded as his brother to steal Isaac's blessing from Esau. Indeed, there are hints that the plaintiff *is* a liar. She is too emphatic that there are no witnesses to refute her, and she knows too many details about the time and cause of death of her neighbor's baby, which presumably took place out of her sight. Moreover, she repeats the word "laid" three times (this is true in the Hebrew, too), as if it is eating at her, as if perhaps it were she who "overlaid" her own baby.

Similarly, readers might hear with Congreve the ring of guilt in the meager grunts of the defendant, whose sparse speech seems characteristic of a sneak who would switch babies in the night. But the defendant could have been truthful though inarticulate, perhaps frightened into speechlessness with more to lose than the fluent plaintiff, who may have had nothing to lose. Indeed, there is a hint that the inarticulate defendant *is* the true mother. For it is likely that she is the one who, lacking speech, possesses honest guts ("for her bowels yearned upon her son"). Of course, the identity of the mother is not meant to be a knowable fact but a challenge to the Hebrew reader. The story's redactors left the question open, probably because imaginative discernment was an incessantly open problem for the ancient Hebrews; they never managed more than a faltering grasp of monotheism's distinctive abstractions, as the Bible's books of chastising prophecy remind us.

Whether the real mother is the plaintiff or the defendant, she is the one who rejects child-sacrifice and hence shows the kind of concerns that Solomon has for the children of Israel in the story's first part. Her maternal nature shows itself in an imaginative capacity to be a mother without a literal baby, while her rival is a materialist who must have the child as a possession. Solomon understands all this about the real mother, and the reader is meant to also, even if the identity of the true mother remains unclear.

Because Solomon served as a model for wise mastery of ancient Hebrew literacy, and because he used this mastery to secure a kind of *pax Hebraica*, he was accorded authorship of the Song of Solomon, which, compiled from love lyrics six hundred years after he died, renders the Land's loveliness in richer detail than any book in the Bible. The Land is polished by streams of cleansing poetry, idealized to the perfection of Solomon's dreams: "I am come into my garden, my sister, my spouse: I have gathered my myrrh with my spice; I have eaten my honeycomb with my honey; I have drunk my wine with my milk; eat, O friends; drink, yea drink abundantly, O beloved" (Song of Solomon 5). Whatever else the Song of Solomon means, it evokes the Land as a representation of a rich civilization. Here again is the "milk" and the "honey" in poetic form, which is what God promised Abraham.

Solomon's language bathes David's warfare and Isaiah's embattled monotheism in a cascade of similes, and perfumes a wilderness with myrrh and frankincense. His imagery rivals Ovid's power of metamorphosis, transforming the hard floor of a martial chariot into a bed of love, the hard hills into Zion:

> Who is this that cometh out of the wilderness like pillars of smoke, perfumed with myrrh and frankincense, with all powders of the merchant? Behold his bed, which is Solomon's; threescore valiant men are about it, of the valiant of Israel. They all hold swords, being expert in war: every man hath his sword upon his thigh because of fear in the night. King Solomon made himself a chariot of the wood of Lebanon. He made the pillars thereof of silver, the bottom therof of gold, the covering of it of purple, the midst thereof being paved with love, for the daughters of Jerusalem. Go forth, O ye daughters of Zion, and behold king Solomon with the crown wherewith his mother crowned him in the day of his espousals, and in the day of the gladness of his heart. (Song of Solomon 3)

This dreamlike sequence of kaleidoscopic images interlaces scenes of peaceful luxury and martial pomp. We sense a "fear in the night" like that of Isaiah's watchman on the towers of beleaguered Jerusalem, and at the poem's fringes we glimpse a pre-Mosaic and pre-Abrahamic "wilderness" into which Zion was always threatening to decline. A "sword" and a "chariot" are ready to spring into action, to bring more violence to the blood-stained Land. Nevertheless the passage manages to transform all into a "gladness" of heart, a rapture of love, a transformation of war. The poetry-making mind of Solomon melts the "chariot of wood" into a marriage bed.

The rabbis struggled hard to find a reason to canonize the beautiful but secular poetry of Solomon. Finally they decided to make the Song of Solomon (Song of Songs, in Hebrew) part of holy writ as an allegory for God's love of his people. Perhaps this is true. But I think the essential point is the one they took for granted, that Solomon's poetry is needed in the Bible because it provides the basis for Solomon's wisdom. The Song of Songs is about the transforming power of the trained imagination, which makes possible the invention of an invisible God and the creation of a new nation. In this Land, "valiant men" of poetry aspire to beat swords into ploughshares, chariots into fruitful wedding beds.

Solomon performs well because his poetry begets ethics and his ethics sharpen poetry. His wisdom is not mere obedience. That he shines in the case of the contested baby matters less than the poetry that teaches him the right approach. Israel is famous for its ethical culture, but in truth its poetry is more impressive, because more fundamental. The rabbis who give us normative Judaism believe that one should do God's will; Jewish mystics believe that one should imitate God's ethics and thereby achieve union with Him; but Solomon thought more subtly. He does the right thing because he has cultivated the poetry of monotheism, which in turn allows him a grasp of the slippery difference between good and evil. Solomon applies the law wisely because he knows Hebrew poetry, and his knowledge of Hebrew law enhances his mastery of poetry.

This recursiveness anticipates a modern intellectual view: laws should reflect values and sharpen minds, so that citizens may make better laws without waiting for God. In this vein, the ancient Hebrews, who helped make our modern culture, warned themselves in Deuteronomy 29 that to go further, to imitate God, led to intellectual failure and landlessness: "And the anger of the Lord was kindled against his land . . . and [He] cast them into another land. . . . The secret things belong unto the Lord our God: but those things which are revealed belong unto us." Monotheism, somewhat paradoxically, is for human beings. It cultivates human minds but does not define God. Thus, Solomon did not follow God in blind obedience, nor did he try to be like God. Rather he made poetry and thus preserved the Land.

At least that was the ideal Solomon. In reality, his materialism overtook him. Trade proved insufficient to finance his grandiose expectations. Debt accummulated. Solomon had planned to keep the Hebrews away from the actual hard labor of his construction projects by commandeering the remnants of the original inhabitants of the Land:

> And all the people that were left of the Amorites, Hittites, Perizites. Hivites, and Jebusites, which were not of the children of Israel, Their children that were left after them in the land, whom the children of Israel also were not able to destroy, upon those did Solomon levy a tribute of bondservice. (1 Kings 9)

But the Jebusites and the others proved insufficient in number. Soon the Hebrews were themselves being taxed with one month's labor out of every three, and the burden did not fall equally. The tribesmen from Ephraim in the North felt they were made beasts of burden in favor of Judah, the tribe of the King in the South. They murmured. Was this not like slavery in Egypt, but worse, because here in the Land?

Matters came to a head with the death of Solomon. Solomon's son Rehoboam did not inherit his father's wisdom. In fact, he took from his father only his materialism, and this as an unexamined birthright. When the men of Ephraim came to Rehoboam for redress of their just grievances, Rehoboam failed to read them correctly, even after consulting with his father's advisors. The Northerners speak bluntly:

> Thy father made our yoke grievous: now therefore make thou the grievous service of thy father, and his heavy yoke which he put upon us, lighter, and we will serve thee. . . . And King Rehoboam consulted with the old men, that stood before Solomon his father while he yet lived, and said, How do ye advise that I may answer this people? And they spake unto him, saying, If you wilt be a servant unto this people this day, and wilt serve them, and answer them, and speak good words to them, then they will be thy servants for ever. But he forsook the counsel

of the old men, which they had given him, and consulted with the young men that were grown up with him. . . . And the young men that were grown up with him spake unto him saying, Thus shalt thou speak unto this people that spake unto thee, saying, Thy father made our yoke heavy, but make thou it lighter unto us; thus shalt thou say unto them, My little finger shall be thicker than my father's loins. And now whereas my father did lade you with a heavy yoke, I will add to your yoke: my father hath chastised you with whips, but I will chastise you with scorpions. (1 Kings 12)

Rehoboam, too stupid to follow his father's advisors, too shallow to invent an answer to serve his selfish needs, relies on the words fed to him by the spoiled young lions at court, themselves foolish in the world though glib of tongue. Soon the tribes of the North secede from the Kingdom, which leads to the collapse of the little empire. Israel becomes a separate kingdom in the North, Judah in the South. As always in Hebrew culture, the dissolution of wisdom leads to the dissolution of the Land. Rehoboam's quip about whips and scorpions, about his little finger being more terrible then his father's thick legs, proves no more than bravado masquerading as poetry, the wisdom of Solomon unraveled. The silly grandiosity of the son, however, expresses something of the problem of the father, a man who, despite his wisdom, exceeded even David in embracing luxury, just as David in his day exceeded the small materialism of Saul.

What happened in the Land thereafter cannot be a surprise:

And Rehoboam the son of Solomon reigned in Judah. Rehoboam was forty ond one years old when he began to reign, and he reigned seventeen years in Jerusalem, the city which the Lord did choose out of all the tribes of Israel, to put his name there. . . . And Judah did evil in the sight of the Lord, and they provoked him to jealousy with their sins which they had committed, above all that their fathers had done. For they also built them high places, and images, and groves, on every high hill, and under every green tree. And there were also sodomites in the land; and they did according to all the abominations of the nations which the Lord cast out before the children of Israel. (1 Kings 14)

"All the abominations of the nations" primarily featured child-sacrifice, the wisdom and poetry of Solomon gone.

Chapter 10

Prophecy in the Land

As a dog returneth to his vomit, so a fool returneth to his folly.
                                        —Proverbs 26

Then the Lord answered Job out of the whirlwind, and said, Who is this that darkeneth counsel by words without knowledge? Gird up now thy loins like a man; for I will demand of thee, and answer thou me. Where wast thou when I laid the foundations of the earth? declare, if thou hast understanding.
                                        —Job 38

FOR MUCH OF THE MILLENIUM FOLLOWING THE DEATH OF SOLOMON IN 922 B.C.E., until the Roman sack of Jerusalem and the great Diaspora, the Hebrews forgot the meaning of the Land they inhabited. In the North, the kings of Israel (or Ephraim), beginning with Jeroboam, grasped Hebrew civilization indifferently and often fell into frank idolatry; their relentlessly declining kingdom was eventually absorbed into the rising Assyrian Empire in 714 B.C.E. In the South, the kings of Judah pursued a similar course from the time of their first king, Rehoboam, until they were overrun by the Babylonians in 586 B.C.E. The two entities, individually corrupt and fratricidal, made matters worse through unending hostility to each other for the duration of their existences:

> And there was war between Rehoboam and Jeroboam all the days of his life. . . . And in the twentieth year of Jeroboam king of Israel, reigned Asa over Judah. And forty and one years reigned he in Jerusalem. And his mother's name was Maachah, the daughter of Abishalom. And Asa did that which was right in the eyes of the Lord, as did David. . . . And he took away the sodomites out of the land, and removed all the idols that his fathers had made. And also Maachah his mother, even her he removed from being queen, because she had made an idol in a grove; and Asa destroyed her idol, and burnt it by the brook Kidron. But the high places were not removed; nevertheless Asa's heart was perfect with the Lord all his days. (1 Kings 15)

Pious but pathetic Asa does the best he can, at least getting his idolatrous queen-mother out of the house and the "sodomites out of the land" (these were particularly vicious idolators), but he can do little about the endemic, low-level idolatry in Judah. The less vile rites of "high places" continued as before. In Israel, matters were even worse:

> And in the thirty and eighth year of Asa king of Judah, began Ahab the son of Omri to reign over Israel: and Ahab the son of Omri reigned over Israel in Samaria twenty and two years. And Ahab the son of Omri did evil in the sight of the Lord, above all that were before him. And it came to pass . . . that he took to wife Jezebel the daughter of Ethbaal king of the Zidonians, and went and served Baal, and worshipped him. And he reared up an altar for Baal in the house of Baal, which he had built in Samaria. And Ahab

made a grove; and Ahab did more to provoke the Lord God of Israel to anger than all the kings of Israel that were before him. (1 Kings 16)

When prophets rose up in protest against this idolatrous worship of Baal, a variant of Molech, Ahab had them murdered by the score. His wife was still more murderous in ridding the land of those who wished to restore monotheism. Obadiah, devoted to the prophet Elijah, manages to save a hundred prophets by hiding fifty in each of two caves where he provides them with bread and water, but for the most part Jezebel had her way, a mere fifty years after the death of Solomon.

In consequence of the brutality and the mindlessness, the prophets who followed Solomon naturally grew shrill. They maintained the long tradition of poetry in the Land, but they moved from lyric and understated story to a more didactic, even peevish, elaboration of Hebrew themes. Their tone became short-tempered as they realized that either nobody was listening or their fellow citizens no longer understood, even when they did listen. The prophets did not abandon the subtle indirection of Hebrew culture, but they began to harp on the loss of Zion's civilization, maintaining a high poetic standard while they hectored.

Hosea, writing two centuries after the kingdom of Solomon fractured, was a Judean who lived in Israel, thus experienced in the degeneracy of both societies. He wrote for Israel a hundred and fifty years after the reign of Ahab, on the eve of its impending destruction. Hosea sets forth clearly the problem of writing poetry for those who think that the cultivation of imagination is merely the art of lying; if there is no literate audience, there will be no place for a poet-prophet, either. The people and the prophet will fall together:

Ephraim compasseth me about with lies, and the house of Israel with deceit. (Hosea 11)

Hear the word of the Lord, ye children of Israel: for the Lord hath a controversy with the inhabitants of the land, because there is no truth, nor mercy, nor knowledge of God in the land. By swearing, and lying, and killing, and stealing, and committing adultery, they break out, and blood toucheth blood. Therefore shall the land mourn, and every one that dwelleth therin shall languish. . . . Therefore shalt thou fall in the day, and the prophet also shall fall with thee in the night. . . . My people are destroyed for lack of knowledge: because thou has rejected knowledge, I will also reject thee, that thou shalt be no priest to me: seeing thou hast forgotten the law of thy God, I will also forget thy children. (Hosea 4)

Hosea understands that his fate as an intellectual monotheist in a resonating Land depends on the literacy of his brethren, and thus he adopts, partly as a literary strategy and partly as a political necessity, a close identification with his audience. He draws an analogy between his personal role as husband to a sluttish wife (this may or may not be based on his actual life) and Israel's unfaithfulness to God. Just as Hosea's wife has gone whoring after other lovers, so has Israel sought idols, forsaking literacy, intellect, law, ritual, and poetry. Hosea names two of his children "Ye-are-not-my-people" and "I-will-no-more-have-mercy," and he pleads with these children to redeem their mother, Israel:

> Plead with your mother, plead: for she is not my wife, neither am I her husband; let her therefore put away her whoredoms out of her sight, and her adulteries from between her breasts; Lest I strip her naked, and set her as in the day that she was born, and make her as a wilderness, and set her like a dry land, and slay her with thirst. And I will not have mercy upon her children; for they be the children of whoredoms. For their mother hath played the harlot: she that conceived them hath done shamefully: for she said, I will go after my lovers, that give me my bread and my water, my wool and my flax, mine oil and my drink. (Hosea 2)

This sly passage simultaneously demands of Israel a sophisticated grasp of simile and accuses it of crass literalism. Israel is expected to have retained just enough literacy to read from these images of whoring that it has sold itself into idolatry and intellectual slavery, that it has forsaken its birthright of literacy in exchange for a bit of flax to wear and bread to eat, as if Israel were a new Esau accepting the old pottage. The idea is that the Land of Israel, rich when its civilization is intact, parches into a "wilderness" and "a dry land" when its intellectual monotheism withers. Without poetry, Zion decays to the state it was in before God showed it to Abraham.

As Hosea's vision continues, a crazed Israel, panting after illusory lovers, grasps at nothing, and makes the Land nothing:

And she shall follow after her lovers, but she shall not overtake them; and she shall seek them, but shall not find them. . . . For she did not know that I gave her corn, and wine, and oil, and multiplied her silver and gold, which they prepared for Baal. Therefore will I return, and take away my corn in the time thereof, and my wine in the season thereof, and will recover my wool and my flax given to cover her nakedness. And now will I discover her lewdness in the sight of her lovers and none shall deliver her out of mine hand.

Thus the prophet again makes explicit the intimate relationship between the survival of intellectual monotheism and the integrity of the Land, whose fruits God will "take away" when mind fails. The idea of the Land goes up in smoke every time the idol-ovens are stoked:

When Ephraim spake trembling, he exalted himself in Israel; but when he offended in Baal, he died. And now they sin more and more, and have made them molten images of their silver, and idols according to their own understanding, all of it the work of the craftsmen. . . . Therefore they shall be as the morning cloud, and as the early dew that passeth away, as the chaff that is driven with the whirlwind out of the floor, and as the smoke out of the chimney. (Hosea 13)

Hosea's poetry, like all poetry in the Hebrew tradition, assumes that monotheism and the very Land that recalls it are "as the morning cloud and as the early dew," gossamer visions seen only by those who cultivate Hebrew civilization, easily lost.

The phrase missing from the ellipsis above is garbled by the King James translators: ". . . all of it the work of craftsmen: they say of them, Let the men that sacrifice kiss the calves." Rather, Hosea's poetry mimics and mocks idolators, who, in the frenzy of idolatry, are made to cry out: "They who sacrifice the men get to kiss the calves." That is, idolators who are onlookers reward men actually performing human sacrifice with the right to kiss the man-wrought cow. In such a mad world, the Land itself, dependent on intellectual power, blows away "as smoke out of the chimney."

The prophet's role, then, as Hosea understands it, is to call Israel back to its intellectual life, to language and to literacy, to the right uses of imagination and to the discernment of idolatry's foolishness.

With the return of "words," Hosea implies, the Land will once again bloom:

> O Israel, return unto the Lord thy God; for thou hast fallen by thine iniquity. Take with you words, and turn to the Lord. . . . They that dwell under his shadow shall return; they shall revive as the corn, and grow as the vine: the scent thereof shall be as the wine of Lebanon. Ephraim shall say, What have I to do any more with idols? I have heard him, and observed him: I am like a green fir tree. From me is thy fruit found. Who is wise, and he shall understand these things? prudent, and he shall know them? for the ways of the Lord are right, and the just shall walk in them: but the transgressors shall fall therein. (Hosea 14)

This plea for wisdom, prudence, and understanding, founded on the belief that the Land's fruitfulness depends on *their* cultivation, finds its most compact formulation in a phrase that occupies the ellipsis in the passage above. I omitted it because, again, it is badly garbled by King James' translators, who give this: "Take with you words, and turn to the Lord; say unto him, Take away all iniquity, and receive us graciously: so will we render the calves of our lips." As it was the custom of Hebrew poets to rhyme ideas rather than sounds, the second half of this verse undoubtedly echoes the first half's plea for "words," for literacy as opposed to literalism and idolatry. The condensed phrase at the end of the verse can perhaps be best paraphrsed like this: "Receive us graciously: we will reexchange our calves for our lips." That is, "We will return to an intellectual relationship with God and tell Him of our readiness to reinstate "lips" (*words, thoughts, conversation with God*) in place of "calves" (*idolatrous sacrifices*).

Hosea's call for a reaffirmation of language and intellect, of loyalty to monotheistic thought, finds its finest elaboration in the great prophecies of Isaiah, which were composed in the Southern kingdom of Judah, perhaps fifty years after Hosea wrote for Israel. By the time Isaiah writes, Ephraim has fallen. The remnants of its population, already decimated by war, disease, and economic failure, were deported by the Assyrians as the "ten lost tribes." Thereafter Judea (which actually had absorbed into it the near neighbors of Benjamin, Simeon, and Dan) was left to represent Hebrew civilization, later called Jewish, after Judah.

Isaiah intimates that if the Hebrews elevate thought they will discover that the Land, a meaningless wilderness to the mindless, becomes a divine garden to the mindful:

> Let the wicked forsake his way, and the unrighteous man his thoughts. . . . For my thoughts are not your thoughts, neither are your ways my ways, saith the Lord. For as the heavens are higher than the earth, so are my ways higher than your ways, and my thoughts than your thoughts. For as the rain cometh down, and the snow from heaven, and returneth not thither, but watereth the earth, and maketh it bring forth and bud, that it may give seed to the sower, and bread to the eater: So shall my word be that goeth forth out of my mouth: it shall not return unto me void, but it shall accomplish that which I please, and it shall prosper in the thing whereto I sent it. For ye shall go out with joy, and be led forth with peace: the mountains and the hills shall break forth before you into singing, and all the trees of the field shall clap their hands. Instead of the thorn shall come up the fir tree, and instead of the brier shall come up the myrtle tree: and it shall be to the Lord for a name, for an everlasting sign that shall not be cut off. (Isaiah 55)

In this passage it is difficult to say where metaphors for an intellectual relationship with God stop and where the literal fruitfulness of the Land begins. But that is Isaiah's point: Land and monotheistic God are inseparable, both equally dependent for their earthly existence on the cultivation of thought, both flowering in the prepared mind, neither possible in the mind of the literalist or the idolator. Isaiah thus spent his career calling for the recultivation of mind.

How difficult it is for the distant descendants of Hosea and Isaiah to grasp the high seriousnes, called prophecy by the Hebrews, which unified monotheism and the intellectual life, connecting both to survival in the Land. For citizens of the modern world, prophecy is not the ability to connect but the capacity for preacher rhetoric. We do not expect our prophets to master poetry and we celebrate our religious poets not for their monotheism but for their language. We admire Gerard Manley Hopkins because his rhythms spring and his phrases alliterate, not because we learn how to connect these techniques with his sense of the grandeur of God. We also assume we can survive without poet or preacher, confining one to the lectern and the other to the pulpit, both nicely subsidized but hardly allowed to shape our course as a people. As T. S. Eliot complained of the divorce between thought and feeling that makes the modern world a wasteland, so Hosea and Isaiah complained of the lost union between poetry and intellectual monotheism, without which the Land becomes a wilderness. Though we no longer remember that this union is possible, Hosea and Isaiah did remember, and they insisted that their congregants remember, that the Land might be sustained.

Their idea was to preserve the Land as an intellectual haven. Today Jew and non-Jew alike often regard the Land as a physical refuge. This is a relatively late idea. The ancient Hebrews thought of Egypt as an uncertain refuge, but the Land by itself was no refuge at all. The Land, stripped of prophetic significance, was land, a wilderness. The only possible refuge was the mind, the intellectual life that invested the Land with a civilization capable of the monotheistic vision. Thus, Isaiah describes the ideal citizen of the Land as one who uses word rather than sword to confront injustice, as one who takes refuge in mind:

> And there shall come forth a rod out of the stem of Jesse, and a Branch shall grow out of his roots: And the spirit of the Lord shall rest upon him, the spirit of wisdom and understanding, the spirit of counsel and might, the spirit of knowledge and of the fear of the Lord; And shall make him of quick understanding in the fear of the Lord: and he shall not judge after the sight of his eyes, neither reprove after the hearing of his ears: But with righteousness shall he judge the poor, and reprove with equity for the meek of the earth: and he shall smite the earth with the rod of his mouth, and with the breath of his lips shall he slay the wicked. (Isaiah 11)

This passage is taken by Christians in a serious way as a foreshadowing of Jesus and sometimes by Jews in a looser way as a harbinger of a messiah yet to come. It seems more likely that Isaiah, who always addressed himself to the common Hebrew, did not mean by "the stem of Jesse" a specific leader of his time or any other time but the entire House of David, which he expected in his own generation and at all times to defer to no messiah in making the Land flower with poetry, godliness, and justice, with "quick understanding."

Jeremiah, too, writing in the time of the Babylonian captivity, insists that Israel and Judah, "this evil people, which refuse to hear my words, which walk in the imagination of their heart" (Jeremiah 13), have fallen because of failed minds, despite the direct cultivation of those minds by God himself:

Because of all the evil of the children of Israel and of the children of Judah, which they have done to provoke me to anger, they, their kings, their princes, their priests, and their prophets, and the men of Judah, and the inhabitants of Jerusalem. And they have turned unto me the back, and not the face: though I taught them, rising up early and teaching them, yet they have not hearkened to receive instruction. . . . And they built the high places of Baal, which are in the valley of the son of Hinnom, to cause their sons and their daughters to pass through the fire unto Molech; which I commanded them not, neither came it into my mind, that they should do this abomination, to cause Judah to sin. And now therefore thus saith the Lord, the god of Israel, concerning this city, whereof ye say. It shall be delivered into the hand of the king of Babylon. (Jeremiah 32)

And like Isaiah, Jeremiah looks forward to the restoration of Zion, which will take place after "seventy years" of Bablonian captivity when Hebrew imagination will reestablish itself.

And at that time they shall call Jerusalem the throne of the Lord; . . . neither shall they walk any more after the imagination of their evil heart. In those days the house of Judah shall walk with the house of Israel, and they shall come together . . . to the land that I have given for an inheritance unto your fathers. (Jeremiah 3)

Because these books of Isaiah and Jeremiah, along with most of the Bible, were edited in the time of the captivity, it was already clear that the initial prophecies had failed; but the hope persisted that prophecy would not continue to fail, that the right use of Hebrew imagination would return.

Eventually the Hebrews came to worry that not even the intellectual life guaranteed a refuge. Thus, they included in their canon the Book of Koheleth (or Ecclesiastes), composed in the third century B.C.E., perhaps four hundred years after Isaiah flourished, in the time of early Hellenism. A tasteful materialism was then pervading the Eastern Mediterranean, and the Land had become a softer place, at least for the worldly. A sophisticated ease was the goal of the Greeks, who undertook intellectual work because it was pleasurable, not because it necessarily brought them closer to God. The writer of Koheleth, known as the Preacher (or the Assembler, in Hebrew), has tried the Greek way and knows that an epicurean life cannot rise above vanity to significance, and so he accepts Isaiah's call to a life of the mind: "I applied mine heart to know, and to search, and to seek out wisdom, and the reason of things, and to know the wickedness of folly, even of foolishness and madness" (Ecclesiastes 2).

But Koheleth is disappointed to find that human imagination is so perverted that it can never predict the future or see into the significance of the creation. Therefore the human mind will never grasp wisdom: "Lo, this only have I found, that God hath made man upright; but they have sought out many inventions" (Ecclesiastes 2). By "inventions" Koheleth means empty lies, imaginative falsehoods masquerading as insight. He broods that wisdom may itself become merely another vanity, despite the ongoing Hebrew claim of value in the high fictions of monotheism:

> Then I saw that wisdom excelleth folly, as far as light excelleth darkness. The wise man's eyes are in his head; but the fool walketh in darkness: and I myself preceived also that one event happeneth to them all. Then said I in my heart, As it happeneth to the fool, so it happeneth even to me; and why was I then more wise? Then I said in my heart, that this also is vanity. For there is no remembrance of the wise more than of the fool for ever; seeing that which now is in the days to come shall all be forgotten. And how dieth the wise man? as the fool. (Ecclesiastes 2)

Nevertheless, even the Preacher remained a devotee of the wise life, writing a book of polished prose that forms part of the foundation of our literary culture, providing titles for *The Golden Bowl*, *The House of Mirth*, and *The Sun Also Rises*. And the Preacher hoped to live nowhere but in the Land of Isaiah, where wisdom and godliness would prevail, where governance would be by measure, and where even the King's setting of a proper dinner hour would signal the mind's capacity for digestion and for discernment: "Woe to thee, O land, when thy king is a child, and thy princes eat in the morning! Blessed art thou, O land, when thy king is the son of nobles, and thy princes eat in due season, for strength, and not for drunkenness" (Ecclesiastes 10).

The Preacher, like many other cynics in ancient Israel, knew too much Hebrew history and too much of human nature to trust in the ephemeral, but the trust he did invest went into the Land and into its civilization of intellectual monotheism, to which he returns at the end: "Let us hear the conclusion of the whole matter: Fear God, and keep his commandments: for this is the whole duty of man."

Chapter 11

Jonah:

Landless and Illiterate

Thou rulest the raging of the sea: when the waves therof arise, thou stillest them. . . . The heavens are thine, the earth also is thine: as for the world and the fulness thereof, thou has founded them.

—Psalm 89

O let the nations be glad and sing for joy; for thou shalt judge the people righteously, and govern the nations upon earth. Let the people praise thee, O God; let all the people praise thee. Then shall the earth yield her increase; and God, even our own God, shall bless us. God shall bless us; and all the ends of the earth shall fear him.

—Psalm 67

FROM THE BEGINNING OF THEIR EXISTENCE AS A NATION, THE ANCIENT Hebrews understood that intellectual monotheism belonged not only to the House of Israel but to "the world and the fulness thereof." That the Law was given at Sinai, in the middle of nowhere rather than in the Land itself, suggested to them that the Law belonged everywhere. A universal God could not belong solely to a small people. Monotheism was intended for all those who could see it. The Hebrews understood, of course, that the world was not quick to see the invisible, but they hoped that more and more nations would grasp monotheistic poetry and root it in their own Lands. Ancient Zionism is a universal voice calling from a particular hill, listening for echoes.

Isaiah, again, best envisions a time when the peoples of the world would take Zion as a model and transform themselves into visionaries and poets:

> And it shall come to pass in the last days, that the mountain of the Lord's house shall be established in the top of the mountains, and shall be exalted above the hills; and all the nations shall flow unto it. And many people shall go and say, Come ye, and let us go up to the mountain of the Lord, to the house of Jacob; and he will teach us his ways, and we will walk in his paths: for out of Zion shall go forth the law, and the word of the Lord from Jerusalem. (Isaiah 2)

Though the prophets anticipated a time when the whole world would recognize the single Creator, the Hebrews realized that it would do no good to hurry the process by dispatching missionaries to those who lived in darkness. The zeal of a hypothetical monotheistic missionary would never substitute for a potential convert's own vision. Thus the Hebrews did not proselytize but waited for intellectual reformation.

Nevertheless there are two books in the Bible that take as their subject monotheism's potential reach. The first is the Book of Ruth, which, as we have seen, describes the intellectual achievement of a single convert. The second is the Book of Jonah, which offers the Hebrews' only recorded theological emissary—and he turns out to be a failure. It is remarkable that the people who expected to be a light unto the nations showed so little faith in the workings of their lighthouses. Perhaps this was so because the Hebrews believed that the other nations were too busy hating Israel to be enlightened by intellectual monotheism (we will later explore that ancient hatred of ancient Zionism). But the main reason given in the Bible for the failure of the nations to enter the Lord's house is not the thorniness of the message nor the obtuseness of the nations but the intellectual failure of the messengers themselves.

The Book of Jonah is the story of a foreign people ready to embrace monotheism and of a Hebrew messenger who has forgotten the intellectual heritage he was expected to convey. The writer is unknown, but from the story's post-exilic Hebrew, strongly influenced by Aramaic, and its Persian customs (the casting of lots, the issuing of royal decrees via a court of noblemen), we can infer a date of composition in the fourth century B.C.E. That the writer makes a fable out of the story of Jonah, an actual citizen of the Northern Kingdom of Israel in the eighth century B.C.E., and that Jonah is portrayed as being sent by God to Nineveh, an Assyrian city known as a center of the civilization that swallowed Israel, leads to the speculation that the writer lived in the northern parts of the Land and took on the thankless task of showing that Isaiah's universalized Zion applied even to Israel's worst enemies.

However this may be, Jonah the son of Amittai appears in 2 Kings 14 as a prophet who brought word to King Jeroboam II that God would restore the part of Israel that had been lost during the reign of his sinful father Joash—who did "evil in the sight of the Lord." The historical Jonah promises that the "coast of Israel" will be restored from "Hamath unto the sea of the plain." This is metaphorical. For neither Hamath, inland in Assyria on the Orontes, nor the Sea of the Arava, a name for the Jordan Valley, are on the coast. As we shall see, the writer of the Book of Jonah wanted an allusion connecting the Land to his fable of the sea, and perhaps he also wanted an allusion to a historical time that seemed but was not hopeless:

> He [Jeroboam II] restored the coast of Israel from the entering of Hamath unto the sea of the plain, according to the word of the Lord God of Israel, which he spake by the hand of his servant Jonah, the son of Amittai, the prophet, which was of Gath-hepher. For the Lord saw the affliction of Israel, that it was very bitter; for there was not any . . . helper for Israel. And the Lord said not that he would blot out the name of Israel from under heaven; but he saved them by the hand of Jeroboam the son of Joash. (2 Kings 14)

That is all we know of the historical Jonah. The fabulous Jonah, the hero of the Book of Jonah, the Jonah who is famous in Western literature, receives the word of God to leave the Land and travel to the Assyrian city of Nineveh, where he is to instruct the idol-worshippers in monotheism. Jonah fears that he will be humiliated or killed among the fierce people of Nineveh, and so he flees by ship to Tarshish, a city of uncertain identity, perhaps in Spain but in any case known to the Hebrews as a faraway place, a distant port during the days of Solomon's argosies. The ship in which he travels tosses dangerously in a storm until he is found by the drawing of lots to be the cause of misfortune. Reluctantly the seamen toss Jonah to the belly of the famous whale, from whence God saves him. At that moment Jonah seems enlightened, and he composes a psalm of great beauty. But even then Jonah takes up the burden of prophecy reluctantly, not really understanding it, even though he does manage to persuade the people of Nineveh to repent. To enrich Jonah's understanding, God enacts a parable for him at the end of the fable, but Jonah still does not understand. The feature of greatest interest for the Hebrews would have been this misunderstanding.

The ancient Hebrews would follow the way the four chapters of the Book of Jonah develop the would-be prophet's failure to become a literary figure. In chapter 1, Jonah flees "from the presence of the Lord," a desperately ridiculous move by a literalist who forgets the placelessness of the monotheist's God. Leaving the rich emblem of the Land, Jonah floats off into a simpler world especially suited to his cast of mind, a world where storms are external and elemental, where responsibility is found in things. The good-hearted, simple sailors cast lots, and the whalebone dice bring Jonah's responsibility for the storm easily to light, though they reduce its meaning to a matter of jettisoning the guilty cargo. When Jonah the material man is cast overboard the sea instantly lies calm. As the literalist-prophet sinks to intellectual depths he becomes doubly immured in matter, inside both his own salvaged carcass and the body of a whale.

Tradition has regarded Jonah's sleeping in the bowels of the ship during the hours of its crisis as a metaphor for moral torpor. But Jonah is more asleep to metaphor than to morality; there is nothing nearly so wrong with his morals as with his dogged literalness. He accepts his responsibility for the sailors' plight as soon as the captain challenges him with the results of the lots, and he gracefully bows to the necessity of being thrown overboard; but he gives no sign of recognizing the folly of literally running from the presence of the Lord. In sacrificing himself for the safety of his shipmates, he does the right thing, but he fails to understand the meaning of the drama he is enacting. He is like Shakespeare's Dogberry in *Much Ado About Nothing*, a morally correct policeman who redeems the day by arresting the right criminal in the middle of the night but who is not sure what the crime is.

Of course there is more to Jonah than to Dogberry. Chapter 2 offers a glimpse of a miraculously transformed, poetic Jonah. With this transformation the literalist's world melts, revealing Jonah's depths. Suddenly, in the belly of the whale, Jonah is no longer merely at sea; he recognizes the sea as metaphor, the weight of water as intellectual swamping and blunder; the darkness of the gastric pit becomes self-imposed benightedness from which self-enlightenment beckons: "For thou hast cast me into the deep, in the midst of the seas; and the floods compassed me about; all thy billows and thy waves passed over me. Then I said I am cast out of thy sight; yet I will look again toward thy holy temple." This aspires to the language of Psalm 88: "Thou hast laid me in the lowest pit, in darkness, in the deeps. Thy wrath lieth hard upon me, and thou hast afflicted me with all thy waves," writes David.* Neither David nor Jonah is talking about the kind of drowning that floods the lungs. Jonah's expression of his poetry-making soul instantly liberates him from the cage of fleshly literalism, bearing him from belly to dry land in a moment of rebirth. Pious readers emphasize Jonah's repentance; however, Jonah's salvation stems not from conventional soul-cleansing but from the repair of metaphor.

In chapter 3 the newly reinspired prophet actually turns the idolatrous citizens of Nineveh to acknowledgment of the One God. Jonah threatens God's vengeance, and the entire populace, from King to cattle, put on sackcloth. What Jonah said to the people of Nineveh is not

---

*Also compare Jonah's psalmistry in the whale's belly with David's celebration of his deliverance from the hand of Saul: "When the waves of death compassed me . . . the sorrows of hell compassed me about . . . I called upon the Lord, and cried to my God" (2 Samuel 22). *Afafooni*, the Hebrew for "compassed me," appears in the Bible only in the poetry of David and Jonah.

quoted. What song must he have sung, what poetic physic must he have instilled in Nineveh's veins, what veils must he have lifted so that gawking eyes might read correctly the theater of idols. Suddenly, the people of Nineveh saw that their old gods were jars of terra cotta, trimmed with mounded breasts made with maws for receiving living babies. Jonah's monotheism begets poetry that begets prophecy that begets monotheism, even in Nineveh, which now—and only now—can be given law and literature and the civilized arts:

> So the people of Nineveh believed God, and proclaimed a fast, and put on sackcloth, from the greatest of them even to the least of them. For word came unto the king of Nineveh, and he arose from his throne, and he laid his robe from him, and covered him with sackcloth, and sat in ashes. And he caused it to be proclaimed and published through Nineveh by the decree of the king and his nobles, saying, Let neither man nor beast, herd nor flock, taste any thing: let them not feed, nor drink water: But let man and beast be covered with sackcloth, and cry mightily unto God; yea, let them turn evey one . . . from the violence that is in their hands.

For Hebrews, "the violence that is in their hands" referred foremost to child-sacrifice. Nineveh is on the verge of becoming another Land, and Jonah, no longer at sea intellectually, is on the verge of becoming a great prophet.

But Jonah cannot appreciate either his gift or its effect. In chapter 4 he regresses; or rather he stands for the regression of each generation of forgetful Hebrews that built a version of the golden calf and dubbed the thing a god. In a curious twist of literalist thinking, Jonah assumes that the converted people of Nineveh, when they discover that they have escaped the promised vengeance, will torment him as a false prophet instead of expressing gratitude:

> And God saw their works, that they turned from their evil way; and God repented of the evil, that he had said that he would do unto them; and he did it not. But it displeased Jonah exceedingly, and he was very angry. And he prayed unto the Lord, and said, I pray thee, O Lord, was not this my saying, when I was yet in my country? Therefore I fled before unto Tarshish: for I knew thou art a gracious God, and merciful, slow to anger, and of great kindness, and repentest thee of the evil. Therefore now, O

Lord, take, I beseech thee, my life from me; for it is better for me to die
than to live.

Jonah's misconstruing of his situation suggests a sudden reversion
to the literary naivete that characterizes his thinking in chapter 1.
Gone is the psalmist's power of chapter 2. He forgets his poetry, like
the Hebrew backsliders who precede and follow him. God speaks to
Jonah in a staged parable, but Jonah fails to interpret, fails even to
appreciate that he is being spoken to in metaphor:

> So Jonah went out of the city, and sat on the east side of the city, and there
> made him a booth, and sat under it in the shadow, till he might see what
> would become of the city. And the Lord God prepared a gourd, and made
> it to come up over to Jonah, that it might be shadow over his head, to
> deliver him from his grief. So Jonah was exceeding glad of the gourd. But
> God prepared a worm when the morning rose the next day, and it smote
> the gourd that it withered. And it came to pass, when the sun did arise,
> that God, prepared a vehement east wind; and the sun beat upon the head
> of Jonah, that he fainted, and wished in himself to die, and said, It is bet-
> ter for me to die than to live.

God is here Himself literary, crafting a story of a gourd that shades
Jonah in his booth and of a worm that eats the gourd, offering Jonah
an opportunity to understand mercy through poetry. Instead Jonah is
disappointed that Nineveh has not been destroyed, according to the
direst interpretation of his prophecy. He cannot rise above the literalist's pleasure in physical vengeance. So while God speaks to him he
sulks. The hot sun penetrates the withered vines and addles his head.
He is in the merely physical world of his own unpleasant feelings, too
busy in his discomfort to attend God.

In the scornful last words of the story, God must interpret His own
parable, filling in for Jonah's failed literary sensibility. As Jonah stares,
God offers literary analysis, which is the soul of prophecy:

> And God said to Jonah, Doest thou well to be angry for the Gourd? And
> he said, I do well to be angry, even until death. Then said the Lord, Thou
> hast had pity on the Gourd, for the which thou has not laboured, neither
> madest it grow; which came up in a night and perished in a night: And
> should not I spare Nineveh, that great city, wherein are more than sixscore

thousand persons that cannot discern between their right hand and their left . . . ? (Jonah 4)

Even after this, Jonah still fails to understand that he has just seen a text and is hearing its reading. Not able to attend, he must hear, or miss hearing, how God lowers the level of the conversation for his benefit. God meets Jonah on a level far beneath that of the repentant people of Nineveh, who may fail to distinguish right and left but would not fail, as Jonah apparently does, to understand value beyond "cattle." Cattle constituted the universal hard coinage of the ancient world (our word "pecuniary" comes from the Latin *pecus*, cow): "And should not I spare Nineveh, that great city, wherein are more than sixscore thousand persons that cannot discern between their right hand and their left; and also much cattle." These are the last words of the story, an anticlimactic cattle-count tossed at Jonah. An exasperated God, who lavished theater, parable, and prophecy on a reluctant poet, must at the end throw up metaphorical hands and count coins. God so much as says, "You may master money, but you lack language; preservation of cattle you grasp, but prophecy is not for you; you tried to tell me this at the beginning, but I misread you, expecting more; this is equally true of your fellow Hebrews, whom you represent."

The ancient Hebrews could enjoy no confidence that the literary tradition they created would survive. They could not foresee a time when the culture of metaphor would be so strong that law and poetry and ritual would try to reign on their own without acknowledging or remembering their connections to monotheism. On the contrary, our forefathers regarded the gifts of metaphor and the monotheism it permitted as flickering candles, easily quenched in a persisting sea of literalism. They told the story of Jonah to remind themselves of the theological blindness and the general stupidity that followed from the loss of these gifts; they told the story in a literary way to serve as an antidote for the literalism of the hero.

Jonah begins his story in a literalist's flight, soars into literary flight, and then falls back from the sublime into a pettiness deserving God's ridicule. One can hardly believe that having donned the garland of metaphor, Jonah would so easily discard it; yet, to believe the old prophets, the Hebrews accomplished this virtually on a daily basis.

The possibility of forgetting metaphor was such a constant threat to ancient Israel that Moses was compelled, by God and redactor alike, to spend his last breaths shoring up imagination and song:

> And the Lord said unto Moses, Behold, thou shalt sleep with thy fathers; and this people will rise up, and go a whoring after the gods of the strangers of the land, whither they go to be among them, and will forsake me, and break my covenant which I have made with them. . . . Now therefore write ye this song for you, and teach it the children of Israel: put it in their mouths, that this song may be a witness for me against the children of Israel. . . . And it shall come to pass, when many evils and troubles are befallen them, that this song shall testify against them as a witness; for it shall not be forgotten out of the mouths of their seed: for I know their imagination which they go about, even now, before I have brought them into the land which I sware. Moses therefore wrote this song the same day, and taught it to the children of Israel. (Deuteronomy 31)

That song never was well learned. Certainly Jonah never learned it well. Not singing well at home, he howls on the road. Out of the Land he is out of his mind. And since the Ur story of Jonah in 2 Kings connects land and sea, we might also say that Jonah represents the Hebrews who were at sea even when they were at home in the Land.

His story ends abruptly. Poetry and prophecy abandon him, leave him squatting in a field far from the Land, a dunce in exile, an ambassador and examplar who foolishly isolated himself because he lost the ability to read the Land's meaning. Thus Jonah serves as the model of a lapsed reader of monotheism. Losing language, Jonah is a man bewildered by metaphor and parable, confused by the literacy that was meant to be his element. It is not commonly recognized how completely Jonah in his booth embodies Isaiah's prophecy of Zion undone: "Zion is left as a cottage in a vineyard, as a lodge in a garden of cucumbers, as a besieged city" (the Hebrew word in Isaiah 1 for "cottage," *succah*, is the same word used for Jonah's "booth").

The image of Jonah forlorn in his booth is the image of Zion abandoned by God. The writer of Jonah implies that Zion—struggling in its post-exilic days, with its better-educated population still in Babylon—would rise to become a beacon to the nations only when it restored its skills in poetry and imagination. Without the old poetry, the Land dried up, like Jonah's gourd. Without the old poetry, prophets became shipwrecked, far from home. This brooding on the consequences of failed imagination permeates late Hebrew civilization. Thus even eleven centuries after the composition of Jonah, the poet Rabbi Elazar ha-Kallir, writing as a member of the dwindling Jewish community in the Land in the eighth century C.E., connects his prayer for dew, to be recited at Passover and afterwards in the dry season, with restoration of Jonah's booth, of Zion, and of Hebrew poetry:

Grant dew for a good year, crowned
With splendid fruit of the land;
Zion now left like a lone booth,
Take her in thy hand like a crown.

Let dew fall on the blessed land;
Bless us with the gift of heaven;
In darkness let a light dawn,
For Israel who follows thee.

Let dew sweeten the mountains;
Let thy chosen taste thy wealth;
Free thy people from exile;
That we may sing and exult.
—From Philip Birnbaum, *Prayerbook for Sabbath and Festivals*

In the Hebrew tradition, Jonah is a failed poet, a scorned schoolboy; he could not reliably "sing and exult." But in Western thought Jonah has become something else, a famous rebel who goes his own way, unashamed to assert his plans over those of the Lord's. He says he will not go, submits only under protest, grumbles into his beard even after enjoying divine redemption from the miraculous belly of the great fish. He is his own man, a Daniel Boone of the long centuries before the advent of demonstrative individualism. But this is not at all the way the ancient Hebrews thought of Jonah.

As the story was understood, the people of Nineveh, Jonah's charges, are stranded, with little hope that they will build a house better than Jonah's hut. If the reformation of the distant nations depended on the Hebrew, those sitting in darkness would have to wait until the lights in the Hebrew Land grew brighter. Though the hope for this was scant, it was never abandoned, for the Hebrews always believed that God might yet relent and reinspire his people, as He did in the time of Joash's son Jeroboam, who received word from Jonah the son of Amittai. Perhaps more importantly, the Hebrews also believed that they might reinspire themselves. Out of these hopes, the Book of Jonah is read in the synagogue on the afternoon of Yom Kippur, the Hebrews' Day of Atonement.

Chapter 12

The Ancient Hatred of Zionism

> . . . *who saw*
> *When this creation was? remember'st thou*
> *Thy making, while the Maker gave thee being?*
> *We know no time when we were not as now;*
> *Know none before us, self-begot, self-rais'd*
> *By our own quick'ning power.*
> —John Milton, *Paradise Lost*

> *Hatred is the coward's revenge for being intimidated.*
> —George Bernard Shaw, *Major Barbara*

PERHAPS MONOTHEISTIC CULTURE SLIPPED AWAY FROM THE PEOPLE OF Nineveh because of the inadequacy of the Hebrew model. Elsewhere Zion had an uncertain impact because it inspired hatred. One might think that intellectual monotheism, which cultivated both mind and Land with poetry and prophecy, might have earned enlightened thanks in the brutish ancient world, or at worst indifference. But Zionism encountered an uncanny hatred from its inception. No rapacious army, no empire-building bully, no glutton for tribute provoked a deeper hatred than the Hebrew poets.

From the beginning, intellectual Zionism implied a confrontation with anti-Zionism. Even in Egypt, as soon as the Hebrews grew in numbers but well before they could establish themselves in their own Land, they were already hated—irrationally and inexplicably—by the new Pharaoh who "knew not Joseph." The poetic analysis of this hatred runs throughout the Bible's presentation of Hebrew national life. Hebrew writers recorded little of what we would today consider the rational and expectable resentment that might have been expressed by those Canaanites who lost cities and fields to the Hebrew invaders. Instead, the Hebrews focused on two kinds of gratuitous hatred, which were far more puzzling than the understandable anger of evicted landholders.

The first was dumb, brutish, and inarticulate, a hatred best exemplified by the Amalekites, who, without provocation—after barely taking a look at the Zionist enterprise—attacked the Hebrews as they camped in the desert on the Canaanite side of the Red Sea. The Amalekites are never quoted in the Bible; they do not appear to have had anything to say. They looked and they attacked. Moses was forced to send Joshua to repel them. "Remember Amalek" became a byword for mean, spontaneous hatred; and the Hebrews were commanded, in a seemingly grim passage with more poetic play than is generally recognized, to blot these bullies out of memory: "And Joshua discomfited Amalek and his people with the edge of the sword. And the Lord said unto Moses, Write this for a memorial in a book, and rehearse it in the ears of Joshua: for I will utterly put out the remembrance of Amalek from under heaven" (Exodus 17).

The antidote to the Amalekites' irrational hatred, if there is one, is the creation of "a book" and of a literary culture. While in part this passage may be a self-serving attempt by writers in generations long

183

after Moses to justify the extinction of the Amalekites, its governing idea is that a literary culture must maintain itself against the hatred of illiterates. Only in a literary culture will the paradox of remembering to suppress the "remembrance of Amalek" be understood as a cerebral ritual designed to dishonor mindlessness.

Amalek's mute hatred provided a context for the kind of irrational hatred that the writers of the Bible found more interesting, namely the intellectual hatred of Zionism. This in turn came in two forms. The first was the non-Hebrew hatred of Hebrews; the second was the hatred of one's own culture.

The intellectual hatred of the Hebrews by foreign nations begins with the Pharaoh of Exodus. Unlike Amalek, Pharaoh thought and said a great deal about what was wrong with the Hebrews; some of this makes superficial sense:

> And he said unto his people, Behold, the people of the children of Israel are more and mightier than we: Come on, let us deal wisely with them; lest they multiply, and it come to pass, that, when there falleth out any war, they join also unto our enemies, and fight against us, and so get them up out of the land. (Exodus 1)

That Pharaoh worries about the Hebrews becoming traitors seems rational, though no evidence is presented that these people, grateful to former pharaohs for having rescued them from famine, would ever join Egypt's enemies. But the passage makes clear that fifth columnists are not really on Pharaoh's mind, as he slides off from sedition into worrying that the Hebrews might merely slip away in time of war. Nor is a potential emigration what concerns him. This becomes clear as the passage above continues with an ironic undermining of Pharaoh's false logic:

> Therefore they did set over them taskmasters to afflict them with their burdens. And they built for Pharaoh treasure cities, Pithom and Ramses. But the more they afflicted them, the more they multiplied and grew. And they were grieved because of the children of Israel. And the Egyptians made the children of Israel serve with rigour: And they made their lives bitter with hard bondage, in mortar, and in brick, and in all manner of service in the field: all their service, wherein they made them serve, was with rigour. And the king of Egypt spake to the Hebrew midwives of which the

name of one was Shiphrah, and the name of the other Puah: And he said, When ye do the office of a midwife to the Hebrew women, and see them upon the stools; if it be a son, then ye shall kill him: but if it be a daughter, then she shall live. (Exodus 1)

If Pharaoh's true intention was to preempt traitors, his strategy makes no sense. The slaying of male babies would diminish the fighting capacity of the Hebrews only in the coming generation and would meanwhile goad the present fathers into action. If the plan was to prevent emigration in order to maintain a vital work force, slaying male babies would only diminish the productivity of the Hebrews. This too makes no sense. If the plan was merely to get free labor, then the gratuitous "rigour" under which the Hebrews were forced to work (first the whip, and later the spiteful and inefficient system of forcing the Hebrews to gather their own straw for making bricks) could only delay the completion of Pharaoh's palace. But the point of the Hebrew writers is that Pharaoh's preoccupations are irrational. Pharaoh meant only to torment the Hebrews, and he couched his hatred in elaborately articulated arguments.

How does one explain Pharaoh's hatred? The ancient Hebrews gave a great deal of thought to this problem. Pharaoh's irrational cruelty was so deep they feared that their monotheism would crack before it. They feared the temptation to separate Pharaoh from creation, to assign him a hell of his own over which he could rule in a Manichean universe. They had to remind themselves that if God created and ruled the entire universe, then somehow Pharaoh's hatred of monotheism had to be part of creation; hence the repeated passages in Exodus in which Hebrew writers make God responsible for Pharaoh by saying, "I will harden Pharaoh's heart."

In Exodus, the Hebrew writers imply that monotheism earns Pharaoh's hatred because it confines his power to his little time on the big river. Monotheism diminishes Pharaoh, as it diminishes every idolator who hopes to rule what he can in this world and then win a mummy's salvation. Though monotheism has many attractions, the Hebrews could understand that Pharaoh would not like its challenge, especially since he was an intelligent man capable of grasping its intellectual content. This stung the Hebrews: monotheism required intellect, but it was precisely the intelligent idolator who hated it most. The writers of the Bible knew there was a sense in which Pharaoh's hatred of the Hebrews was not irrational at all: Pharaoh hated them because he understood them. And because he understood, he could not merely rid Egypt of the Hebrews (the one thing he could not do, despite ten plagues, is let these people go) but had to humiliate them.

The intellectual whose hatred of Israel most fascinated the Hebrews was Balaam. Balaam the son of Beor came from the nomadic tribe of Midian, which in the time of Moses spread itself westward across the northern Arabian desert into Sinai and eastward into Mesopotamia, nibbling at the underbelly of the fertile crescent. Despite remaining on the outskirts of civilization, the intelligent Midianites accumulated wealth and some power, though leadership of their far-flung tribe had to be divided between "five kings." When Moses commits murder as a young man in the House of Pharaoh, it is to the Midianites he must flee, out at the fringes. Moses recognizes kindred spirits in Midian, and he takes a wife from among them. When his father-in-law, Jethro, advises him on the establishment of law courts, Moses recognizes the man's wisdom. Thus the Hebrews would not be surprised to find that Balaam, the most intelligent of the wise Midianites, understands the Hebrew enterprise, nor would they be surprised that Midian wisdom allows Balaam to rise as a prophet to the rank of the five kings themselves; in Numbers 31, he is mentioned in one breath with them.

Balaam's story, told at length in Numbers 22–24, is pointedly inserted just as the Hebrews are preparing to enter the Land. Balak, King of Moab, sees the Hebrews camping in the plain below his mountainous stronghold, which overlooks the gateway to Canaan. The Hebrews are not troubling him. Balak even knows that they specifically plan not to disturb him on the way to their promised Land. Yet he hates them. He sends for Balaam, the justly famous prophet, to curse that which he hates. And it turns out that Balaam's venomous intellect is, indeed, one of the great obstacles to life in the Land.

Over the centuries, Balaam has won many favorable comments for his grasp of poetry and of the Hebrew vision, but the rabbis saw that it was precisely his mastery of the tools of monotheism that powered his hatred. In a world without monotheism, Balaam rose high—a great sorcerer, a marvel of wisdom, a mentor to kings. In the face of monotheism, he was reduced to his own understanding, made little in his own view. He is famous for being mocked by the ass on which he rode, but this is probably meant as a poetic representation of the mockery he made of himself in the light of monotheism. Thus he hated the Hebrews.

Balak, King of Moab, gives sanctuary to Molech, who guarantees greatness to little men. Intuitively Balak recognizes that the Hebrew ideas undermine him, that monotheism is a threat to all idolators. He also knows that he needs intellectual help to combat the intellectual menace:

> He sent messengers therefore unto Balaam . . . to call him, saying, Behold, there is a people come out from Egypt: behold, they cover the face of the earth, and they abide over against me: Come now therefore, I pray thee, curse me this people; for they are too mighty for me: peradventure I shall prevail, that we may smite them, and that I may drive them out of the land: for I wot that he whom thou blessest is blessed, and he whom thou cursest is cursed.

Balaam wants to oblige, but "God said unto Balaam, Thou shalt not go with them; thou shalt not curse the people: for they are blessed." I think we can understand God's speaking to Balaam as a poetic way of saying that Balaam's own insight told him it was useless to wave away intellectual monotheism. Initially, he refuses the mission. Still he wants to oblige. He wants to curse. If he can't curse, if his magic has no power, if monotheism is intellectually more powerful than his sorcery, then he is finished. He must give his curses a last chance, as pointless as he knows this to be. After Balak sends more emissaries, Balaam agrees to come to Moab and try his luck. He saddles his ass, placing himself in a situation whose simultaneous foolishness and total seriousness helps create one of the Bible's drollest passages:

> But the angel of the Lord stood in a path of the vineyards, a wall being on this side, and a wall on that side. And when the ass saw the angel of the Lord, she thrust herself unto the wall, and crushed Balaam's foot against the wall. . . . And the angel of the Lord went further, and stood in a narrow place where was no way to turn either to the right hand or to the left. And when the ass saw the angel of the Lord, she fell down under Balaam: and Balaam's anger was kindled, and he smote the ass with a staff. And

the Lord opened the mouth of the ass, and she said unto Balaam, What
have I done unto thee, that thou has smitten me these three times? And
Balaam said unto the ass, Because thou hast mocked me: I would there
were a sword in mine hand, for now would I kill thee. . . . Then the Lord
opened the eyes of Balaam, and he saw the angel of the Lord standing in
the way, and his sword drawn in his hand: and he bowed down his head,
and fell flat on his face. (Numbers 22)

The ass, which perhaps represents Balaam's bridled sense of reality,
sees clearly what Balaam will not allow himself to see; Balaam would
like to kill the ass. The Hebrew reader would not miss the double
irony here. They would find asinine Balaam's fancy that he might
silence his sense of reality with a sword (if he only had one), and they
would laugh at his need for a sword to kill his ass even while he has set
out without weapons to slay monotheism with bare hands. Though he,
in part, recognizes the irony of his own situation, though he momentarily sees "the angel of the Lord" and bows in recognition of the fee-
bleness of his curses, he goes forward anyway, promising to bless Israel
but still angling for a way to curse.

The Hebrew writers probably mean to draw a contrast between
Abraham and Balaam. Abraham sets off in Genesis 22 to sacrifice
Isaac by saddling his ass and taking along "two of his young men."
Similarly Balaam "saddled his ass . . . and his two servants were with
him." This may appear accidental until we realize that Abraham
thought to exterminate the House of Israel as it then existed in possibility—in God's promise to make of Isaac a nation as numerous as the
stars—while Balaam struggled with the plan to exterminate that
nation as it lay before Balak in its actual numbers. While Abraham was
glad to regain his hope for his son and for nationhood to be, Balaam is
happy to curse. Abraham needed to be told only once to desist, but
Balaam pushes foreward despite many warnings. The intellectual skills
that made Abraham rapt, make Balaam rabid, yet there is hardly a
hairbreadth's difference between them, so close is this hater of Zion
to Zion's founding father. Those who embrace the covenant most
intelligently and those who hate it most deeply are made of much the
same stuff—then and now. It is part of the Hebrew task to distinguish
between them.

Balak builds altars and a stage for Balaam's curses. But Balaam delivers only blessings, phrased in lovely poems, for he can see no flaw in the Hebrew idea, no reason to doubt the wisdom of monotheism. He tells Balak that the Hebrew God will not permit him to curse. Balak, another of the Bible's many literalists, moves the altars around, assuming that Balaam's difficulty in producing curses is a technical matter, a problem of visual perspective. He moves the altars from a high place that overlooks the full Hebrew congregation, to a place from which Balaam will "see but the utmost part of them," and then to a place from which the Hebrews cannot be seen at all, as if to confess that the literalist's hatred of Zion persists even without the presence of the Zionists. And Balaam indeed does try with each configuration of altars to curse the Hebrews. But his own intellect, his own gift of poetry, and his grasp of monotheism permit only blessings and inspired vision, no matter how the altars are arranged:

> And Balaam lifted up his eyes, and he saw Israel abiding in his tents according to their tribes; and the spirit of God came upon him. And he took up his parable, and said, Balaam the son of Beor hath said, and the man whose eyes are open hath said: He hath said, which heard the words of God, which saw the vision of the Almighty, falling into a trance, but having his eyes open: How goodly are thy tents, O Jacob, and thy tabernacles, O Israel. As the valleys are they spread forth, as gardens by the river's side, as trees of lignaloes which the Lord hath planted, and as cedar trees beside the waters.

This passage, incorporated into later Hebrew liturgy, reminds us that the Hebrews are on the cusp of moving into the Land's metaphorically lush valleys of aloes and cedars, where people will fall into intellectual trances, but with eyes open, capable of the monotheistic "vision of the Almighty." But that is not really where Balaam's mind wants to go. He is not ready to be a little man in a little Land with a big idea. He walks away, still hoping to salvage his career as a sorcerer, hating Israel for reminding him of his littleness. He tells Balak he is going home, but that is not where he goes. The last we hear of him he is in the field with the Midianite warriors. Knowing that the Hebrews are able to curse themselves even if they cannot be cursed, Balaam apparently directs the Midianites to use holy prostitution to seduce the Hebrews away from monotheism. Because of this,

God commands Moses to spend his dying energy destroying the Midianites and their advisor, Balaam. In Numbers 31, Balaam dies at the sword of those he hated, still trying to curse the only people he ever met who were worthy of his intellect, trying to curse them because they limited his mind to the merely human.

Balaam wins a prominent place in the Bible not only because he represents the stranger's intellectual hatred of Zionism but because his hatred of the Zionist enterprise turned up at home among the Hebrews, too. That Moses married into the Midianites was itself reason enough to take Balaam's hatred as a version of self-hatred. Korah in the time of Moses offers a good example of the native Hebrew version of Zion's intellectual enemies. As in the cases of Pharaoh and Balaam, monotheism makes Korah feel small. He expresses this troubled feeling by attacking Moses for being too big:

> Now Korah . . . took men: And they rose up before Moses, with certain of the children of Israel, two hundred and fifty princes of the assembly, famous in the congregation, men of renown: And they gathered themselves together against Moses and against Aaron, and said unto them, Ye take too much upon you, seeing all the congregation are holy, every one of them, and the Lord is among them: wherefore then lift ye up yourselves above the congregation of the Lord? (Numbers 16)

Korah appears to be leading a democratic insurgency against the tyranny of Moses. He is supported in his demand for a kind of Magna Carta by "men of renown" who say that they wish a legitimate share in power. Among these are Dathan and Abiram, who accuse Moses of deluding the people into making him a prince by promising a distant Land when in reality Egypt was the true place of milk and honey:

> And Moses sent to call Dathan and Abiram, the sons of Eliab: which said, . . . Is it a small thing that thou hast brought us up out of a land that floweth with milk and honey, to kill us in the wilderness, except thou make thyself altogether a prince over us? Moreover thou hast not brought us into a land that floweth with milk and honey, or given us inheritance of fields and vineyards: wilt thou put out the eyes of these men?

Though Moses has indeed been slow to get the Hebrews to the Land as a consequence of the people's own stiffnecked worshipping of the golden calf, the wildness of Dathan and Abiram's accusations is apparent from their idealization of Egypt and their reduction of the Hebrew enterprise to a mere ploy of Moses to become Prince of Wandering.

The writers of the Bible have been careful to show that Moses, no arrogant King John, has already taken steps, partly on the suggestion of his father-in-law, toward democracy:

> And Moses chose able men out of all Israel, and made them heads over the people, rulers of thousands, rulers of hundreds, rulers of fifties, and rulers of tens. And they judged the people at all seasons: the hard causes they brought unto Moses, but every small matter they judged themselves. (Exodus 18)

But Dathan and Abiram are not really interested in democracy, and neither is Korah. The writers of the Bible treat Korah as if he were articulating democracy only as a ruse to overthrow Moses and enlarge his own cramped sphere. Moses is given to penetrate Korah's psychology exactly, accusing the democrat of needing a larger domain than that afforded by his already elevated role in monotheistic practice. Moses notes that Aaron, against whom Korah also rails, has no higher role than Korah himself, who is also a priest; it must be, infers Moses, not exclusion from power but the monotheistic vision itself that makes Korah feel small:

> And Moses said unto Korah, Hear, I pray you, ye sons of Levi: Seemeth it but a small thing unto you, that the God of Israel hath separated you from the congregation of Israel, to bring you near to himself to do the service of the tabernacle, and to stand before the congregation to minister unto them? And he hath brought thee near to him, and all thy brethren the sons of Levi with thee: and seek ye the priesthood also? For which cause both thou and all thy company are gathered together against the Lord: and what is Aaron, that ye murmur against him? (Numbers 16)

Moses implies that Korah would not be satisfied even if he were elevated above his office as Priest to High Priest, for how much greater can Aaron be that Korah murmurs against him? Like Pharaoh and Balaam, articulate Korah is fit only for idols; in worshiping them he might be as large as the stars, providing that no hated Hebrew mocked the moans from Molech's ovens. Moses forces Korah to enact his idolatry by arranging a kind of duel, in which the true service of Aaron will be pitted against the false fire of Korah:

And Moses said unto Korah, Be thou and all thy company before the Lord, thou, and they, and Aaron, to morrow; And take every man his censer, and put incense in them, and bring ye before the Lord every man his censer, two hundred and fifty censers; thou also, and Aaron, each of you his censer. And they took every man his censer, and put fire in them, and laid incense thereon, and stood in the door of the tabernacle of the congregation with Moses and Aaron. . . . And the Lord spake unto Moses and unto Aaron, saying, Separate yourselves from among this congregation, that I may consume them in a moment. . . . And it came to pass . . . that the ground clave asunder that was under them: And the earth opened her mouth, and swallowed them up, and their house, and all the men that appertained unto Korah, and all their goods. They, and all that appertained to them, went down alive into the pit, and the earth closed upon them: and they perished from among the congregation.

For sedition to the Hebrew enterprise and for the false fire of his implied idolatry, Korah is swallowed up in the earth.

One might argue that Pharoah's and Balaam's hatred of ancient Zionism is a cautionary tale invented by Hebrew poets to encourage xenophobia, the better to keep the Hebrews from foreign temptation. But the story of Korah reminds us that the hatred of Zionism grows out of its own nature and is not limited to foreigners, whom the Bible in no way stigmatizes merely for being *other*—as demonstrated by the stories of Ruth and Jonah. Astonishingly, the Hebrew poets accepted as a sad irony that the Land could stand not only for a God-minding civilization but also a hateful civilization, especially to those like Milton's Satan, who believe they plant their own seed, beget, and raise themselves.

That Korah was swallowed in a hole in the ground did not sink the persisting hatred against Zionism. The family of Ahab, for example, managed to illustrate both Hebrew self-contempt and the foreign hatred of Zion. Hebrew Ahab, ruler of the northern Kingdom of Israel, was by no means a stupid man; he was wily and resourceful in his campaigns against the Syrians. Yet his mind could not hold the Hebrew enterprise, for which he developed a revulsion. He "reared up an altar for Baal in the house of Baal, which he had built in Samaria," but this was not insult enough. Ahab married Jezebel, a princess of Phoenicia from the tribe of Zidonians, who took a crafty pleasure in murdering the prophets of Zion and imposing the religion of Zidon; many Hebrews received it as if there were little difference (*Tsidon* and *Tsion* differ by a single Hebrew letter). Ahab's and Jezebel's daughter Athaliah married Joram, ruler of the southern Kingdom of Judah, thus spreading the contempt of Zion into its old center in the City of David. When the reformist Jehu killed the backsliding Joram, Athaliah slaughtered her grandchildren, "all the seed royal," and seized the throne, forcing the religion of Baal on the hateful Hebrews who protested. One of her grandchildren, however, was hidden in the Temple as a baby, and when the boy reached the age of seven he was brought forward by the High Priest Jehoiada as the rightful King of Judah. For the moment Zion was rescued from its enemies:

> And when Athaliah heard the noise of the guard and of the people, she came to the people into the temple of the Lord. And when she looked, behold the king stood by a pillar, as the manner was, and the princes and the trumpeters by the king, and all the people of the land rejoiced, and blew with trumpets: and Athaliah rent her clothes, and cried, Treason, Treason. But Jehoiada the priest commanded . . . Let her not be slain in the house of the Lord. And they laid hands on her; and she went by the way by the which the horse came into the king's house: and there was she slain. And Jehoiada made a covenant between the Lord and the king and the people, that they should be the Lord's people; between the king also and the people. And all the people of the land went into the house of Baal, and brake it down; his altars and his images brake they in pieces thoroughly. (2 Kings 11)

But that of course did not end the matter of the hatred of Zion. Throughout the period of the Bible and to this very day some Hebrew and non-Hebrew intellectuals continued to find their own station too small and little Zion too big. When after fifty years of exile in Babylonia the returning Hebrews were trying to rebuild the Temple under the guidance of the priest Ezra, those Hebrews who had not gone into exile—including many who had intermarried with foreign tribes—feared the reinstitution of Zion, seeing it as a threat to their position. At first the local "chancellor" and "scribe" tried to attach themselves to the building project, hoping to influence it in their direction. But their low motives were recognized at the outset, and they were rebuffed:

> Ye have nothing to do with us to build an house unto our God: but we ourselves together will build unto the Lord God of Israel, as king Cyrus the king of Persia hath commanded us. Then the people of the land weakened the hands of the people of Judah, and troubled them in building, And hired counsellors against them, to frustrate their purpose. . . . Rehum the chancellor, and Shimshai the scribe wrote a letter against Jerusalem to Artaxerxes the king in this sort: . . . Be it known unto the king that the Jews which came up from thee to us are come unto Jerusalem, building the rebellious and the bad city, and have set up the walls thereof, and joined the foundations. Be it known now unto the king that, if this city be builded, and the walls set up again, then will they not pay toll, tribute, and custom, and so thou shalt endamage the revenue of the kings. (Ezra 4)

The Hebrew enemies of Zion, and "the rest of their companions" among the Elamites and other tribes that had been imported into the Land, cited "bad" Jerusalem's history as a rebel against domination by foreign kings. But Ezra outflanked those who opposed the rebuilding of the Temple by citing another view of Jerusalem's history as a beacon of good will, a "house of God" that Cyrus wanted rebuilt. Ezra prevails for the moment. His colleague Nehemiah, the new Hebrew governor of the Babylonian province of Judah, carries out the building, but he has to defend the project with armed force against Hebrew harassment: "And it came to pass . . . that half my servants wrought in the work, and the other half of them held both the spears, the shields, and the bows, and the habergeons" (Nehemiah 4).

Nehemiah is appalled by the hatred of his fellow Hebrews, and he prays to free Zion from this burden:

> Hear, O our God; for we are despised: and turn their reproach upon their own head, and give them for a prey in the land of captivity: And cover not their iniquity, and let not their sin be blotted out from before thee: for they have provoked thee to anger before the builders. So built we the wall; and all the wall was joined together unto the half therof: for the people had a mind to work. (Nehemiah 4)

Thus those with "a mind to work" in Zion have limped along, fighting off those who hate them from far and near, spending half their energy in building and the other half in defending themselves, struggling to maintain monotheism and the tiny Land that represents it, hoping to avoid the worst of disasters, which is to be landless and in captivity.

Chapter 13

Esther:

The Hebrew Mind in Diaspora

Get wisdom, get understanding. . . . *Forsake her not, and she shall preserve thee: love her, and she shall keep thee. Wisdom is the principal thing: therefore get wisdom: and with all thy getting get understanding. Exalt her, and she shall promote thee: she shall bring thee to honour, when thou dost embrace her.*

—Proverbs 4

DURING THE CENTURIES AFTER THE DEATH OF SOLOMON, THE HEBREWS, despite their haters and apostates, struggled to maintain intellectual monotheism in the Land. One cannot say they did a good job, but that they did any job at all is remarkable. When at the end of a thousand years they were dispersed, the haters of Zion probably had little to do with Zion's fall. True, the Roman Emperor Hadrian, initially inclined to favor the Hebrews, grew to loathe these thorns in the East. After he destroyed Jerusalem during the rebellion of Bar Kochba in 135 C.E., he spitefully erected an equestrian statue of himself in the innermost sanctum of the Temple, the Holy of Holies, and renamed Israel *Syria-Palaestina*, after Israel's old enemies, and Jerusalem *Aelia Capitolina*, after himself. Nevertheless, Israel fell not because of any special hatred toward the Hebrews but by way of standard Roman practice. The rabbis blamed the final collapse of Hebrew civilization in the Land on Jewish backsliding; however, that probably was not the problem, either. The great Roman machine, ready to use monotheism and idolatry alike as an instrument of governance, crushed Hebrew independence. The culture of the Land then went into the great Diaspora, where it was preserved in the minds of Jews who for two thousand years truly inhabited a cerebral version of the Land. Images of Zion pervaded the daily liturgy and imagination of the scattered Hebrews, engendering a longing that itself became a substitute for a rooted civilization.

Eventually, almost two millenia after the Roman destruction, Zion was reestablished in the Land with its premises still intact. The Jews from the great Diaspora, from every quarter of the world—from all the lands around the Mediterranean, from northern Europe, from Russia and the Ukraine, from Persia and Iraq, from China and India, from the New World where they had voyaged with Columbus—reassembled in the old Land, a historical movement as unlikely and as miraculous as getting a genie back in the bottle. Jews no longer needed to cling to a longing for the Land, but they acquired new versions of old problems. In returning to Israel, Jews faced the charges that their attachment to the Bible and its anachronistic rituals was itself a form of fanatical idolatry and that their insistence on return was a usurpation, as the Land had become settled by others during their long absence. Was longing for return an evil, a perverse clinging to the past? Was returning a greater evil, itself a kind of idolatry in which the

Land figured as the idol? Were assimilation and persecution in the Diaspora a greater good?

We will return to these questions in the concluding chapter. Here let us note that a version of these problems is presented in the Bible itself. For Zionism had suffered an earlier diaspora. In the sixth century B.C.E., a conquering Babylonia shipped most of Israel's intelligentsia to the Tigris and the Euphrates, where they spent a half century before being allowed to return. This ancient diaspora shares certain features with the great Diaspora. For the experience of Babylonia was not one of mere suffering or even subsistence. Jews thrived in Babylonia, and when Cyrus told them they could return most Hebrews remained, proud of their businesses and their cultural accomplishments. The academies they built later produced the Babylonian Talmud, which was far superior to the Jerusalem Talmud, compiled as it was by descendants of the threadbare scholars who did return to Israel. Some of these academies survived from the days of the redaction of the Talmud in the fifth century C.E. into the twentieth century when they were destroyed by the Iraqis, who expelled the old princes of the diaspora back to Israel after a twenty-five-century sojourn.

Jeremiah went with the Hebrew aristocracy to the rivers of Babylon, as did Ezekiel and the later Isaiah. These men ignored the material attractions of Babylon, rather focusing their prophetic visions on the contrast between a forlorn life in a nonsignifying land and a rich fulfillment in the Land: "Go ye forth of Babylon, flee ye from the Chaldeans, with a voice of singing declare ye, tell this, utter it even to the end of the earth; say ye, The Lord hath redeemed his servant Jacob" (Isaiah 48). For Israel's great prophets, the idea of exile, the catastrophe of having no Land at all, was the chief point to be made, and thus they held forth the hope of returning to a spiritually resplendant Zion.

But the material diversions from Zion were also part of the experience of exile in Babylon, just as they would be in Spain before 1492, in Turkey before 1700, and in the West now. The prophets largely ignored the wealth of Babylon, not even raising it to the level of a noticed temptation, insisting rather on the cultivation of the intellectual skills necessary to the preservation of monotheism and the return to Zion. But other writers explored the temptations of assimilation into the riches of Babylonia. The Books of Daniel and Esther remain from what must have been a plentiful Hebrew literature on the glitter of Babylonia. The Book of Daniel, for example, not only portrays with disdain the idolatry of King Nebuchadnezzar but evokes his sumptuous wealth, which was itself a snare:

> Nebuchadnezzar the King made an image of gold, whose height was threescore cubits, and the breadth thereof six cubits: he set it up in the plain of Dura, in the province of Babylon. . . . Then an herald cried aloud, To you it is commanded, O people, nations, and languages, That at what time ye hear the sound of the cornet, flute, harp, sackbut, psaltery, dulcimer, and all kinds of musick, ye fall down and worship the golden image that Nebuchadnezzar the king hath set up. (Daniel 3)

The gold and the dulcimers kept the Jews in Babylonia even when they shunned the golden idols. The Book of Esther also evokes a world of tempting wealth. The story is set during the days of Xerxes, known to the Hebrews as Ahasuerus and famous in the West for his wars against the Greeks in the fifth century B.C.E.:

> In the third year of his reign, he made a feast unto all his princes and his servants; the power of Persia and Media, the nobles and princes of the provinces, being before him: When he shewed the riches of his glorious kingdom and the honour of his excellent majesty many days, even a hundred and fourscore days. And when these days were expired, the king made a feast unto all the people that were present in Shushan the palace, both unto the great and small, seven days, in the court of the garden of king's palace: where were white, green, and blue hangings, fastened with cords of fine linen and purple to silver rings and pillars of marble: the beds were of gold and silver, upon a pavement of red, and blue, and white, and black marble.

As we shall see, the attraction of this wealth is part of the meaning of the Book of Esther. Yet the writer of this compact book, working perhaps in the second century B.C.E., also focuses on what preoccupied the prophets in exile—the Hebrews' capacity to renew their intellectual life in the Land. Where Jonah illustrates the intellectual disaster that might befall a Hebrew prophet far from Zion, Esther exemplifies the kind of mind that could reestablish a monotheistic culture in the Land, should she escape the luxury in which she has become enmeshed as queen and be allowed to return to Zion. Her story earns a telling because her mind possesses the requisite tone and power to hold monotheism and to escape the cloying wealth of Babylonia, not because she is beautiful and pious, which have come to be her traditional virtues.

Let us follow the intelligent Queen Esther of Babylonia (or Persia), who is often celebrated only for a mindless beauty and a heedless heroism. She is, in fact, presented as one of the most insightful characters in the Bible. Her adversary, Haman, an intelligent hater of the Hebrew enterprise, provides a contrast to Esther's heroic intelligence. And her husband Ahasuerus, who also becomes an adversary of sorts, provides another kind of contrast, a mindless materialism. The story is exquisitely written in a Hebrew that works by hint and suggestion, except in the bloodthirsty chapter 9, which explains everything at least twice and in clumsy language—hence probably a late insertion of spurious text.

King Ahasuerus, the rich lord of 127 lands but still trying to get the feel of power in the third year of his reign, decides to prop up his magnificence with a drinking party lasting 180 days and followed by a more intimate spree in the castle that goes on for seven days. Vashti, his wife, gives a separate party for the ladies that is equally dazzling. The King, a sensualist well into his cups, finds it necessary to make further demonstrations of his sensual prowess, for that is what power means to him. He commands the beautiful Vashti to show herself, to advertise the object of the mighty king's lusts. Thinking she knows her usually indolent husband, Vashti refuses to appear on call, forgetting that a weak man with limitless power will trade his lazy sensuality for explosive cruelty when his weakness is made public (of this, more later). King Ahasuerus, drunk, baffled, angry, doesn't quite know how to answer his wife's disobedience, until his advisors tell him to get another wife. This entices the man: he can reinflate his prowess in his habitual sphere, trying a new woman every night for a year. Vashti is dismissed, and the parade of women begins.

Esther, the Jew, pleases the sensualist best. The text is understandably reticent about just how Esther wins the King's love, but clearly it is not because of her mind; that is not what engages this pleasure-loving man of neither brain nor brawn. Power for him is sensual power. Esther must understand this; she has sensual power over the sensualist. In Hebrew her name is Hadassah (*myrtle*), but to Ahasuerus she is Esther, after Astarte, goddess of sex.

While the Queen exerts her sexual power, the King's chief advisor, Haman, who is preoccupied with power of a different kind, plots the destruction of the Jews. Haman wants to be worshipped as a god. When Esther's uncle, Mordecai, refuses to bow down to him, Haman is enraged. This refusal, and the Jewish monotheism behind it, reminds him of the truth he knows but wishes to forget, namely that he is not a god. A crazed act of social repression follows from a crazed attempt at psychological repression: Haman must kill all the Jews to remove his doubts about himself. Indifferently, the King approves Haman's plans, which have no bearing on his sensuality and are therefore not interesting to one whose attentions never wander into statecraft. Meanwhile, Mordecai has saved the life of the King by aborting an assassination attempt, but the King knows nothing of this. Because the King is oblivious, Haman for the moment is allowed to define Jews as monsters, the loyal act of an actual Jew notwithstanding.

Mordecai now begs Esther to intercede with the King. Although not summoned, she bravely goes to the royal chamber, an interruption punishable by death if the King so chooses. The King, however, hears her out, for he cares more for her beauty than the rules of court. Jewish tradition gives her great credit for this breathless action, but most readers miss the true heroism, the ingenious plan that Esther puts into play after she knows that she will not be killed for intruding on the King. The plan is founded on intelligence, which is to say on Esther's knowledge of what motivates both the King and his evil advisor.

"What wilt thou Queen Esther? and what is thy request? it shall be given thee to the half of the Kingdom," says the pleasure-loving King to the trembling Queen. He cares nothing for the Kingdom, as long as he is able to indulge his appetites. She, surprisingly, does not blurt out, "Save the Jews," as we might expect if that were the extent of her plan. Rather, she invites the King and Haman to a private feast. Why she does this is not clear, at first. How will this help?

Haman and the King come to the banquet. Haman sees that this adds to his self-aggrandizement. It is not clear yet what the King sees. Esther now invites the two to yet another banquet, further delighting Haman, who brags to his wife: "Yea, Esther the queen did let no man come in with the king unto the banquet that she had prepared but myself; and tomorrow am I invited unto her also with the king." But it is still not clear what effect this is supposed to have on the King and how the Jews might be saved by her plan.

Then we get a hint on how to read Esther's stratagem, which is based on her insight into the King's character. Between banquets the King is unable to sleep. Why? The answer is implicit. Haman thinks Esther is honoring him as a demi-god, but the King sees her attentions to Haman differently. He is jealous of Haman, worried about why Esther keeps inviting the chamberlain, so much smarter and more worldly than the King himself. Thinking that Esther loves sensuality as much as he does, the King must worry that she invites Haman because she finds him attractive. The King is unable to sleep for fear of cuckoldry.

Sleepless, the King distracts himself by reading old royal chronicles and discovers in them that Mordecai had once quietly saved his life. Because this discovery is necessary to certain ironic aspects of the story, naive readers assume that a clumsy writer had the King develop a case of insomnia in order to bring in this matter at the appropriate time. But the King's insomnia is a characteristic response to Esther's attentions to Haman, part of Esther's astute plan, and therefore part of the writer's well-made plot. Esther deliberately sets the King to brooding about Haman in the middle of the night.

At the second banquet, the King again asks Esther what she wants. Seeing that the King is now wary of Haman, Esther finally takes this opportunity, her third, to deliver a musically phrased alarm (mellifluence might catch the ear if not the conscience of the pleasure-sated King) at an exquisitely well-composed moment: "We are sold, I and my people, to be destroyed, to be slain, and to perish." The stuporous and jealous King, having forgotten that he himself approved the plan, asks, "Who is he, and where is he, that durst presume in his heart to do so?" And Esther says, casting her language in clear blacks and whites for this King, "The adversary and enemy is this wicked Haman," pointing him out.

This stratagem would not have worked on the King before his mind was prepared for it—not in his royal court, not at the first banquet, only now, after a night of insomniac jealousy, in his wife's private chambers.

And the king arising from the banquet of wine in his wrath went into the palace garden: and Haman stood up to make request for his life to Esther the queen; for he saw that there was evil determined against him by the king. Then the king returned out of the palace garden into the place of the banquet of wine; and Haman was fallen on the bed whereon Esther was. Then said the king, Will he force the queen also before me in the house?

The jealous King, wrought on by Esther, much as Othello was led by Iago to see fornication where none existed, seems to be assuming that Haman has been violating the Queen in private and is about to do it again before his very eyes.

Now we see clearly what is on the King's mind, implanted there by Esther on the eve of his insomnia, that he should so misread a desperate man's plea for his life as a sexual assault. Apparently the King, after the first banquet, went to his chambers, ran Esther's invitations to Haman through his mind and condemned Haman for the very conquest that he bragged about to his wife. Of course, Haman would never notice the possible sexual interpretation of Esther's interest in him, because he no more thought in sensual terms than the King thought politically; Esther could count on this blindness of Haman and be certain of his failure to notice that bait had been laid.

Further, Esther could count on Haman to throw himself on her couch or behave rashly in some other way, even when he well might have saved himself by merely leaving and allowing the King to calm down as he walked in the garden, a process that ordinarily would not have taken long. Esther could reasonably hope that Haman, threatened by loss of glory—the only sphere in which his otherwise sound judgment is warped—would act imprudently. In a flash, like the instant in which Vashti was divorced, the furious King orders Haman hanged on the gallows erected for Mordecai.

To have devised a plan that left the King cool or gave Haman time to think would have been to lose the game, either to the King's indolence or Haman's cleverness. But the woman knew her men. The text says she fasted two days before putting her plan into action; pious readers may assume that the Queen was praying. More probably she was thinking, plotting, working out a plausible and effective strategy. She needed time to think, for her intelligence was of the slow and dogged type, like that of Gibbon and Darwin, even Einstein, who brooded for years. The writer of the Book of Esther wanted us to know that she was not a quick study, bothering to include in the story her initial misreading of Mordecai's attempt to communicate with her in her sequestered chambers. When Mordecai first hears of Haman's plan to destroy the Jews, he knows he must enlist the help of the powerfully placed Esther. But how is he to reach her? He stages a play of his own in the palace courtyard: he puts on sackcloth and wails, hoping she will get the message of the Jews' plight; she thinks he has fallen on hard times and sends clothes. Only when the clothes come back does she, with her slow but sure intelligence, realize that Mordecai is saying something else, and she clandestinely sends messengers to discover his meaning. She is conventionally given credit for her prayers and her boldness but not for her patient intelligence, her carefully worked-out plot, without which nothing could have been accomplished, perhaps not even by God, who is never mentioned in these secular maneuverings.

Esther illustrates the qualities of mind the Hebrews valued most, the ability to see beyond what is directly in front of one's nose and the conviction to act on an intelligent vision. The monotheistic belief in an unseen God required these qualities. Esther earns her place in the Bible not for her godliness but for possessing the kind of mind that could be educated to monotheism and restored to citizenship in the Land. She thus provides an antidote to the kind of mind, like Haman's, that can be educated only to idolatry and to hatred of the monotheistic enterprise. By implication, Esther also is shown to possess the kind of mind that rises above the insensate materialism of Ahasuerus, which reveals itself as another obstacle to Hebrew national life by the King's approval of Haman's plot.

It turns out that the Land and its monotheistic civilization are not far below the surface of the Book of Esther, even though its setting is distant. The passage at the crux of the story, where the King reveals that he regards Haman as a sexual rival, thus consummating Esther's carefully wrought plan, turns on a highly charged word: "Will he *force* the queen also before me in the house?" The Hebrew verb that is rendered by "force" is *lichbosh*, "conquer." This word has roughly the same range of meanings as it does in English, a "conquest" being either a military or a sexual triumph (prudishly, the great nineteenth-century Hebraicist Wilhelm Gesenius, citing our passage in Esther, gives the sexual meaning of the Hebrew verb in Latin). *Lichbosh* also means "to tread," which has aggressive and sexual connotations, both in English and in Hebrew.

But in Hebrew, the most charged meaning of *lichbosh* refers to the conquest of the Land. The word cannot be used, now or in antiquity, without evoking the Land. *The* conquest is Joshua's conquest, just as *the* land is Israel, and all conquests in Hebrew culture allude to gaining possession of the Land. Thus the King's spluttering question, "Will he force the queen," overwrought and misconstrued though it be, summons the attentive Hebrew reader to a level of meaning above the King's head. Without knowing what he says, the King turns the scene of Haman on Esther's couch into an allegory. He asks, as it were: Shall Hatred conquer Intellect, the Jewish Queen? Shall the possession of the Land and the installation there of an intellectual culture, of which Esther is the bearer, be violated by ambitious spite? From above the line of text, the allegory answers: Not while Intellect, Queen of the Jews, applies herself to the protection of Israel. And a further question is implied above the text: Shall the return to the Land be thwarted by the splendid indolence of the likes of Ahasuerus? The answer is again no: Not while the Queen of intellect demonstrates herself superior to the King of marble. Thus do the ancient Hebrew writers draw their readers back from diaspora to the potential recovery of the Land via Esther's intellect.

And because the Land represents man's relationship with God, God cannot be left out of Esther's story, even though He is never mentioned. In the allegory (which is inaudible to both Haman and the King), we hear Mordecai, by indirection, begging Esther to view herself as an instrument of providence:

> For if thou altogether holdest thy peace at this time, then shall there enlargement and deliverance arise to the Jews from another place; but thou and thy father's house shall be destroyed: and who knoweth whether thou art come to the kingdom for such a time as this?

Who knows! What an astonishing thing to find in the Bible. But the ancient Hebrew was expected to know Who might know, and Who might help. And there *is* divine help, unmentioned but suggested. For Esther has an unsuspected co-conspirator, acting in tandem with her.

Haman's wife is unknowingly cast in the play that will hang her own husband!

Haman's wife, Zeresh, learns that Haman has been humiliated. The King has discovered that Haman's enemy Mordecai is an unhonored hero of the realm, and he wants to see this rectified. Without any awareness that Mordecai is a Jew and thus Haman's enemy, the King asks Haman to parade Mordecai about on a royal horse and to honor him in other ways. So while the King is worried that Esther finds other men attractive, Haman must worry that the King will find other servants more worthy than he. Haman is particularly bothered that it is Mordecai who may supplant him, and he takes his worries to Zeresh. Zeresh helps guarantee that Haman, having been humiliated, comes to Esther's second banquet unnerved, jittery, and primed to play the role that Esther has prepared:

> And Haman told Zeresh his wife and all his friends every thing that had befallen him. Then said his wise men and Zeresh his wife unto him, If Mordecai be of the seed of the Jews, before whom thou hast begun to fall, thou shalt not prevail against him, but shall surely fall before him. And while they were yet talking with him, came the king's chamberlains, and hasted to bring Haman unto the banquet that Esther had prepared.

Who arranged this well-timed prophecy? Not Esther, who already has her hands full. Someone else has cast Zeresh in a helpful role.

So Haman comes trembling to Esther, and she knows how to seize her opportunity. Haman is hanged. But there remains a difficulty. The King has no objection to sparing the Jews, but he does not know how to accomplish this, since that "which is written in the king's name, and sealed with the king's ring, may no man reverse." Though the King be a toy of opportunists like Haman, his royal decrees are perfect. He is unable to imagine how his previous edict might be circumvented, but he gives Mordecai the right to try. "Write ye also for the Jews as it liketh you." Mordecai composes an edict empowering the Jews to defend themselves if attacked, and this seems to head off the disaster:

> The Jews had light, and gladness, and joy, and honour. And in every province, and in every city, whithersoever the king's commandment and his decree came, the Jews had joy and gladness, a feast and a good day.

And many of the people of the land became Jews; for the fear of the Jews fell upon them.

That is the way the original story probably ended. Chapter 9 goes on to retell the story and ends it with a bloodbath, the Jews killing multitudes of those who are willing to follow Haman's original order even if they must now take their chances in pitched battle. In either version, the Jews are, by implication, spared by God, for despite the coyness of the writer, the "fear of the Jews" that wins converts among Haman's "people" can only be for Hebrews the awe that Jews show God. The Hebrews would see through the absence of God's name as a literary device and recognize He who converted the people of Nineveh as the redeemer of the Persians. It seems clear that the original writer wanted to end with this "light," not with the murder in chapter 9 of Haman's ten sons and their minions.

Thus the Book of Esther points its readers upward, into the realm of the Creator as well as to the Land representing Him, beyond the ken of Ahasuerus—who rules 127 lands and understands nothing— beyond the faraway land of Babylonia, which in the end is of little concern to the Hebrews. It also points its readers forward to a long line of future Hamans who would rival God Himself. While Ahasuerus gives to Mordecai the signet ring of power he once gave Haman, the Hebrews would have recognized that such a gift was certain to be bestowed by kingly caprice and foolish materialism on yet another Haman in time. The line of Pharaoh and Balaam could not reasonably be expected to cease. In every generation the Jews, in the great Diaspora and now back in the Land, listened for the whine of Haman, the peevish note of a little man who turns violent as he discovers that monotheism makes him even smaller. And they listened for the indifferent snores of the materialist Ahasuerus, who might tempt them with every luxury, just as he once promised Esther everything she could desire.

To signal the need for returning to the civilization of the Land, and escaping exile, where both the lethal hater and the stupified materialist shadowed them, the Hebrews instituted the annual holiday of Purim. The holiday is deeply ambiguous, starting from its name, which is taken from Haman's idolatrous practice of throwing lots, or *pur*, to determine the date of the Hebrew demise. Purim is a day of misrule, a day of drinking in the manner of Ahasuerus. The rabbis recommended inebriation to the point of failing to distinguish Haman from Mordecai. In this, they are seemingly following the writer of the original story. He shows a triumphant Mordecai who cannot be distinguished, at least physically, from the glorious Ahasuerus: "And Mordecai went out from the presence of the king in royal apparel of blue and white, and with a great crown of gold, with a garment of fine linen and purple; and the city of Shushan rejoiced and was glad."

The day of Purim is spent in putting on plays, donning elaborate costumes, and inventing nonsensical interpretations of Torah. Those who now dress in Mordecai's dazzling robes may not realize they are imitating the Jew who mimicked the foolish Ahasuerus, crown and ring and all, but the writer of Esther would have appreciated this irony. The blurring of Haman and Mordecai and Ahasuerus is precisely what Jews have always tried to avoid, what they did avoid when they were in the Land and attending its song. The misrule of Purim is the misery of the diaspora incarnate, a day that Hebrews were thankful to celebrate but once a year. There is a sly suggestion along these lines even in the outrageous chapter 9: Jewish life in the diaspora, a place where the name of God cannot be breathed, can be defended only with a bloodbath.

Thus there was consensus among Jews in post-exilic times that the return to the Land was to be desired above any temptation to remain in the diaspora. The Hebrews, then as now, displayed a good deal of hypocrisy on this score, but they included in their Bible only those stories reminding them that their destiny as a people required a return to the Land that represented their peoplehood. The writer of Esther, surveying the situation of the Land in the second century B.C.E., recognizing the thriving Jewish communities in Babylon and Alexandria, aware of the possibilities of an expanded diaspora in the Hellenistic empire, still wished to put at the center of his story a mind capable of the intellectual conquest of the Land. That a little Land might mean so much is part of the meaning of Purim. "These days should be remembered and kept throughout every generation . . . that these days of Purim should not fail from among the Jews, nor the memorial of them perish from their seed."

Chapter 14

Zohar

And, behold, the Lord passed by, and a great and strong wind rent the mountains, and brake in pieces the rocks before the Lord; but the Lord was not in the wind: and after the wind an earthquake; but the Lord was not in the earthquake: And after the earthquake a fire; but the Lord was not in the fire: and after the fire a still small voice.

—1 Kings 19

What Europe owes to the Jews? Many things, good and bad, and above all one thing that is both of the best and of the worst: the grand style in morality, the terribleness and majesty of infinite demands, infinite meanings, the whole romanticism and sublimity of moral questionabilities.

—Friedrich Nietzsche, *Beyond Good and Evil*

IN THE BOOK OF ESTHER, HAMAN'S CRAZED HATRED IS INTERTWINED with superstition and magic. He fixes the date for the murder of the Jews by casting lots; later he trembles as his wife augurs his ruin from Mordecai's royal advancement. He is an irrational man, intelligent yet steeped in the primitive thinking of the ancient world. For the Hebrews, Haman is another version of Mesha, King of Moab, who "took his eldest son that should have reigned in his stead, and offered him for a burnt offering upon the wall." That Haman lost his own life and the lives of his ten sons in his mad pursuits would strike the Hebrews as the expected outcome for a committed idolator. The Hebrews commonly associated Haman's kind of magical thinking with the idolatrous hatred of monotheism; hence the struggle to remove witchcraft, sorcery, and divination from their own lives. The Land, representing rationality, was to be peopled by rationalists. Intellect was to be Queen of Israel, magic banished.

"Come now, and let us reason together," says Isaiah to his fellow Hebrews, on his very first page. And God tells Isaiah to tell those who prefer conjuring that if they wish "for signs and for wonders in Israel" they should seek a living God and his rational law, "which dwelleth in mount Zion":

> And when they shall say unto you, Seek unto them that have familiar spir-
> its, and unto wizards that peep, and that mutter: [Say unto them], Should
> not a people seek unto their God? [Why should the living seek among the
> dead? Refer them rather to] the law and to the testimony: if they speak
> not according to this word, it is because there is no light in them. (I
> rephrase the King James translation, which garbles Isaiah 8.)

It was from this perspective that Saul had to be mocked for consulting the Witch of Endor.

Deuteronomy 18 formally bans divination and magic, linking the observance of rationality to a sustainable life in the Land:

> When thou art come into the land which the Lord thy God giveth thee,
> thou shalt not learn to do after the abominations of those nations. There
> shall not be found among you any one that maketh his son or his daughter
> to pass through the fire, or that useth divination, or an observer of times,
> or an enchanter, or a witch, Or a charmer, or a consulter with familiar spir-
> its, or a wizard, or a necromancer. For all that do these things are an

abomination unto the Lord: and because of these abominations the Lord thy God doth drive them out from before thee.

Balaam puts to verse this distinction between the nations and the Hebrews; the former have magic, the latter have God:

Surely there is no enchantment in Jacob, neither is there any divination in Israel: accordingly, in every moment [when other nations are offered enchantment], it shall be said to Jacob and to Israel, What hath God wrought! (King James mistranslates from Numbers 23, Surely there is no enchantment *against* Jacob, neither is there any divination *against* Israel.)

Nevertheless, despite the insistence on rationality and the prohibition against sorcery, magic found a prominent place in Hebrew civilization. According to the history that the ancient Hebrews constructed for themselves, God himself commanded Moses to match Hebrew magic against Pharaoh's wizards:

And the Lord spake unto Moses and unto Aaron, saying, When Pharaoh shall speak unto you, saying, Shew a miracle for you: then thou shalt say unto Aaron, Take thy rod, and cast it before Pharaoh, and it shall become a serpent. And Moses and Aaron went in unto Pharaoh, and they did so as the Lord had commanded: and Aaron cast down his rod before Pharaoh, and before his servants, and it became a serpent. The Pharaoh also called his wise men and the sorcerers: now the magicians of Egypt, they also did in the like manner with their enchantments. For they cast down every man his rod, and they became serpents: but Aaron's rod swallowed up their rods. (Exodus 7)

This kind of magic weaves through the Hebrew narrative. For Moses, the bush burns without being consumed; the Red Sea gapes; Manna appears; the rebel Korah is magically swallowed into the earth. Joshua makes the sun stand still in the Valley of Ajalon, so that the day lasts long enough to complete a victory; the prophet Elijah challenges the prophets of Baal to a battle of sorceries, which he wins on behalf of monotheism, just as Aaron did in Pharaoh's court. The Book of Esther, too, though it mocks Haman's slavery to *purim* and to his wife's crystal ball, itself partakes in magic. Though Esther's plan is brilliantly rational, it is a desperate longshot, and its success is uncanny, miraculous, magical, the begetter of Purim, an annual All Fools' Day, during which revelry, drunkenness, and masquerading reign alongside the solemn reading of Esther's story in the synagogue. Thus the Hebrews preserved the magical with the logical.

The sober arbiters of ancient Hebrew culture not only tolerated a certain kind of magic but cultivated it. They wove magic into their stories not because they were backsliders but because they saw a sophisticated use for it. Just as mere chronicles bloomed into history in their hands, legal codes became the Law, and lands became the Land, so the superstition of idolators and the sleight-of-hand of sorcerers were also redeemed and transformed. The Land became the home of a sublime magic—the deep transforming magic of divine imagination—which was not meant to displace reason but to elevate and broaden it. In fact, the Land became a magical place, bringing poetry and civilization to the minds of those who encountered it.

There is no good word in English for this higher form of magic. *Metaphysics* captures the aspect of transcendance, but it departs too far from reason to characterize the Land. *Artistry* and *poetics* cast too pale a magic. Perhaps the Hebrew word *zohar*, used as a title for Judaism's medieval books of mysticism, comes closest. *Zohar* means "brightness," "teaching," and "warning." The Land enlightens, teaches, and warns those who can read it; and *zohar* is the response of those who do. The magic of the Land is thus the magic of art's influence on a perceptive audience.

Bristling with stern warnings to idolators, fraught with the Law's obligation, heavy with history, the Land nevertheless levitated, sparkled as if composed of the fiery air that baked its hills. To the esthetic eye, the Land danced:

> When Israel went out of Egypt, the house of Jacob from a people of strange language; Judah was his sanctuary, and Israel his dominion. The sea saw it, and fled: Jordan was driven back. The mountains skipped like rams, and the little hills like lambs. What ailed thee, O thou sea, that thou fleddest? thou Jordan, that thou wast driven back? Ye mountains, that ye skipped like rams; and ye little hills, like lambs? Tremble, thou earth, at the presence of the Lord, at the presence of the God of Jacob; Which turned the rock into standing water, the flint into a fountain of waters. (Psalms 114)

This exuberant language, which was later translated by the young Milton in his first poem, reflects a reality of experience. From Abraham forward, enlightened readers of the Land lifted dancing eyes to contemplate the meanings they found there. As the brightness of Chapman's Homer moved Keats to "wild surmise," like an astronomer "when a new planet swims into his ken," so the brightness of the Land startled the literate Hebrew. The Land *was* a new planet, a grand work invested with art's power to transform the encountering mind. The Hebrews elevated forbidden sorcery to capture the startling experience of that planet.

The well-wrought story of Elijah's competition with the magicians of Baal illustrates the function of *zohar*. The story, told in 1 Kings 18, contrasts two kinds of magic, just as the story of Abraham's break with Lot contrasts two kinds of intellect. We recall that Ahab, ruler of the northern Kingdom of Israel, has married Jezebel, who brings with her from Phoenicia the old magic of her people, as practiced by the baby-burning priests of Baal. Jezebel murders the graduates of David's seminaries, stamping out the monotheistic dissent that rises against her. She enjoys success, since the Hebrews, who always find Abraham's vision difficult to maintain, again turn to idolatry and hardly mind the extermination of their teachers, who had an unwelcome habit of nagging them to support monotheism.

Soon, the only prophet left in Israel is Elijah. He evades arrest, flitting here and there, popping up to excoriate Ahab, then slipping into a grove or cave. His very elusiveness wins him a reputation for sorcery, but this fame does not please him. The magic that interests Elijah is not intended to evoke the admiration of fanatics but to inspire rational fidelity to Abraham's vision.

Elijah predicts a drought, which comes to pass. The Land degenerates into a wilderness. Ahab redoubles his efforts to capture the prophet, whom he calls the "troubler of Israel," as if all would be well in Israel if the prophet had predicted rain instead. Unable to comprehend that the drought is a commentary on his own intellectual sterility, Ahab cannot physically apprehend Elijah either. But when the grass is parched and the cattle lean, Elijah goes to Ahab, knowing that the King will not kill him. For Ahab, in secret from his wife, now doubts the magic of Baal and will give audience to the foresaken God of Israel. Elijah proposes a public duel between himself and Jezebel's prophets, and Ahab, whose choices in the parched Land have dwindled, must go along. Elijah orders him to gather 450 prophets of Baal and 400 prophets of Asherah, a sister goddess of Baal, along with the children of Israel, on Mount Carmel, where Elijah will perform:

> And Elijah came unto all the people, and said, How long halt ye between two opinions? If the Lord be God, follow him: but if Baal, then follow him. And the people answered him not a word. Then said Elijah unto the people, I, even I only, remain a prophet of the Lord; but Baal's prophets are four hundred and fifty men. Let them therefore give us two bullocks; and let them choose one bullock for themselves, and cut it into pieces and lay it on wood, and put no fire under: and I will dress the other bullock, and lay it on wood, and put no fire under: And call ye on the name of your gods, and I will call on the name of the Lord: and the God that answereth by fire, let him be God. And all the people answered and said, It is well spoken. (1 Kings 18)

It appears that Elijah is about to sink to the level of the idolatrous priests. Will Elijah or the Baalites excel at the magical production of fire? But the story is careful to distinguish what Elijah does from what the magicians do. The Baalites get their opportunity first, in the manner of this kind of story, and we know that they are sure to be upstaged. Nevertheless it is worth attending to their song and dance, for literary care is devoted to their foolishness:

> And they took the bullock which was given them, and they dressed it, and called on the name of Baal from morning even until noon, saying, O, Baal, hear us. But there was no voice, nor any that answered. And they leaped upon the altar which was made. And it came to pass at noon, that Elijah mocked them, and said, Cry aloud: for he is a god; either he is talking, or he is pursuing, or he is in a journey, or peradventure he sleepeth, and must be awaked. And they cried aloud, and cut themselves after their manner with knives and lancets, till the blood gushed out upon them. And it came to pass, when midday was past, and they prophesied until the time of the offering of the evening sacrifice, that there was neither voice, nor any to answer, nor any that regarded.

The Hebrew verb for this dancing of the Baalites is *pasach*, "to limp," the same verb that Elijah uses a few sentences earlier when he accuses his brethren of "halting" between idolatry and monotheism.

The Baalite dancers, in fact, externalize the limping, self-mutilating thoughts of the Hebrews themselves. In this dance and in these thoughts there is no magic, no fire, no imagination. No god answers the Baalites, nor is there one who could. Elijah's scorn is at once harsh and humorous as he urges the Baalites to yell louder for the god who is, perhaps, out to lunch; in Hebrew, this mockery shines and winks in a row of tiny words: *kee see-ach v'chee seeg lo v'chee derech lo* (Yell louder to your god, for perhaps "he chats or chases or makes calls").

Now it is Elijah's turn. He sets up as if he too were a trickster, bathing his sacrifice three times in water and then surrounding it with a moat of more water, so that the divine fireball will impress all the more. But the point of the drama is not to bring about a display of magic but to quench intellectual drought and rekindle esthetic delight in the Land. Indeed, Elijah is careful to direct attention away from his role as magician to his larger purpose of reuniting Israel's tribes in a Land fired by monotheism. Insisting that he himself has no power, he begins by rebuilding the toppled altar to the One God, using stones that represent each tribe:

And Elijah took twelve stones, according to the number of the tribes of the sons of Jacob, unto whom the word of the Lord came, saying, Israel shall be thy name: And with the stones he built an altar in the name of the Lord: and he made a trench about the altar, as great as would contain two measures of seed. And he put the wood in order, and cut the bullock in pieces, and laid him on the wood, and said, Fill four barrels with water, and pour it on the burnt sacrifice, and on the wood. And he said, Do it the second time. And he said, Do it the third time. And they did it the third time. And the water ran round about the the altar; and he filled the trench also with water. And it came to pass at the time of the offering of the evening sacarifice, that Elijah the prophet came near, and said, Lord God of Abraham, Isaac, and of Israel, let it be known this day that thou art God in Israel, and that I am thy servant, and that I have done all these things at thy word. Hear me, O Lord, hear me, that this people may know that thou are the Lord God, and that thou has turned their heart back again. Then the fire of the Lord fell, and consumed the burnt sacrifice, and the wood, and the stones, and the dust, and licked up the water that was in the trench. And when all the people saw it, they fell on their faces: and they said, The Lord, he is the God; the Lord, he is the God. . . . And

Elijah said unto Ahab, Get thee up, eat and drink; for there is a sound of abundance of rain. (1 Kings 18)

The high drama here, marvelously paced, pauses only briefly on the magic of divine flames licking up bullock, water, rocks, and all. The bright fire burns on a plane higher than magic. The emphasis falls on the reawakening of monotheism and on the fertile rain that falls as its aftermath. That the children of Israel heed Elijah's warning marks their rekindled imaginations; that God "has turned back their heart again" is what matters, not the magic. Mere magic makes wonder serve literalism ("Oh, the stones really burned"), while *zohar* moves in the opposite direction, making magic metaphoric, in the service of wonder and intellect ("The Lord, he is the God"). At the end, Elijah stands not as a miracle worker but as an intellectual, a restorer of the vision of Abraham, on whom he calls. He is tough-minded, wry, witty, stinging, teaching, warning. His sophisticated story repudiates those who view religion as miracle and the conjuring of stones.

But of course not everybody can find *zohar* in the Land. Lot, we remember, missed it. Manoah missed it. Jephthah missed it. Ahab missed it. Even most of the spies whom Moses sent from Sinai to make an early survey of the Land missed it. The spies are nevertheless useful because they cast light into *zohar*'s darker depths, even though dim themselves:

And they brought up an evil report of the land which they had searched unto the children of Israel, saying, The land, through which we have gone to search it, is a land that eateth up the inhabitants thereof; and all the people that we saw in it are men of great stature. And there we saw the giants, the sons of Anak, which come of the giants: and we were in our own sight as grasshoppers, and so we were in their sight. (Numbers 13)

In their fear of the wild inhabitants of Canaan, these spies cannot read the greatness of their culture in the Land. The land they glimpse merely diminishes them. Short-sighted rather than short of stature, they belittle themselves as grasshoppers and assume that the Canaanites will flick them away. Their self-described insignificance makes them spiteful. They try to turn their brethren from the Land by telling lies.

The spies are mocked, but their deeper utility lies in the mirror they hold up to thinking Hebrews, who could also be stunned by the work of apprehending the Land and its poetry. Through the story of the spies, the Hebrews brood on the possibility that the Abrahamic vision of the Land might merely terrify, that *zohar*, which arises from the Land and sustains it, might unnerve the stoutest soul. This realization, eating at all people who realize they live only by what the mercurial mind holds, challenged the Hebrews particularly, because their idea of God, their valued literacy, their very sense of being, all depended on a terrifying and lonely cultivation of mind in a world where mind was largely unknown. God at Sinai is portrayed as a terrifying figure partly to capture what happens when a cultivated mind apprehends a Divinity who delivers Law as poetry.

Even Moses is terrified by *zohar*, though he is a near master of it, as is any poet anywhere who looks at mind. Moses is overwhelmed by *zohar* in the early story of his son's circumcision, told briefly in Exodus 4. In order to escape the consequences of a murder he committed in defending a fellow Hebrew from an Egyptian, Moses has fled to Midian. In Midian he sees the burning bush, and in its presence he learns that he must lead the Hebrews out of slavery. God shares with Moses the grand but bizarre plan to harden Pharaoh's heart and make this an excuse for killing the royal firstborn in a ten-plague, operatic manner. That the shuddering Moses is also told those who sought his life are now dead and he is thus free to return to Egypt can hardly comfort him, for he must now go, a known killer, to threaten Pharaoh himself:

> And the Lord said unto Moses in Midian, Go, return into Egypt: for all the men are dead which sought thy life. . . . And thou shalt say unto Pharaoh, Thus saith the Lord, Israel is my son, even my firstborn: And I say unto thee, Let my son go, that he may serve me: and if thou refuse to let him go, behold, I will slay thy son, even thy firstborn. And it came to pass by the way in the inn, that the Lord met him, and sought to kill him. Then Zipporah took a sharp stone, and cut off the foreskin of her son, and cast it at his feet, and said, Surely a bloody husband art thou to me. So he [God] let him go: then she said, A bloody husband thou art, because of the circumcision. And the Lord said to Aaron, Go into the wilderness to meet Moses.

Told in hallucinatory language and inserted into a passage otherwise written in plain prose, this story is almost universally misread. The rabbis dutifully seek Moses' sin to understand why God should try to kill him, and they find it in his having delayed Gershom's circumcision. Even Harold Bloom, the author of *The Book of J* and a critic who takes nothing literally, thinks it outrageous that God would want to kill his own elect, especially when Moses is even now undertaking His frightful mission. But almost certainly we are not meant to take as narrative fact the fantastic statement that God met Moses at the inn and sought to kill him.

For one thing, the story that "the Lord met" Moses, especially as I have framed it, emphasizes *human* meeting and seeking: the Egyptians who "sought" Moses's death are now dead, and Aaron comes "to meet" Moses. Thus when we read that "the Lord met him, and sought to kill him" we might wonder if God meets Moses not because God seeks but because the human Moses dreams. Perhaps these are nightmarish images fabricated by a terrified servant in the middle of the wilderness, in the middle of the night. Indeed the flitting appearance of Zipporah as she throws the foreskin at the feet of Moses seems more dreamlike than covenant-related, and her repeated accusation against the "bloody husband" sounds less like the customary ritual of circumcision and more like a madly repeated dream element. Magically, as in a dream, Zipporah's incantations dissolve the rage of God, just as Jacob's dream-work dissolves the grasp of the angel with whom he wrestles in his sleep at Penuel (indeed, the language of Gershom's circumcision alludes to Jacob's dream, helping us recognize what it is).

How natural it would be for Moses to dream of his own firstborn on the night after accepting the command to threaten the death of Pharaoh's son; how fitting that his dream repeats God's phrase regarding the death of those Egyptians who sought his life, for this expresses his more current fear that God is seeking his life by sending him to threaten Pharaoh. Is it not apt that Moses exploits the circumcision of his son (it probably took place *already*) to represent both a threat that he himself feels and a wish-fulfillment that he be spared the worst of God's searing power. For is not a circumcision a token castration, a symbolic substitution for the sacrifice of Isaac and for the maiming that an encounter with God might otherwise entail?

Is not Zipporah herself a terrifying dream figure, both a protectress and a knife-wielding mother who menaces both Moses and his son?

Such a lurid magician cannot be meant as an actual appeaser of the God of Abraham. What Hebrew reader would accept at face value the claim that this harpy dissuades a berserk God from squeezing Moses' throat? That God "let him go" (the idea though not the exact word is again from Jacob's dream at Penuel) probably represents Moses's own dream wish that Pharaoh will indeed let the Hebrews go and that Moses himself will be let go without being doomed as a false prophet or a failed servant. Perhaps the repetition of "bloody husband" represents Moses' fear that in bonding himself to God he is repeating, this time personally and more ominously, the bloody rituals of his son's circumcision.

If we read Moses as dreaming of circumcision, we learn what an awful commitment he has made—to found Hebrew civilization on imagination and to accept the burden of *zohar*, which circumcision partakes in as a marker of the covenant. If we read Moses merely as the victim of the rabbis' reluctantly vengeful God or of Bloom's rascally God, then the story has little power to command our attention. If *zohar* had not produced in Moses a profound terror that touched his deepest childhood fantasies, from which the power of imagination springs, it could not have a roused in him the flights of understanding for which he later earned reverence. Without *zohar*, he would not have had the wherewithal to found a new nation, headed en masse for David's literate Zion. The Hebrews accepted the terrors of the imagination because nothing less would bring them to the promised Land. They realized that if they sanitized the intellectual life they would remain in the wilderness, diminished. The best one can do with wild *zohar* is to set its poetry within strong borders.

Zohar can also be contained in ritual, like all important aspects of Hebrew culture. One ritual especially captures the nature of *zohar*: deeply paradoxical, full of poetry, and concerned with life and death. We learn in Numbers 19 that a red heifer, "without spot," must be burnt with her blood and dung along with "cedar wood, and hyssop, and scarlet [thread]." Spotlessness clashes with dung, loveliness of scarlet with horror of blood. Finally a "water" is produced that the high priest can sprinkle on those who defile themselves by touching a corpse; the defiled are thus purified. Yet all those who prepare the water are themselves defiled, in need of purification! The rabbis, for whom *zohar* was already fading, thought this ritual so self-contradictory that they shrugged and followed the unintelligible hocus pocus simply because God willed it. Yet the meaning of the red heifer is not so difficult to interpret in the context of Hebrew poetry, which values literary ambiguity even when it arouses terror. Poetry redeems the mind from intellectual death, but it also defiles, overruns the mind with mad dreams; this was probably the fearsome thought that the red heifer recalled to those pre-rabbinic Hebrews who knew why Moses and the spies shuddered.* The Hebrews did not need deconstructionism to teach them that poetry tends to run amok and dissolve meaning altogether; but where moderns have no anchor, the Hebrews had the civilization and rituals of Zion.

In making the red heifer rote, the rabbis enact the quintessential Hebrew belief: though the only God we can have is a God we invent, we must obey Him because he fashioned us. This fearful symmetry of recursive subjectivities, in which the Hebrews imagined themselves able to create the Creator because He created them in His image, became in its independent Western manifestation the conundrum of subjectivity—from Plato's cave to Kant's categorical imperative.

---

*The paradox of the red heifer finds its natural home among the Hebrews, whose poetry juxtaposed unreconcilables. That Adam is required to make distinctions without the capacity to tell good from evil, that Abraham is willing to preserve the covenant by sacrificing its fruit, that Balaam's imagination allows him both to praise and to hate the Hebrews, that the cunning of David both advances and undermines the culture of the covenant are all part of the worldview of the Hebrews. The rabbis accepted these paradoxes with resignation, but their forebears embraced them with a deeper brooding, apparently concluding that the Creator made the world in such a puzzling way that mankind's capacity for monotheism rested on the imagination of human dust, while the substance of the world itself rested on the creative powers of an immaterial God. As the human mind embraces these contradictions, it approaches the mind of God and defiles itself with imaginings.

The poetry of paradox suffuses the Bible. Jonah possesses moral power, moving his shipmates to offer "a sacrifice unto the Lord" and the Ninevites to "cry mightily unto God," yet he is obtuse. Similarly, the priest Eli misreads Hannah's prayer for a son as the murmurings of a drunkard, failing to appreciate the spiritual transformation that will enable Hannah to give birth to the prophet Samuel (1Samuel 1). God says, "The imagination of man's heart is evil from his youth" (Genesis 8), yet He rests His covenant precisely on imagination. And amazingly, that imagination, failing Jonah, blinding Eli, even hampering the great rabbis, has nevertheless preserved to this day the culture capable of the terrifying poetry of the red heifer.

While the Greeks and their intellectual descendents explored the inescapable nature of human subjectivity, the Hebrews cultivated the recursiveness of monotheism in the Land. This was all the philosophy they had. They produced no Berkeley with his worried solipsism and no Hegel with his megalomaniacal Absolute Idea, nor did they think such mental endeavors necessary, having stopped with the "still small voice" of *zohar*, which they thought terrifying enough.

Zohar, no more complex than the elaboration of poetics in the West over the last twenty-five hundred years, is still too rich for many sensibilities. Because it contributes to the tenacity with which Israel clings to its signifying Land, it is sometimes found offensive. But critics who object to the poetics of Zion as atavistic should offer an alternative, one that is nobler and more tolerant, if that is possible. One cannot hope to exceed the high standard of Isaiah, whose poetry shines on an idealized nation, incandescent with *zohar*, at peace within the small space in which jewels and poems are customarily set, where border markers are reduced (and thereby enlarged) to the scale of sapphires:

> Behold, I will lay thy stones with fair colours, and lay thy foundations with sapphires. And I will make thy windows of agates, and thy gates of carbuncles, and all thy borders of pleasant stones. And all thy children shall be taught of the Lord; and great shall be the peace of thy children. (Isaiah 54)

Those who demean Zion (Zionism is racism, said the United Nations, then grudgingly reversed themselves) and fail to comprehend Isaiah's vision of nationhood must tell us how the substitutes they propose will improve the various kinds of wilderness that prevailed before the poetry of Zion was invented.

Chapter 15

A Bough Over the Wall

Each blade of grass has its spot on earth whence it draws its life, its strength; and so is man rooted to the land from which he draws his faith together with his life.

—Joseph Conrad, *Lord Jim*

THOUGH ABRAHAM HAD THE GIST OF THE LITERARY CULTURE HE WAS spawning, and though the Bible treats Zionism as if it were an unchanging ideal, the full expression of Zionist civilization required the intellectual work of centuries. But even early on, ancient Hebrews could feel the full force of the culture they had rooted into their Land, taking pleasure in the legal and literary traditions, the history and the historicism, the rituals and the rites that emerged from the Land and converged on monotheism. The culture of monotheism, through the intimately related idea of Zionism, became a national culture, inseparable from the Land. Exile was the worst of disasters.

It is surprising, then, to note that the ancient Hebrews considered the possibility of willingly uprooting themselves. They understood that their intellectual training was a moveable feast, that if they wished they could take intellect abroad, separate it from the work of monotheism, and apply it to other affairs. They saw that the skills of ancient Zionism were of universal value, that Hebrews could do well everywhere. Yet they stayed at home. They hoped that monotheistic culture would find local expression elsewhere, perhaps in Nineveh, perhaps in places Jonah never dreamed of, but they believed the use of Hebrew intellect outside the Land eventually led to sterility. This discussion enters into the stories concerning Joseph in Egypt, told in the last fourteen chapters of Genesis. The Hebrews reminded themselves that the idea of sending the seed of Abraham into Egypt originated with God. They also noted, however, that Joseph seemed overly willing to apply Hebrew intellect to Egyptian purposes.

Joseph is a master of the pillars of ancient Israel's civilization. He knows both fiction making and distinction making. Like Solomon and David, he is imaginative, a dreamer, and a reader of dreams. Able to pierce the future, he can hold in the mind what is invisible to others. He is also a man of great discernment, who can both anticipate the grain market and make crucial distinctions between one man's character and another's. Yet this most celebrated son of the patriarch Jacob is an ambiguous figure in the lore of the ancient Hebrews, the only one to have his name struck from among the tribes of Israel. No region in the Land bears his name. He is, further, the only one not listed among the sons of Jacob at the beginning of Exodus. Though his name is appended after a half verse with the terse comment that Joseph was "also" in Egypt, and though the great commentator Rashi explains this setting aside as an honor, the quiet segregation of Joseph has an ambiguous quality.

Joseph is ambiguous precisely because he applied his great intellectual skills only in Egypt, never in the Land, except for the period of his youth. He preferred to marry an Egyptian priest's daughter, to raise his family in Egypt, and to be embalmed there in the Egyptian manner. Indeed, his burial, described in the last words of Genesis, prepares the way for the Hebrew enslavement and is itself a comment on Joseph's choice of Egypt: "And they embalmed him, and he was put in a coffin in Egypt." Immersed in foreign ways to the end, making an idol of his own dead body, Joseph, unlike his father who insisted upon burial in Israel, comes to rest in an Egyptian coffin, which is also, in the ambiguous Hebrew, a coffin that *is* Egypt.

Joseph actually creates the very institution of slavery that became the living coffin for his descendants, thinking he was doing himself and his family a favor:

> And Joseph bought all the land of Egypt for Pharoah; for the Egyptians sold every man his field because the famine prevailed over them: so the land became Pharaoh's. And as for the people, he removed them to cities from one end of the borders of Egypt even to the other end thereof. Only the land of the priests bought he not; for the priests had a portion assigned them of Pharaoh. (Genesis 47)

The rabbis praise Joseph for sparing the lands of the Egyptian priests from his acquisitiveness, for this allowed the Hebrew priests to study the Law when their time came to be slaves. This hopelessly anachronistic reading (the Law did not exist yet) fails to note the bitter irony of clever Joseph outsmarting himself as he converts Egypt from a land of freeholders to a place prepared for Hebrew enslavement. Thus, Joseph is unaware of an irony that he helps express: his brothers unknowingly created the conditions under which he was sold into slavery (they threw him into a pit, from whence the Midianites pulled him out and sold him to the Ishmaelites, who carried him down to Egypt), and he unknowingly returns the favor.

But let us return to Joseph's admirable qualities. The rabbis, after all, called him "the righteous." Joseph's deep imagination and discernment, those primal Hebrew values, are particularly evident in his ability to dream and to interpret dreams, a Hebraic skill that will secure him advancement in Egypt. Like his father, Joseph as a young man is smug about his acute intelligence. He uses his wits at first merely to ferret out his brothers' misdeeds so that he may report them to his father, and to tell of dreams that will annoy his brothers:

> Now Israel loved Joseph more than all his children, because he was the son of his old age: and he made him a coat of many colours. And when his brethren saw that their father loved him more than all his brethren, they hated him, and could not speak peaceably unto him. And Joseph dreamed a dream, and he told it his brethren: and they hated him yet the more. And he said unto them, Hear, I pray you, this dream which I have dreamed: For, behold, we were binding sheaves in the field, and, lo, my sheaf arose, and also stood upright; and, behold, your sheaves stood round about, and made obeisance to my sheaf. And his brethren said to him, Shalt thou indeed reign over us? or shalt thou indeed have domination over us? And they hated him yet the more for his dreams, and for his words. And he dreamed yet another dream, and told it his brethren, and said, Behold, I have dreamed a dream more; and, behold, the sun and the moon and the eleven stars made obeisance to me. And he told it to his father, and to his brethren; and his father rebuked him, and said unto him, What is this dream that thou hast dreamed? Shall I and thy mother and thy brethren indeed come to bow down ourselves to thee to the earth. And his brethren envied him. (Genesis 37)

Jacob recognizes Joseph's capacities, and he singles him out for special attentions. This naturally evokes the enmity of the other brothers, whose clumsy plottings lead to Joseph's being sold into Egypt, where he soon stumbles into the sexual snares of Potiphar's household. Unjustly convicted of attempting to rape Potiphar's wife, Joseph is soon in prison. Now at the very bottom of Egyptian society, shackled in a dungeon, Joseph begins his climb out of the pit into which his own brothers have cast him. He does this by using what he learned in the Land:

> And it came to pass after these things that the butler of the king of Egypt and his baker had offended their lord the king of Egypt. And Pharaoh was wroth against two of his officers, against the chief of the butlers, and against the chief of the bakers. And he put them in ward in the house of the captain of the guard, into the prison, the place where Joseph was

bound. . . . And they dreamed a dream both of them, each man his dream is in one night, each man according to the interpretation of his dream, the butler and the baker of the king of Egypt, which were bound in prison. (Genesis 40)

This passage shows a good deal of psychological sophistication. Each man dreams "his dream," which suggests a dream that reflects his own insights and fears, his own character. Joseph, who attributes the interpretation of dreams to God, is less a pietist and more an early Freud—it is not surprising that the ancient Hebrews, interested in mind, anticipated modern psychology here and elsewhere in the Bible. Joseph is able to read each man's dream knowing that the dream reveals the man and therefore something of his future.

And Joseph came in unto them in the morning, and looked upon them, and, behold, they were sad. And he asked Pharaoh's officers that were with him in the ward of his lord's house, saying, Wherefore look ye so sadly to day? And they said unto him, We have dreamed a dream, and there is no interpreter of it. And Joseph said unto them, Do not interpretations belong to God? Tell me them, I pray you.

There is a small but crucial literary point here. The text contrasts the officers, who speak of a single dream (this is true in the Hebrew, too), and Joseph, who speaks of dreams ("them") and of interpretations, in the plural. He reads the faces of his dreamers and finds both "sad," but he goes on to read more deeply, discerning not one dream but two: two men, two natures, and two fates. If "interpretations belong to God," it is because God gives people the ability to interpret by reading what they see. The Egyptians appear to believe that God makes dreams and their interpretations, but Joseph, trained in the literacy of monotheism, realizes that there is more to dreams than that.

And the chief butler told his dream to Joseph, and said to him, In my dream, behold, a vine was before me; And in the vine were three branches: and it was as though it budded, and her blossoms shot forth; and the cluster thereof brought forth ripe grapes: And Pharaoh's cup was in my hand: and I took the grapes, and pressed them into Pharaoh's cup, and I gave the cup unto Pharaoh's hand. And Joseph said unto him, This is the interpretation of it: The three branches are three days: Yet within three days shall Pharaoh lift up thine head, and restore thee unto thy place: and thou shalt deliver Pharaoh's cup into his hand, after the former manner when thou wast his butler.

Again Joseph draws more on psychology than palmistry. This literary text notes, and so must Joseph, the butler's naive exuberance. He steps briskly forward, while the baker hangs back to see what Joseph knows. The butler shines. As his vine bursts forth with grapes, his dream beams with an eagerness to serve. He can hardly wait to pour for Pharaoh. Unlike the baker, who advertises his own importance ("I also was in my dream"), the butler submerges himself ("a vine was before me"), just as he is eager to submit himself to Pharaoh's service. It is easy for Joseph to see that Pharaoh, if he is at all rational, and this one is, will soon want the hardy butler back, especially with a birthday coming up in three days. And so events prove: "And it came to pass the third day, which was Pharaoh's birthday, that he made a feast unto all his servants. . . . And he restored the chief butler unto his butlership; and he gave the cup into Pharaoh's hand." Joseph can anticipate that on his birthday Pharaoh will not forsake the butler's cheer, nor will he do injustice on the day that celebrates his connection to the eternal world.

With the baker, matters are different. Both the literate Joseph and the trained readers of ancient Israel can see why:

> When the chief baker saw that the interpretation was good, he said unto Joseph, I also was in my dream, and, behold, I had three white baskets on my head: And in the uppermost basket there was of all manner of bakemeats for Pharaoh; and the birds did eat them out of the basket upon my head. And Joseph answered and said, This is the interpretation thereof: The three baskets are three days: Yet within three days shall Pharaoh lift up thy head from off thee, and shall hang thee on a tree; and the birds shall eat thy flesh from off thee. And it came to pass the third day, which was Pharaoh's birthday, that he made a feast unto all his servants: and he lifted up the head of the chief butler and . . . he hanged the chief baker: as Joseph had interpreted to them.

The baker is not forthcoming. He is hiding something. Only the uppermost of his three baskets contains bakemeats for the Pharaoh; the emptiness of the lower two is hidden. He steps forward only when he sees that Joseph is delivering favorable interpretations. Something troubles him that does not trouble the butler. His dream contains no imagery of serving Pharaoh and nothing of the butler's cheer. Rather, the baker's meager dream, niggardly told, betrays a preoccupation with the punishment he has likely brought down on his own head. He imagines birds eating sweets from off his head, reflecting, as Joseph would recognize, his own experience as a spectator at public hangings, where birds peck at dead eyes. The baker must know that his faults, not the butler's, provoked Pharaoh's anger. Accordingly, his skulking and his anxious dream make easy reading for the discerning Joseph, who humbly attributes the interpretation to God but demonstrates that he himself is no mere conduit but a master of literacy.

The butler is saved as Joseph predicts but forgets his promise to mention Joseph's plight to the Pharaoh. However, two years later the Pharaoh himself has a troubling dream, which nobody can or will interpret:

> And Pharaoh awoke, and, behold it was a dream. And it came to pass in the morning that his spirit was troubled; and he sent and called for all the magicians of Egypt, and all the wise men thereof: and Pharaoh told them his dream; but there was none that could interpret them unto Pharaoh. (Genesis 41)

The magicians remaining silent, the butler, good-hearted at bottom, now remembers the skillful reading of the poor Hebrew in prison. Joseph is fetched. Dressed in elegant robes, he gets his chance to show off the skills of his culture. Of course he succeeds, using the same literary principles as before. He does not *divine* Pharaoh's dream; rather he *reads* its entire context, letting the dreamer and his situation provide a rational meaning:

> And Pharaoh said unto Joseph, In my dream, behold, I stood upon the bank of the river: And behold, there came up out of the river seven kine, fatfleshed and well favoured; and they fed in a meadow: And, behold, seven other kine came up after them, poor and very ill favoured and lean-fleshed, such as I never saw in all the land of Egypt for badness. And the lean and the ill favoured kine did eat up the first seven fat kine: And when they had eaten them up, it could not be known that they had eaten them; but they were still ill favoured, as at the beginning. So I awoke. And I saw in my dream, and behold, seven ears came up in one stalk, full and good:

And, behold, seven ears, withered, thin, and blasted with the east wind, sprung up after them: And the thin ears devoured the seven good ears: and I told this unto the magicians; but there was none that could declare it to me. (Genesis 41)

A monotheist who can discern an underlying unity, Joseph appreciates that while the baker and the butler each dreamed his own dream, Pharaoh's two dreams are one, the products of one mind. He understands that the dreams reflect Pharaoh's troubled situation, which is probably what the Egyptians magicians understand, too. What is it in these dreams that is so troubling Pharaoh? Surely he doesn't run to his magicians with every dream. And why are the famous magicians of Egypt, who always have some answer, now standing there, shuffling their feet? Joseph sees in an instant that the dreams concern precisely what they appear to concern, and that Pharaoh, like the baker, knows more than he wants to acknowledge, as do the magicians.

It is obvious that Pharaoh sees encroaching famine, a recurrent nightmare in the ancient Near East. There is nothing recondite in his imagery. As Pharaoh dreams the dream repeatedly; Egypt suffers famine again and again. Pharaoh may wish the problem but a dream, but he also knows that famine is inescapable in waking life—this is probably the meaning of Pharaoh's startling himself awake between dreams. Too intelligent to think that these cycles will cease or that his magicians can stop them, Pharaoh broods. The magicians, too shrewd to contradict Pharaoh's insight, too clever to display the impotence of their magic, remain silent in their knowledge.

Joseph knows what the problem is, too. His great-grandfather and grandfather had been dislodged by famine, and his father and brothers are soon to follow. What he sees in the dreams is obvious to everyone. But he reads more in the whole situation. He sees the court's paralysis. Where the magicians are reduced to impotence, Joseph discerns a way to exploit both the coming famine and the political vacuum; he sees that he can make a killing with the use of his Hebrew intellect. No need for the Land, when one can acquire all of Egypt:

And Joseph said unto Pharaoh, The dream [i.e., the two dreams] is one: God hath shewed Pharaoh what He is about to do. . . . Behold there come seven years of great plenty throughout all the land of Egypt: And there shall arise after them seven years of famine; and all the plenty shall be for-

gotten in the land of Egypt; and the famine shall consume the land. . . .
Now therefore let Pharaoh look out a man discreet and wise, and set him
over the land of Egypt. Let Pharaoh do this, and let him appoint officers
over the land, and take up the fifth part of the land of Egypt in the seven
plenteous years. . . . And the thing was good in the eyes of Pharaoh, and in
the eyes of all his servants. And Pharaoh said unto his servants, Can we
find such a one as this is, a man in whom the Spirit of God is? And
Pharaoh said unto Joseph, Forasmuch as God hath shewed thee all this,
there is none so discreet and wise as thou art: Thou shalt be over my
house, and according unto thy word shall all my people be ruled: only in
the throne will I be greater than thou. (Genesis 41)

Having insinuated himself into the office he himself proposed,
Joseph goes on to acquire great wealth, as he sells his hoarded grain
for exorbitant prices, for cattle and houses, for all the land in Egypt,
for the very bodies of the Egyptians, who are now forced to enslave
themselves. Very clever. But for the Hebrews, Joseph's self-advance-
ment involves a great forgetting of the proper use of monotheistic literacy. Possession of immense wealth was nothing compared to the
possession of Hebrew culture. Without comment but with quiet irony,
the editors of the Bible tell us that Joseph shaved his head in the manner of Egyptians, married a priest's daughter, and had two sons, the
first significantly named Manasseh, which means *forgetting* ("For God
. . . hath made me forget all my toil"), and the second Ephraim, which
means *fruitful* ("For God had caused me to be fruitful in the land of
my affliction"). Joseph's new fruitfulness is all material, and he forgets
not only his Egyptian suffering but his inheritance—his birthright.

Joseph later takes pride that God arranged for him to be in Egypt
during the great famine so that he could "save much people alive," as
he says in the closing verses of Genesis. But, in fact, he prepares for
Israel's slavery in materialist Egypt, as we quickly learn, turning the
page to Exodus. Nor was Joseph's father, Jacob, fooled by his son's
posturings. Jacob sees the ambiguity in Joseph, the misuse of Hebrew
intellect, the misapplication of literacy. He sees the forgetting and the
the sterility and therefore does not like the idea of Joseph raising
Manasseh and Ephraim. Jacob takes his grandchildren into his own
house, and he finds it necessary to remind Joseph of the old fruits of
imagination, the forgotten covenant, and its relationship to the Land:

And Jacob said unto Joseph, God Almighty appeared unto me at Luz in the land of Canaan, and blessed me, And said unto me, Behold, I will make thee fruitful, and multiply thee, and I will make of thee a multitulde of people; and will give this land to thy seed after thee for an everlasting possession. And now thy two sons, Ephraim and Manasseh, which were born unto thee in the land of Egypt before I came unto thee into Egypt, are mine; as Reuben and Simeon, they shall be mine. And thy issue, which thou begettest after them, shall be thine. (Genesis 48)

Forever afterward, the tribes of Israel contain the names of Ephraim and Manasseh, but not the name of Joseph. With the conquest of the Land after the Exodus, Ephraim and Manasseh are assigned their own territories, but no possession is named after Joseph. By expunging Joseph's name, Hebrew tradition perhaps implies disappointment with the way Hebrew skills were transmuted by Egyptian aims. However successfully Joseph adapted Hebrew culture to Egyptian economics, it is Ephraim and Manasseh who will transmit the heritage of intellectual monotheism, under Jacob's guidance. Jacob unenthusiastically tells Joseph that he can raise his other, Egyptian children himself, knowing that these children, never named, would all fall into an Egyptian oblivion, outside history, outside the Land. And they did.

Even though Jacob sees that Joseph can not be permitted to raise his own children, he knows that Joseph possesses the qualities of mind that monotheists most need. Joseph's literacy must be cherished. Thus, when it comes time for the dying patriarch to assess and bless his twelve children, Jacob saves the longest blessing for Joseph, the longest by far, highlighting the brilliant son's gifts and barely alluding to his excesses, but not neglecting the ambiguity:

Joseph is a fruitful bough, even a fruitful bough by a well; whose branches run over the wall: The archers have sorely grieved him, and shot at him, and hated him: But his bow abode in strength, and the arms of his hands were made strong by the hands of the mighty God of Jacob; (from thence is the shepherd, the stone of Israel): Even by the God of thy father, who shall help thee; and by the Almighty, who shall bless thee with the blessings of heaven above, blessings of the deep that lieth under, blessings of the breasts, and of the womb: The blessings of thy father have prevailed above the blessings of my progenitors unto the utmost bound of the everlasting hills: they shall be on the head of Joseph, and on the crown of the head of him that was separate from his brethren.

The tension here between admiration and anxiety is poignant. Jacob notes that Joseph's arms were made strong "by the hands of the mighty God of Jacob," but the father seems to fear that urgent "blessings," greater than those bestowed on his "progenitors" are required to rescue the assimilated Joseph from oblivion. Jacob tries to justify Joseph's departures from the Hebrew tradition by recalling the hostility of his brothers, "the archers" who "hated him." But Jacob's metaphors also suggest that Joseph was separated from his brothers not only by foul play but by his own inclination to grow "over the wall," which is to say outside the Hebrew enclosure, beyond the right uses of intellect. Jacob's blessing is loaded with references to the Almighty, by many names, as if Joseph could be called back from an Egyptian coffin by the mere incantation of the monotheist's God. By lingering over Joseph's blessing, Jacob perhaps hopes to substitute for Joseph's sterile success in Egypt the fruitful womb of Zion. The "blessings of the breasts and of the womb" and blessings from the "utmost bound of the everlasting hills" refer not to the breasts and mountains of Egypt but to the Land which Joseph has neglected.

The dying Moses, in his farewell address in Sinai, echoes the ambivalence of Jacob when he, in turn, blesses the tribes. Again Joseph gets the most complicated blessing, and again the fact that he was "separated from his brethren" weakly explains his disinheritance in favor of his sons; Joseph gets a double portion and no portion at all:

> And of Joseph he said, Blessed of the Lord be his land. . . . And for the precious fruits brought forth by the sun, and for the precious things put forth by the moon. And for the chief things of the ancient mountains, and for the precious things of the lasting hills. . . . let the blessing come upon the head of Joseph, and upon the top of the head of him that was separated from his brethren. . . . his horns are like the horns of unicorns . . . and they are the ten thousands of Ephraim and they are the thousands of Manasseh. (Deuteronomy 33)

Like Jacob, Moses praises Joseph's mind by praising the abundance of "his land"—which Joseph ignored. Again Joseph's portion is named after Ephraim and Manasseh, whom Jacob saved from Egyptian sterility.

Joseph dreamed that the sun, the moon and all the stars bowed down to him, but in Moses's reversal of this dream the fructifying sun and the harvest moon do not bend to the prince of Egypt but shine down on the "lasting hills," which make no more room for Joseph than a grave.

Throughout his successful career in Egypt, Joseph allows himself to hear only distantly the call of Jacob and of Zion. He makes no attempt to reawaken his connections with his father and the Land, remaining aloof even after his gaunt brothers show up with the message that Jacob is suffering. He spends many months tormenting his distant father with the threat of first Simeon's and then young Benjamin's death; he has planted on Benjamin false evidence of theft. The brothers try to defend Benjamin, but Joseph feigns unmovablility. Unaware that he is a plaything in Joseph's cruel story, Judah approaches the man he takes to be the Egyptian vizier and tries to mollify him; he uses his lesser mastery of Hebrew story telling and offers to substitute himself for the imprisoned Benjamin, who after Joseph is his father's favorite, the only other son of the beloved Rachel. "Oh my lord, let thy servant, I pray thee, speak a word in my lord's ears," begs Judah of Joseph, "And let not thine anger burn against thy servant; for thou art even as Pharaoh":

> My lord asked his servants, saying, Have ye a father, or a brother? And we said unto my lord, We have a father, an old man, and a child of his old age, a little one; and his brother is dead, and he alone is left of his mother, and his father loveth him. And thou saidst unto thy servants, Bring him down unto me, that I may set mine eyes upon him. And we said unto my lord, The lad cannot leave his father: for if he should leave his father, his father would die. And thou saidst unto thy servants, Except your youngest brother come down with you, ye shall see my face no more. And it came to pass when we came up unto thy servant my father, we told him the words of my lord. And our father said. Go again and buy us a little food. And we said, We cannot go down: if our youngest brother be with us, then will we go down; for we may not see the man's face, except our youngest brother be with us. And thy servant my father said unto us, Ye know that my wife bare me two sons; And the one went out from me, and I said, Surely he is torn in pieces; and I saw him not since: And if ye take this also from me, and mischief befall him, ye shall bring down my gray hairs with sorrow to the grave. (Genesis 44)

As Judah tells his story he sees that the vizier begins to melt. He does not know the reason for his success, that Joseph is beginning to hear once again the call of his father. He does not even know that he is talking to Joseph. He knows merely that he might now succeed with his selfless proposal:

> Now therefore, I pray thee, let thy servant abide instead of the lad a bond-man to my lord; and let the lad go up with his brethren. For how shall I go up to my father, and the lad be not with me? lest peradventure I see the evil that shall come on my father.

Judah accomplishes far more than he intends. His story works on far deeper levels than this near-literate brother can fathom. Joseph hears how his father was told that he was torn to bits by a wild animal, and he reads from the way Judah alludes to this fabrication that the wise fox his father has quietly doubted Joseph's death all these years. For according to Judah it seems that Jacob took to appending to the tale of Joseph's supposed death the otherwise unnecessary phrase "and I saw him not since"—as if that is the only part of the story that he believes. Joseph hears about his mourning father and he breaks.

Up to this moment, Joseph has thought of his brothers as the characters and the audience of his story, but now he suddenly finds himself the audience; *he* is now a character, directed by Judah. As such, Joseph surrenders to the repressed longing for Jacob and to the power of the Hebrew story:

> Then Joseph could not refrain himself before all them that stood by him; and he cried, Cause every man to go out from me. And there stood no man with him, while Joseph made himself known unto his brethren. And he wept aloud: and the Egyptians and the house of Pharaoh heard. And Joseph said unto his brethren, I am Joseph; doth my father yet live? (Genesis 45)

This belated inquiry bespeaks Joseph's ambivalence, as does his belated submission to Hebrew narrative. Why did he delay? He yearns for Jacob, but the unwelcome memory of his life in Zion distracts him from his success in Egypt, shames him with neglected uses of his intelligence. He does not like being reminded that Egypt is a pit even deeper than the one into which his brothers cast him. So he pushes Jacob out of his mind. But at a price. Like David who was to follow him, he vents his shame through acts of sadism. He torments his family, including Benjamin, who had no part in Joseph's sufferings, and even Jacob, whom he would not have abused with the threat of Benjamin's execution were his motive solely the punishment of those guilty of throwing him into the pit. The Hebrew Joseph yearned for Jacob, but the successful Egyptian recoiled and thus had to punish Jacob for reminding him of his yearning.

But after hearing Judah's story Joseph feels pulled back to his brethren. He is now submissive to their purpose. Though his brothers throw themselves at his feet, terrified that he will avenge the evil they committed against him, he instead prostrates himself before them, an often unnoted reversal of the reversal that a moment earlier left the brothers groveling before the Joseph they once humbled. Joseph had dreamed in symbols that his brothers would bow to him, and he brazenly irked them by telling them so; little did he dream that he would bow to Judah, nor did he notice the fact when it came to be, oblivious too that time would elevate the name of Judah and erase Joseph from Israel's map.

Thus the fruitful bough, the clever but wayward son, slips away from the longing father's rescue, away from Hebrew culture, into a grave over which his descendants would slave. Joseph is brought back to Zion only in the form of dry bones, in the time of the Exodus, to be reintered in the Land, which offers the only context that can give his story significance. To the Hebrews the meaning of Joseph's ambiguous Egyptian success was clear: the exploitation of Hebrew intellect outside the Land falters, because it cannot transmit the literary culture on which it relies. Ephraim and Manasseh cannot be entrusted to the wizard of Egypt, who himself falls into the illusion that slavery in materialist Egypt constitutes a saving of life. Rather the sons of Joseph must be raised by Jacob, whose other name is rooted in the Land of Israel. The stories of Joseph thus bring us back to the Hebrew conviction that Hebrew intelligence requires the Land, where mind is free, yet harnessed to the Zionist enterprise.

Chapter 16

Dry Bones:
Zion as Tragicomedy

They made me keeper of the vineyards; but mine own vineyard have I not kept.

—Song of Solomon 1

ACCORDING TO ONE JEWISH TRADITION, EZRA PRESERVED THE BIBLE while the Hebrews sat in exile in Babylonia. He is said to have arranged the disparate Hebrew materials and to have determined the canon. But he, or somebody like him, or perhaps it was a group of scholars, achieved much more than putting the Bible in order. The Bible appears deeply edited, given a perspective that is strongly marked by exile. Even the Torah, whose authorship Jewish tradition assigns to God, seems deliberately brought into harmony with the view from exile. Sitting by the waters of Babylon, Ezra and the Hebrew scholars traced the invention and tribulations of Zion from the perspective of its most recent failure. Indeed, they saw the whole arch of Zion's history as a tragicomedy of repeated failure.

They kept before them the story of the recent destruction of Zion by Nebuchadnezzar's armies as representative of the big picture:

> Nebuchadnezzar king of Babylon came, he, and all his host against Jerusalem, and pitched against it; and they built forts against it round about. And the city was besieged unto the eleventh year of King Zedekiah. And on the ninth day of the fourth month the famine prevailed in the city, and there was no bread for the people of the land. And the city was broken up, and all the men of war fled by night. . . . And the army of the Chaldees pursued after the king, and overtook him in the plains of Jericho: and all his army were scattered from him. So they took the king, and brought him up to the king of Babylon to Riblah; and they gave judgment upon him. And they slew the sons of Zedekiah before his eyes, and put out the eyes of Zedekiah, and bound him with fetters of brass, and carried him to Babylon. (2 Kings 25)

The ninth day of Av, commemorating the breach of Jerusalem, became a national day of mourning and a fast day, annually observed down to the present. But what happened after the breach of Zion's wall was even more dreadful:

> And in the fifth month, on the seventh day of the month, which is the nineteenth year of king Nebuchadnezzar king of Babylon, came Nebuzaradan, captain of the guard, a servant of the king of Babylon, unto Jerusalem: And he burnt the house of the Lord, and the king's house, and all the houses of Jerusalem, and every great man's house burnt he with fire. . . . Now the rest of the people that were left in the city . . . did

> Nebuzar-adan the captain of the guard carry away. But the captain of the guard left of the poor of the land to be vinedressers and husbandmen. And the pillars of brass that were in the house of the Lord, and the bases . . . did the Chaldees break in pieces, and carried the brass of them to Babylon. (2 Kings 25)

The markers of their civilization broken up into so many pieces of brass, their scholars and teachers carted off, the remnant of Israel was degraded to the most menial and literal relationship to the Land, to "vinedressers and husbandmen," gardeners to a distant emperor, Zion out of mind.

The writer of the Book of Lamentations recalls the catastrophe in Jerusalem, the city burned, corpses in the street, children abandoned:

> The elders of the daughter of Zion sit upon the ground, and keep silence: they have cast up dust upon their heads; they have girded themselves with sackcloth; the virgins of Jerusalem hang down their heads to the ground. Mine eyes do fail with tears, my bowels are troubled, my liver is poured upon the earth, for the destuction of the daughter of my people; because the children and the sucklings swoon in the streets of the city. They say to their mothers, Where is corn and wine? when they swooned as the wounded in the streets of the city, when their soul was poured out into their mothers' bosom. (Lamentations 2)

The wailing children are not victims of chance and misfortune. Rather, the recurrent Hebrew failure to maintain the idea of Zion has pulled them from the bosom:

> Jerusalem hath grievously sinned; therefore she is removed: all that honoured her despise her, because they have seen her nakedness: yea, she sigheth, and turneth backward. Her filthiness is in her skirts; she remembereth not her last end; therefore she came down wonderfully; she had no comforter. (Lamentations 1)

Thus the redactors remembered the fall of Zion. With these vivid details before them, even if distanced by time and art, it is hard to believe that they did not despair. But they did not. They remained hopeful of Zion's restoration. Oddly, they took a tragicomic view of Zion. If tragedy shows that our defenses fail to protect our values from the complexity of the human situation, comedy shows the opposite, the survival of our values against all odds. Comedy affords us the relief that we can fail without being destroyed, and this relief provides the energy for our laughter when what we care about falters. We laugh at the survival of what we value.

In the comic tradition the Hebrews in exile reassured themselves that their noble heritage, this idea of Zion, would survive despite an unending series of complications and disasters. The depth of disaster of the recent exile darkened their comedy, so that we may call it tragicomedy. Nevertheless, the Hebrews in exile colored the narrative of Zion's history with a remarkable comic humor, starting from its beginning in the imagination of Abraham. The founding patriarch, we remember, made a straightforward bargain to hold the One God in his mind in exchange for the gift of Canaan, which he would in good faith make represent the culture of monotheism. That this deal quickly shaded into a promise of slavery in Egypt and other complications, including the binding of Isaac, is a kind of joke on Abraham, but one he can survive, because the idea he carries is indestructible. At least that is the comic conviction of the redactors in Babylonia.

So, too, can Joseph survive the joke played on him. He thinks he has saved many lives by establishing the Hebrews in Egypt, where they will become slaves. In a way he is right about saving lives, for a multitude of Hebrews does return to the Land after four hundred years of slavery. Though that is not what he had in mind, Joseph gets carried up to the Land anyway. For the Land has survived his neglect and is there to provide him a grave. That Joseph thrives in exile but returns to the Land merely as dry bones is another joke on him, but the idea of Zion can survive this, too.

Joseph's burial in the Land begins national life but foreshadows the reversibility of that life, brought on at least in part by the national adoption of Joseph's impulse, to turn one's back on Zion. Astonishingly, the Hebrew redactors let their beginning represent their end, or possible end; they may have created the only national culture that made Land stand both for eternal peoplehood and for the opposite, for the exile that they knew would come. Yet they remained confident, persuading themselves in the comic mode that they would overcome the ruin of Zion, again and again if necessary.

In the Hebrew imagination, Joseph was buried four times, each time elevating his station in the world. First he was left for dead in the

Canaanite pit where his brothers cast him, from whence he was reborn into the opulent exile of Potiphar's house; then he was interred in Pharaoh's jail, from whence he was reborn as all-powerful vizier; then he was mummified and immured in Egypt, from whence he was carried up to Zion, to be laid to rest at last in the Land. Here his old bones signal a fruition higher than any possible in the fertile Egyptian mud, but not so high as to escape the ebb and flow of Hebrew understanding. In the view of the redactors in Babylon, Joseph's old bones earn earthly reincarnation in a Zion that is renewable whenever Jews master the patriarch's understanding but eschew his choice to be embalmed in Egypt. In this comic view, the House of Joseph can be buried and resurrected again and again.

Because Jerusalem's destruction is regarded as only a temporary loss, the author of Lamentations still preserves the old poetry of Zion, even as he paints her physical and cultural collapse:

> The Lord hath purposed to destroy the wall of the daughter of Zion: he hath stretched out a line, he hath not withdrawn his hand from destroying: therefore he made the rampart and the wall to lament; they languished together. Her gates are sunk into the ground; he hath destroyed and broken her bars: her king and her princes are among the Gentiles: the law is no more; her prophets also find no vision from the Lord. (Lamentations 2)

The image startles us. God the surveyor stretches out a measuring "line" over the tumbled wreck of Zion, as if He were founding the fortress of David's city. Instead, he is committed to the opposite, the end of "law" (Torah) and "vision," for which Zion stood. Thus in a single image of the macabre surveyor do we have the sum, the beginning and the end, of an unsentimental civilization that can yet hope for another beginning.

The redactors in Babylonia projected back onto Moses the realization that Zion was doomed to fail, but not in a deeply tragic and permanent way. In the view of Moses and his editors, the Hebrews might forget the idea of Zion at any time, but the memory of Zion could always be renewed. At the end of his life, within sight of the new Land awaiting his people, Moses is made to position himself in the future and to look back on relapsing monotheists who failed their beginning and came to a bad end, or at least to a hiatus, requiring another beginning; he can already foresee how the Hebrews will anger God, who will then expel them to Babylon:

> They sacrificed unto devils, not to God; to gods whom they knew not, to new gods that came newly up. . . . They have moved me to jealousy with that which is not God; with their vanities: and I will move them to jealousy with those which are not a people; I will provoke them to anger with a foolish nation. . . . The sword without, and terror within, shall destroy both the young man and the virgin, the suckling also with the man of gray hairs. . . . I said I would scatter them into corners, I would make the remembrance of them to cease from among men. (Deuteronomy 32)

What other people would predict that, having invented intellectual nationalism, they would be destroyed by those who "are not a people," of no nationality beyond a horde, as punishment for embracing "that which is not God"? What other people would make the glory of their beginning stand for the ignominy of their likely end? Only those who suffered ignominy and still believed they might return to a fruitful national life would record such a history.

For Moses and the Babylonian Hebrews, a bleak future might be averted by the preservation of intellect. But this, as the wry Moses realizes, is too much to expect. "For they are a nation void of counsel, neither is there any understanding in them. O that they were wise, that they understood this, that they would consider their latter end." By *understanding* Moses means the wisdom of Abraham, of David and Solomon and Esther, of Elijah and the prophets, who would maintain the national civilization and avoid destruction. Moses knows that the whole mighty edifice of ancient Zionism, powerfully founded on mind though it was, would tumble when understanding failed, as it eventually must in a comic world.

So Moses is made to know that the Babylonian exile is to come, that there is no guarantee that the Land will be owned in perpetuity. In fact, Moses specifically teaches that the Land is not to be owned at all. The Land is a symbol, not a property, and as such it can be as powerful or flimsy as the minds that do or do not recognize it. This principle itself became part of Mosaic Law, the better to remind the Hebrews that no plot, let alone the whole Land, could be a permanent possession. This is the law of the jubilee, the mandatory expiration of all deeds of ownership every fifty years: "The land shall not be sold for ever: for the land is mine; for ye are strangers and sojourners with me. And in all the land of your possession ye shall grant a redemption for the land" (Leviticus 25). But this law was not observed regularly, so of course it could not serve as a reminder. The Hebrews grabbed land and lost the Land. Remarkably, the sharpest meaning of the Land was the eventuality of landlessness, as a consequence of ignoring all the other meanings of the Land.

Moses himself had to die outside the Land for his own failed understanding. Perhaps the joke on him is even more poignant than the joke on Abraham and Joseph. Moses is promised by God that if he challenges Pharaoh he will triumph. He will lead the children of Israel into the promised Land and make of them there a great nation. Instead he has to wander with the quarrelsome Hebrews who worshipped the golden calf while he received the Law on Mount Sinai. The Hebrew idolatry was not his fault, but he too has to endure the wandering. During these forty exasperating years he finally loses his patience, striking a rock to bring forth water when reverence was required, and God holds him accountable in the end:

> And the Lord spake unto Moses . . . Get thee up into this mountain Abarim, unto mount Nebo, which is in the land of Moab, that is over against Jericho; and behold the land of Canaan, which I give unto the children of Israel for a possession: And die in the mount whither thou goest up, and be gathered unto thy people . . . Because ye trespassed against me among the children of Israel at the water of Meribah-Kadesh, in the wilderness of Zin; because ye sanctified me not in the midst of the children of Israel. (Deuteronomy 32)

Even as he predicts the Hebrews' eventual failure of mind, Moses recalls his own lapse, and he lets his exile stand for that which is to come, surely the only founder forbidden at the outset to enter his own country. Moses's death alone on Mount Nebo is a touching yet comic falling short, and it is a signifying beginning for his followers.

The story of Moses' exclusion from Zion is subtle and poignant. In Exodus 17, while in the "wilderness of Sin," Moses is told by God to satisfy the murmuring Hebrews' thirst by striking a rock with his staff; he does so, and all goes well. In a repetition, in Numbers 20, where the Hebrews are again groaning of thirst, the scene is now set in the "desert of Zin," certainly the same place with a different spelling. This time God asks Moses to *speak* to the rock, to use Hebrew intellect rather than force. But Moses is irritable:

> And Moses and Aaron gathered the congregation together before the rock, and he said unto them, Hear now, ye rebels; must we fetch you water out of this rock? And Moses lifted up his hand, and with his rod he smote the rock twice; and the water came out abundantly, and the congregation drank, and their beasts also. And the Lord spake unto Moses and Aaron, Because ye believed me not, to sanctify me in the eyes of the children of Israel, therefore ye shall not bring this congregation into the land which I have given them.

Mocking the Hebrews' cry for miracles, Moses is snide, contemptuous of the miracle he will perform yet claiming it as his own rather than God's ("must we fetch you water"). This is not *zohar* but magic. In no condition to "sanctify" a God of literacy, he strikes the rock in a pique of literal-mindedness. Thus Moses fails in just the way that he predicts his congregants will do, by turning his back on the central purpose of the Zionist enterprise, which is to raise oneself to the level of the abstract Creator. Stooping to the physical beating of rocks, he earns the legacy of Zin, suffering exile to the wilderness as warning to the Hebrews not to sate their holy thirst with actual water. The spelling change from Sin to Zin (*Sin* is Sinai, the wilderness), which rather mystified the rabbis, suggests his exclusion from Zion (Zion and Zin share the same root). This is a mean trick on Moses, to switch Zin for Zion, meaner than the trick played on Abraham. Astonishingly, Moses' fate at the beginning of national history is that of Zion herself, as in Isaiah 64: "Thy holy cities are a wilderness, Zion is a wilderness, Jerusalem a desolation." But both the reputation of Moses and the meaning of the Land survive the wilderness in which Moses dies, as is the way of tragicomedy.

At the end, Moses makes peace with his role, which provides living proof that literalists get Zin, not Zion. He does so even though he knows that his martyrdom on Mount Nebo, an awful echo of the forbidden human sacrifices atop leafy high places, will not stem the Hebrew drift into forgetfulness: "For I know thy rebellion, and thy stiff neck: behold, while I am yet alive with you this day, ye have been rebellious against the Lord; and how much more after my death?"

(Deuteronomy 31). The great-minded man, however, does not stop with a prediction of blindness and permanent exile. Moses has a few more words to say before he dies alone, outside the Land: "Happy art thou, O Israel: who is like unto the, O people saved by the Lord." In the end, or in a fresh beginning, monotheism might again triumph, inspirited anew by the God who moved Abraham. God might rekindle Hebrew imagination and thereby permit recultivation of the Land.

In the high comic view, Isaiah describes God Himself as calling for this renewal:

> Remember the former things of old: for I am God, and there is none else; I am God, and there is none like me. Declaring the end from the beginning, and from ancient times the things that are not yet done, saying, My counsel shall stand, and I will do all my pleasure. . . . I will place salvation in Zion for Israel my glory. (Isaiah 46)

The God who is the beginning and the end, the God who created all, planting the end in the beginning, has made Zion appear to come to an end only in the manner of a winter tree, with a new flowering not far away:

> For I will pour water upon him that is thirsty, and floods upon the dry ground: I will pour my spirit upon thy seed, and my blessing upon thine offspring: And they shall spring up as among the grass, as willows by the water courses. One shall say, I am the Lord's; and another shall call himself the name of Jacob; and another shall subscribe with his hand unto the Lord, and surname himself by the name of Israel. (Isaiah 44)

Thus the possibility of renewing the Land, both as a place of parched fields and as a desiccated civilization, is very much a part of ancient Zionism. In an eerie allusion to the reburial of Joseph's old bones, Ezekiel creates the most famous image of Zion's redemption:

> The hand of the Lord . . . set me down in the midst of the valley which was full of bones. . . . Then he said unto me, Son of man, these bones are the whole house of Israel: behold they say, Our bones are dried, and our hope is lost. . . . Therefore prophesy and say unto them, Thus saith the Lord God; Behold, O my people, I will open your graves, and cause you to come up out of your graves, and bring you into the land of Israel. (Ezekiel 37)

One may hope for a replanting and quickening of seed, both in the mind and in the Land. For both Ezekiel and Isaiah, ancient Zionism, subject to eternal cycles of loss and renewal, waits in exile after exile for the rekindling of poetry in a fallow Land and in a cultivated mind.

A cultivated mind vitalizes any intellectual civilization, especially in ancient Zion, where it redeems all, helped along by the Almighty. This is where Isaiah's national poetry begins and ends:

> Have ye not known? have ye not heard; hath it not been told you from the beginning? have ye not understood from the foundations of the earth? (Isaiah 40)

> Come now, and let us reason together, saith the Lord: though your sins be as scarlet, they shall be as white as snow; though they be red like crimson, they shall be as wool. If ye be willing and obedient, ye shall eat the good of the land. (Isaiah 1)

A prepared mind, in the visions of the prophets, ushers in the messianic age, which will arise not in a gossamer world-to-come, not in a metaphysical or universalized state, but in Zion, the physical Land of Israel, whose transcendent soil produces intellectual fruits even though it remains the literal dirt of Ephron's field. Messianic thought in later Judaism, and even more in Christianity, uprooted itself from the soil of ancient Zion, but this was not so in the poetics of Israel's prophets, who were committed to the Abrahamic vision wherein physical landscape stands for the profoundest of ideas. Ezekiel, in imagining the end of days after apocalyptic battles, foresees a final rebirth of the old Land, now the actual center of civilization. "Gog and all his multitude" will encounter "the mountains of Israel," where they will turn upon themselves, slaying each other so that their corpses exceed the appetite of "ravenous birds" and requiring the astonished Hebrews to labor seven months to bury the heaped-up nations and to harvest their abandoned weapons, which are to supply firewood without end:

> And it shall come to pass on that day, that I will give unto Gog a place there of graves in Israel, the valley of the passengers on the east of the sea, and it shall stop the noses of the passengers. . . . And the passengers that pass through the land, when any seeth a man's bone, then shall he set up a sign by it, till the buriers have buried it in the valley of Hamon-gog. (Ezekiel 39)

This grisly vision of another Valley of Dry Bones turns on a pun. The burial squads, passing through the stinking Land, will set up the bones of the hostile multitudes as a "sign" that here lies yet another corpse of one who once opposed the humane vision of Zion. On a still higher level, this bone sign is a symbol of Zion itself. The Hebrew word for "sign" is *tsioon*, virtually the same word as *tsion*, the Zion that is as real as a bone in the dirt and as powerful as an idea on which one might refound a nation for now and for eternity, at least according to the poetry of Ezekiel.

Ezekiel's punning on the bone sign lends a comical air to the renewal of Zion. It is not surprising, then, that the first efforts to rebuild Jerusalem a half-century after Ezekiel's death were bumbling though sincere. The returning Hebrews had forgotten Hebrew, and they required the Levites to translate the Law into Aramaic, slowly and "distinctly," so that they might understand. They were in a muddle about whether to celebrate or to weep, and they did not know whether to weep on account of their awe or their forgetfulness. Ezra and Nehemiah permit them to wipe their tears and to celebrate:

> So they read in the book in the law of God distinctly, and gave the sense, and caused them to understand the reading. And Nehemiah . . . and Ezra . . . said unto all the people, This day is holy unto the Lord your God; mourn not, nor weep. For all the people wept, when they heard the words of the law. . . . Go your way, eat the fat, and drink the sweet. (Nehemiah 8)

There was not much to celebrate for these faltering Hebrews. But the story of Zion, as in all comedies, is meant to end with true joy and celebration. And that is the way Isaiah ends his book, offering us a vision of Jerusalem's orphans comforted and of her boneyard come back to life in a nonspecified future:

> Who hath heard such a thing? who hath seen such things. Shall the earth be made to bring forth in one day? or shall a nation be born at once? for as soon as Zion travailed, she brought forth her children. . . . Rejoice ye with Jerusalem, and be glad with her, all ye that love her; rejoice for joy with her, all ye that mourn for her. . . . For thus saith the Lord, Behold, I will extend peace to her like a river, and the glory of the Gentiles like a

flowing stream: then shall ye suck, ye shall be borne upon her sides, and be dandled upon her knees. As one whom his mother comforteth, so will I comfort you; and ye shall be comforted in Jerusalem. And when ye see this, you heart shall rejoice, and your bones shall flourish like an herb. (Isaiah 66)

Chapter 17

Ancient Zionism and Its Modern Competitors

To wish the greatness of our own country is often to wish evil to our neighbors. He who could bring himself to wish that his country should always remain as it is, would be a citizen of the universe.

—Voltaire, "Country," *Philosophical Dictionary*

THE RENEWED HEBREW CULTURE THAT NOW ROOTS IN THE LAND OF Israel may not have pleased Isaiah and Ezekiel. Nevertheless it is a direct descendant of the prophets' unique and literate civilization. Abraham's coupled visions of a universal God and a signifying Land produced a seed from which poetry, law, and history flowered in an intellectual garden, nurtured by invention and discernment. Often this culture, more a potential than a realized Eden, stooped to literal-mindedness and to looting, but the seed was transmitted to every generation. Offshoots of ancient Hebrew civilization now flower in other cultures and now again in Israel. Many have cause to thank the ancient Hebrews for the concept of using place to signify value, thus raising nationalism to poetry.

But there are also many who, while admiring the French and English ideas of *La Belle France* and Albion, condemn the Jews for using Israel to represent their ancient culture. The world is full of craven national ambition, of which Zionism is often cited as an example. All over the world, in Russia and El Salvador, in Egypt and Iran, the scurrilous *Protocols of the Elders of Zion* continues to sell briskly. Translations of this nineteenth-century forgery are ongoing. This is poor thanks for having invented intellectual nationalism. If we now distinguish base from thoughtful nationalism; if we now recognize, as Shakespeare did, that King Henry V of England had no right to the French crown despite the glorious rhetoric of his invasion; if we deny that Kuwait is a lost province of Iraq and believe that the Aryan nation is no such thing; if we agree that Kurdistan is probably a nation and that Yugoslavia was not; if we see that Somalia, even in its homogeneity under Islam and close-knit clanship, lacks a national idea, this is because ancient Zionism has taught us to think more deeply about what nations ought to be.

Let us briefly survey the ways in which we now regard the relationship between people and land, placing ancient Zionism in its modern context. There are at least six ways to think of land. In the West, most people at one time or another have adopted them all, shifting from one to another as convenient, but it is worth distinguishing them. The first is the principle of non-ownership, which we might call primitive, although it is quite sophisticated. This is best illustrated by the ideal of native American Indians, who understand that the land is sacred, radiating with spiritual meanings, and cannot be a possession. American Indians were willing to sign treaties ceding rights to their lands because they never understood that the white man would actually take possession and evict them. We admire this view now that we understand it, and we have given it a modern slant; the environmental movement, for example, emphasizes stewardship of the land. But since the world is now carved into owned properties and national entities, we are unlikely to see this tribal view dominate anywhere. Even in ancient Zion, where the Hebrews regarded themselves as tenants of a signifying Land, property was held and national claims protected.

The second way of thinking about land is the simple notion of a man's right to the field he farms. The land is literal and nonrepresentational in this view, which is not at all sophisticated, not part of a national idea or any other idea. A man owns the field that his ox plows, and that is the end of the matter. But since the idea of property rights is itself complex, requiring a culture to embody it, the right to a field dissolves in a world without nations and law. Without a civilization of law, a field can be maintained only by might. Because this has never proved satisfactory, we look to a more complex idea of land to avoid eternal feuding. Still the notion that every person is a sovereign in his or her own castle finds a protected niche in our thinking, and it provides the basis for claims by those who have suffered the misappropriation of property. This is the banner under which West Germans now claim their old homes in East Germany and the descendants of Spanish Moors bequeath to heirs in Algeria their 500-year-old keys to houses in Granada. The Arab refugee's claim to lost houses in Israel also falls into this category.

The third is the idea of land as part of a set of business arrangements. In this view, perhaps best represented by Lichtenstein and Hong Kong, the land is made to represent simple rules of doing business and protecting property. The rules do not constitute an entire civilization; this must come from outside. In the view from Hong Kong, it might not matter whether the civilization is British or Chinese, or whether either is of any value, as long as the climate of efficient business is protected. In the United States we sometimes adopt this perspective, forgetting our larger values of being a land of freedom and a haven for the oppressed when it appears that too many immigrants are bad for business. Lot's and Boaz's businessman cousin would do well in Hong Kong, as long as somebody else put together the sustaining civilization of Britain.

The fourth is the idea of empire, the old notion that land can be made to represent the glory of a civilization if only enough of it is acquired. This was the driving force behind Hellenistic Greece, imperial Rome, and Islam. In the West we repudiate this ethic, yet adopting it to protect our perceived interests, as on occasion in the Philippines or Viet Nam or Latin America. We do not admire ourselves at these times, and we retreat with some shame. We know that empires collide with one another, that their armies clash by night, and that they always die, whether their armies win or lose. We have learned not to let our civilization rest on empire, even if we sometimes cheat on our values as when we sent on expeditionary force to Grenada. In these moments we pretend that we are operating under the banner of democracy or selfless humanitarianism, but it doesn't wash.

The fifth way of thinking about land is the idea of Zion, the model of intellectual nationalism that we have been discussing. Other examples are the Greek polis and the United States whose purple mountains' majesty represents the Bill of Rights and other enlightened values. Ancient Zion and the Greek polis insisted on making a small place represent a large civilization, but even in America, where the fantasy of manifest destiny allowed us to seize a continent to mark our values, we have realized that a border does not cramp us but defines us.

The sixth way is a bluff, a ruse. Every schoolroom globe is covered by "nations," each shown in a distinct color, as if each were equally constituted. But some places are nonplaces that pretend to represent a distinct civilization when no such synthesis has taken place on the ground. Saddam Hussein's Iraq is an example of this craven nationalism: the Kurds in the north require a no-fly zone to protect them from gassing, while the Shiites in the south require a no-fly zone to protect them from tanks. Somalia has Islam but this rich civilization is an import unconnected to the land and therefore unable to make the place cohere. Much of Africa suffers from this failure to meld the idea of the land with the local culture. We suspect that the idea of a greater Serbia is largely fake. The idea of a Palestinian nation is also a ruse, created as a club against Israel. Of course Palestinian Arabs possess the rich civilizations of Islam and Arabia, but these are not legitimately represented by the Land of Israel (of this more later). In the West, craven nationalism raises its ugly head whenever demagogues dissolve intellectual nationalism and replace it with the claptrap of McCarthyism and its like. Sometimes we allow ourselves to mainstream our craven nationalism, as in our jingoistic polemics against Japan. And as the press is happy to remind us, craven nationalism occurs in Israel too, where in the past it has attached itself to the Sinai as part of a greater Israel and to the lunatic project of blowing up the mosques that were built on the Temple Mount. The scale of craven nationalism in Israel, however, never reaches the imperial, for the simple reason that Israel is tiny.

The modern view of land and nationhood, it should be apparent, is to adopt none of the above with conviction but all of the above situationally. In America we admire ourselves most when we recall that we were founded on the principles of ancient Zion as they were brought to this land by the pilgrims, who believed they were making a New Jerusalem, and by the deists, who thought they were instituting the culture of ethical monotheism. But what makes us modern is our freedom to move among all the ways of thinking of land and nationhood. We would not be able to take care of business if we limited ourselves to the idea of Zion. Similarly, modern Israel, insofar as it is modern, departs from its origins to make deals and accommodations that appear necessary. At times Israel has imported foreign values, trying for example to make herself part of the socialist revolution or part of the international business community. Alternatively, Israel on occasion makes herself represent new home-grown values, convenient to the moment but not derived from ancient Zionism, such as the creation of a secular pioneer movement and the building of a refuge for embattled Jews in the Diaspora.

But this modern freedom to flit among the possibilities presupposes that somebody bothers to uphold the kind of civilization that was created by ancient Zionism. Of the six ways of thinking about land, only the model of ancient Zion can provide the standard that keeps the plowman in possession of his field and the Hong Kong businessman safe in his skyscraper. If there is no Britain (which is herself founded on a civilization like that of ancient Zion) and no principled civilization of China, Hong Kong cannot survive. The idea of the Indians' unpossessable plains, the idea of the individual's right to land, the idea of the business state, the idea of empire, and the pretense of nationhood cannot maintain the earth as a place of peaceful habitation. These competitors of ancient Zionism are impractical or sterile.

The modern freedom to move as necessary between different ideas of nation and land can be dressed up as an ideal itself, especially when bathed in a liberal and tolerant ideology. But eventually the ideology of flexibility and tolerance founders on its own lack of backbone. If specific lands need not represent specific cultures, a blur of mixed ideas about nationhood eventually creates chaos on the ground. The modern practitioner of flexibility ultimately winds up living as a Latvian when Latvia is being overrun by Russia, or as a Russian when Latvia is expunging reminders of the Soviet Union. To live in Latvia as a Latvian in a world that recognizes Latvia as the symbol of Latvian civilization is a safer and richer prospect. Of course, Russians living in Latvia may be threatened by the Latvian idea, but this is not reason enough to abandon the idea of Latvia, or for that matter the idea of Russia. Similarly, if one doesn't want to take the risk of living in a Hong Kong that is being dismantled by a fierce cultural revolution, the idea of founding one's nation on a ninety-nine-year lease should give way to intellectual nationalism. Situational nationalism is as problematic as the individual situations themselves.

Thus Israel does not rely on modern pragmatism but draws her strength from her ancient roots, which nourish intellectual nationalism. Its modern accommodations are fitful and finally irrelevant. The idea that Jews might choose a tolerant and liberal diaspora is a parallel irrelevancy, for the choice to remain flexible about one's homeland proves as fatal for Jews as does the choice of adopting situational nationalism. Both take one out of Zion for something less durable. Eventually, one winds up with the wrong strategy at the wrong time or in the wrong place at the wrong time, either in Roman Israel attempting to cope with the Emperor Hadrian or in Poland in the time of the Nazis.

What is most remarkable about Israel is not its modern agriculture or its modern absorption centers for refugees but its ancient Zionism. Perhaps the Jews who take their Zionism the most seriously, the ones who have made the fewest accommodations to modern pragmatism and business, are the Jewish inhabitants of the West Bank. These much maligned "settlers" in the tiny heartland of ancient Israel may have much more to offer us than conventional wisdom or the popular press allows. It is easy to find the lone fanatic among them, but fanaticism is never sanctioned by that group. They do not participate in international terrorism or in drug running. They do not organize or condone missions of assassination to the Olympic games or to the World Trade towers. They do not meet in their councils to approve airliner bombings and machine-gun attacks on children. They do not send their children to hurl stones as Molech's mighty soldiers. The settlers stay home.

These dedicated Zionists, the vast majority of whom are decent and nonviolent, have chosen to rebuild the ancient civilization of the Bible. For them, this is an intellectual enterprise, as it was for their ancestors. They make of the Land neither a fetish nor an idol but live in it as a symbol of a civilization to whose rational discipline they submit themselves. They have no wild plans to launch rockets into Baghdad. Their attachment to the Land is self-limited, according to the tenets of their culture. They know all about David's corruption of his own ideal into craven nationalism, which they repudiate. They know that Rabbat-Ammon does not belong to them, and they do not covet it, let alone Granada and Cordoba. They believe that God deliberately gave the Law outside the Land in Sinai, and so they are content to have made peace with Egypt in exchange for that wilderness. They are committed to reclaiming their ruined Land, but they are opposed to the absorption of anybody else's wilderness. Envious of no other people, they are happy to see Arabs make Arabia flower. If those who assail these settlers kept their own ambitions and envy to the settlers' scale, the earth would abound with tiny nations eager for peace.

That these settlers have been made to represent their own antithesis is their most salted wound. The smear persists that they and the Zionist enterprise provide the standard of fanaticism. Thus Henry Louis Gates, Jr., sincere and well-meaning, tells us on the Op Ed page of *The New York Times* for March 27, 1994 that "the West Bank fanatic" is in the vanguard of those who "march to a single drum" of "messianic hatred." The settlers in fact march to no drum, rather shouldering the much more complex burden of rebuilding Zion. In their view, none of the other possible ways of regarding land would secure them the kind of cultural stability and meaning that Mr. Gates enjoys in his office in the new Jerusalem. Mr. Gates recommends a vague "liberalism of heart and spine"—a kindly version of situational nationalism—but the settlers know that is no way to build Jerusalem. The Constitution of the United States has substantial content which the United States helps represent, but one suspects a liberalism of heart and spine has minimal contents, with little heart to contain it and no spine to support it.

The West Bank settlers endure the additional smear that they have displaced another civilization that is said to root in the same land. This is a little notion pushed forward as a big lie. A Palestinian Arab claim to the Land of Israel cannot rise above a claim to houses lost from the larger Arab empire. Neither Moorish homes in Cordoba nor Arab homes in Jerusalem can reasonably constitute lost nations. Jewish houses in Iraq were similarly lost, and Jews still claim them, but this does not constitute lost nationhood either, as West Bank settlers whose families were displaced from Baghdad after one hundred generations would acknowledge, for they know Zion. They know, and we now know, that homeland represents the grafting of a specific place with a specific national idea. No Palestinian idea beyond the claim to land or other lost property has ever been articulated. Borrowed and usurped nationhood does not count. The idea of a "Palestinian Covenant," which in Arab hands is a credo to damn Zion to yet another end, is lifted from the Christian term for the Deuteronomic threat of exile (see, for example, the Scofield Reference Bible on Deuteronomy 29 and 30). The "Palestinian Diaspora" is similarly borrowed from the dispersion of Zion.

One might argue that Palestinian Arabs have no obligation to articulate or even possess a national idea, for the idea of a national concept is Jewish, later European, perhaps even Chinese, but not at home in the world of Islam and pan-Arabism, where a mixture of the local and the universal bypasses Western ideas about national identity. We might simply take Palestinian Arabs at their word and accord them nationhood because they claim it on the basis of having lived in the area of the Turkish Empire called Palestine. Even if Palestinian nationalism is, according to Edward Said, its most vocal advocate in English, "unusual," "cubistic," without a defining idea, with "obtruding planes jutting out into one or another realm," who but Palestinians should say what nationhood means to them? Even if, as Said concedes (I am quoting from *The Question of Palestine* [Vintage, 1979], pp. 118–124),

"Palestinians made their world-historical appearances largely in the form of refusals and rejections," even if their "multiplication of selves" still seeks a cohesive identity, even if "Palestinians are still perceived— even at times by themselves—as a collection of basically negative att- tributes," should not their "wildly multiple Palestinian actuality" be granted "the goal of getting a place, a territory, on which to be located nationally"? We might simply accord them their "entity"—as they describe the Jewish state—under the rubric of a claim to lost fields.

But Palestinian Arabs have staked their claim to nationhood in Western terms, probably because they can see, better than those Westerners who take their own living nationhood for granted, that a "cubistic" nation is a fractured community, that "basically negative attributes" do not make a positive nation. Thus Palestinian Arabs insist that their brotherhood with other Arabs and other Moslems is beside the point. They claim a specific national idea as the true and displaced nation of Israel or, under the new peace, as a second true nation of Israel, with its own covenant and diaspora, with a fusion of land and idea. For a while the idea of Palestine was presented as that of a secular democratic state, but this has not floated well in the West, where a mockery of Western ideas can be recognized even if the mockers are still taken seriously. Besides the absence of examples of secular democratic states in the Arab world, there is the larger difficulty of recognizing a nation that is based on so light a notion, unsupported by the constitutional law and the constituting myths that may make the majesty of *particular* purple mountains represent the rule of a thriving national democracy.

The problem with Palestine, the question of Palestine, is precisely the lack of a national idea despite the pretense that one exists. "Pressure on Israel," meaning terrorist assault, substitutes for the absent "Palestinian psyche," at least in this passage, where Said—with a sneer and a magician's sleight of hand—waves away the inquiry into the nature or existence of a Palestinian national soul:

> . . . the various Palestinian communities, each with its own defined priorities, must be kept in touch with one another, tensions reduced or eliminated, alliances promoted. And on top of all this there is always the goal of maintaining the pressure on Israel, whose borders, to the Palestinian exiles, seem far and hard to get to. Thus whatever problems we may wish

to discover in the Palestinian psyche—a new object for scrutiny among Palestinians and other "experts" in national character analysis—will, I think seem relatively ephemeral alongside this string of competing material imperatives for action. (Said, *The Question of Palestine*, p. 124)

The "material imperatives" that supersede inquiry into the Palestinian psyche are the assault on Israel's borders and the dampening of internecine "tensions." This suggests that Palestinians themselves and other "experts" may be right when they doubt the existence of a Palestinian "national character." An inquiry into the Palestinian psyche is in order, even if Said brands the pursuit "ephemeral." For the soul of a nation is what lasts, what counts at the beginning and what counts when all is said and done.

The West Bank settlers see no reason to accord nationhood to a non-nation. And though they are ready to compensate Arabs for lost land, they are not willing to elevate to national status the claim to lost fields. They think Arabs did not and should not inherit Jerusalem for the same reason that Jews failed to inherit Baghdad: Jerusalem stands for Jewish ideas and Baghdad for Arab ideas. Jerusalem can be made to stand for Arab empire, but it cannot with justice be made to stand for the secular democratic state or any other come-lately, soulless fabrication. In the Middle East at the beginning of the twentieth century, as the Turkish Empire gave way to national states, the Jewish national idea was again allowed to count. Not to count the people who invented intellectual nationalism would have been to convert the Turkish empire back into an Arab empire at a time when the age of empires was passing. A Palestinian province in an Arab empire is not a nation, even if it is dressed up under the heading of "self-determination."

The settlers understand the Arab accusation that modern Israel was introduced into an area of the world that was largely Arab. But they think this is true only in the most narrow-minded sense. Israel was always there, and when it "returned" it left the Middle East still largely Arab in ninety-nine percent of the Turkish empire. The problem was not the imposition of tiny Zion, or the ejection of Arabs from Jerusalem and Jews simultaneously from Baghdad, but the failure to found authentic nations in addition to Zion. Perhaps the non-Arab Kurds in the north of Iraq would not require a no-fly zone to protect them from the murderous Sadaam had the energy that whipped up

Palestine gone into the realization of nationhood for Kurds. Perhaps a Middle East made up of states akin to Zion, each radiating its own culture, would find peace natural. But this would have meant the unthinkable, the giving up the Arab empire.

In the Arab view, the only nation missing from the modern Middle East is Palestine, the nation that has most defined itself by hatred of Zion and sympathy with the fabled Arab nation. But the Arab nation is unrealized because unrealizable, a "nation" without a national idea precisely because of its imperial pretensions. Palestine is probably similarly unrealizable, because its founding purpose was to destroy the inventor of nationhood and its defining act was the cheering of Sadaam, whose rockets rained on Israel even as his craven soldiers despoiled Kuwait. Palestinian Arabs, who see as little value in an independent Kuwait as they do in an independent Israel, will not likely join the family of thoughtful nations.

But the power of the ideas behind Mecca and Medina might inspire a true peace, not the one between Israel and a hollow Palestinian Liberation Organization, but between Israel and Islam, which may yet recognize Zionism as kin. This process may already be under way. The recent Arab recognition of the idea of Zion, if that is what we are hearing, may force Palestinian spokesmen to articulate their own idea of Palestine or to acknowledge that there is none. Everybody welcomes peace, but it is a hollow peace that is made by hollow nations.

One can imagine on this point a Palestinian prophet with a vision. "Enough," he might say. "Let us return to the traditions of our father Abraham and our brother Israel. Let us permit the Jews their Land. Let us give land for peace. We kept the world on its ear because our people claim a nation on top of Israel. This is a fable. We have fulfilled the prediction of our prophet Moses that the Jews would be hounded by those who 'are not a people.' We mouth words of freedom fighters and covenant makers, as if we were Jews or Americans. But in fact we are mainly Arabs, free to mingle in Tunis and Tripoli, where some of us have fled to welcoming crowds after committing atrocities in Israel or Europe.

"If such a claim were made to any other part of the Arab world we would dismiss it as a ruse, a kind of bullying, a claim to lost houses, not a nationality. The lost Arab houses in Israel arouse a communal pang, but that does not a nation make. It is true that the new Zionists behaved badly when they pretended that no Arabs lived in Palestine, cruelly when they pretended that they were not evicting these nonexistent Arabs during our wars against the Jews. But since we do not pretend that our eviction of Jews from Aleppo and Alexandria was decisive in melding the Jews into a nation, we should not claim that the eviction of Arabs from Israel created a new Arab people. We invented Palestine in order to destroy Israel, not because we believed that this outpost, captured as an Arab province and then managed as a Turkish colony, had ever created a distinct nation. From the Turks we reinherited a vast empire and created many Arab nations, which give no place to Jews or Kurds; why then should we complain when the one percent of the Turkish empire that went to the Jews makes inadequate room for Arabs or for Islam?"

As if in a dream, our prophet might continue. "It is true that the fiction of Palestine is no longer believed to be a ruse by the Palestinian Arabs who indulge it. Nevertheless, Palestine remains a ruse. Palestinians no more make a separate nation than do the Arabs of Detroit, and we Palestinian Arabs are even less likely to cohere than the mixed and combative citizenry of Lebanon, whom we resemble, both in our religious mixture and in our political factionalism. We have persuaded ourselves that the House of Israel is made up of colonists from elsewhere, even though from ancient times they constituted a local kernel of meaningfulness. We are the colonists, having built great mosques on their ancient Temple, pretending otherwise.

"Israel, too, is a fiction, imposed on the modern Middle East just as it was once imposed on the ancient world, just as Islam was imposed on a large part of the globe. But, like other great national cultures, Israel is a noble fiction, intended not to destroy any nationhood but to offer intellectual nationalism, from which we ourselves benefit. And Israel remains tiny, overenlarged in our imaginations. The whole country would fit into a small American state, while the disputed West Bank rivals Rhode Island. Though we carry on about the menace of Israel as if it is large and we greatly reduced, we triumph from the Atlantic to the Indian Ocean, not really diminished by those who cut Israel from our grasp.

"Let Palestine pass, even though it now wins more support than ever, as our posturing breeds minions to please us. Let us draw a border with the Jews, something they require of themselves, and let us settle amongst our brethren, in Jordan and in Gaza, and in those parts of the West Bank that will inevitably not be part of Israel. Let the Jews have their corner. Let us develop our extensive Arab lands, which rightfully represent Islamic culture to us, just as Israel represents Zion to Israelis. The idea of Zion is beautiful, balancing as it does stone clods with a bold idea of God, a bordered land with a discriminating civilization. Let us make for ourselves, from our own poetics, other such lands, elsewhere. Let us acknowledge that the Jews taught us the use of national poetics. Our swords we too will beat into metaphors, which might nourish our Land with literacy and law, with history and poetry."

Of course there are no Arab prophets who talk this way, and perhaps that bespeaks a failure of prophecy in Arab populations. Current efforts at peace notwithstanding, Arabs in their vast lands remain almost universally hostile to little Israel in the manner of the Bible's description of those who hate Zion. There are also no settler prophets who are speaking in poetic tones of compromise, partly because they feel that Israel has little to give away, and partly because there is little understanding of the Hebrew idea coming from the other side, all the efforts at peacemaking notwithstanding. But let us imagine such a settler prophet in the near future, one who might begin thus: "If Arabs recognize Israel as the home of one of the world's rich national cultures, if they concede land, especially in Jerusalem, they will demonstrate that they too understand the principles of Zion, which are universally applicable. They will understand that the Palestinian claim should be addressed as a proprietary claim and not as an attempt to reinstate a deracinated civilization. They will see the benefits of distinguishing between claim and culture, and they will cease to demand nationhood for claimants of land. In return, Israel will recognize, as she always has, the Arab nations that have already come into being outside of Israel as capable of intellectual achievement, in the past and now."

Our settler prophet might continue: "Our worst fear is that Zionism will not be the basis for peace. Some businesslike arrangement will be superimposed, one without soul and doomed to failure. The idea of Arab empire or the notion of lost Arab fields will play a disproportionate role. This might well lead to a kind of peace, in which a Palestinian state struggles with its identity and a circumscribed Israel seems to trouble the world less. But in such a peace,

Palestinian Arabs may create a Lebanon-like arena of endless claims, thus diminishing for all Arabs what Arab nationalism might mean. Arabs, falling from what they could be, will thus come that much closer to the ancient haters of Zion, dispatching Land back to Lot."

The settler prophet might conclude: "But by adopting the principles of ancient Zion, our Arab cousins will achieve the blessing of their own nationhood, as was promised to Abraham our father on behalf of Ishmael his son. By adopting the vision of Abraham's signifying Land, they will fulfill the prophecy that in Zionism all the nations of the earth be blessed. And because we are instructed that Zionism is meant even for our former enemies as it was once meant for our oppressors the Assyrians in Nineveh, we will do our part to make peace with our cousins. We will not quibble over every field in Judea and Samaria. We will draw a border, and we will make it represent peace."

Acknowledgments

Many friends have contributed to this book, which arose from conversations brief and extended, around kitchen tables and over texts, sometimes in formal study. I am particularly indebted to Cynthia Ozick, without whose encouragement and brilliance I would have committed little of my table talk to writing. Norma Rosen, Robert Rosen, and Bernard Hallote enriched me in ways they could hardly have realized, as we went along. Edward Alexander, Rabbi Chaim Dov Beliak, Jack Litewka, and Jonathan Rosen generously shed their intelligence on the manuscript. William Meyers, Nahma Sandrow, Henry Wollman, Eli Wertman, and David Silbersweig inspired me with their capaciousness of mind. Students and faculty at Queens College, when I was a professor there, stimulated this or that thought, now so jumbled with my own broodings that I no longer remember the difference. Rabbi Philip Weinberger, blessed with a wise soul, may find his own insights reflected or distorted here, without attribution. Rabbi John Hellman teaches *Talmud* to me and to Bruce Francis, Sheldon Goldberg, Jourdan Gottlieb, Scott Pollock, and Jason Schneier, while I quietly appropriate all their thinking. The suggestions of Adam Bellow, a wise editor and best of readers, have much enriched this book; I am deeply indebted to him.

Index